*This study was conducted in
the Bureau of Study Counsel,
Harvard University*

PARTICIPANTS

Staff of the Bureau of Study Counsel 1953–1964

Daniel M. Fox	Robert Schwitzgebel
Peter K. Gunness	John L. Sloanaker
Peter B. Gustafson	Grace R. Smith
Roderic C. Hodgins	H. Eric Solomon
Frank J. Jones	Norman A. Sprinthall
Kiyo Morimoto	Albert E. Trieschman, Jr.
Thomas F. A. Plaut	Charles P. Whitlock
Donald P. Reutlinger	John W. Wideman
Saul Rogolsky	Edward T. Wilcox
William J. Schwarz	

With the assistance of the following editors, judges, and statisticians:

D. Mowbray Allan	Robert G. Kirkpatrick
M. Royden Astley, Jr.	Susan B. Letzler
Barbara Benson Barrall	Paul Lohnes
David A. Cathcart	Jerry L. Mills
Arthur S. Couch	Beatrice Nelson
Gordon A. Dudley	David W. Panek
Chisholm Gentry	Helen H. Pringle
William L. Godshalk	Richard W. Tillinghast
Judith P. Gregory	Fred F. Weiss
Norman Hoffman	William C. Young

Forms of Intellectual and Ethical Development in the College Years

William G. Perry, Jr.

Introduction by L. Lee Knefelkamp

Forms of Intellectual and Ethical Development in the College Years

A Scheme

JOSSEY-BASS
A Wiley Company
www.josseybass.com

Published by

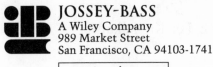

JOSSEY-BASS
A Wiley Company
989 Market Street
San Francisco, CA 94103-1741

www.josseybass.com

Jossey-Bass books and products are available through most bookstores. To contact
Jossey-Bass directly, call (888) 378-2537, fax to (800) 605-2665, or visit our website
at www.josseybass.com.

Substantial discounts on bulk quantities of Jossey-Bass books are available to
corporations, professional associations, and other organizations. For details and
discount information, contact the special sales department at Jossey-Bass.

We at Jossey-Bass strive to use the most environmentally sensitive paper stocks available
to us. Our publications are printed on acid-free recycled stock whenever possible, and
our paper always meets or exceeds minimum GPO and EPA requirements.

Jossey-Bass also publishes its books in a variety of electronic formats. Some content that
appears in print may not be available in electronic books.

Library of Congress Cataloging-in-Publication Data

Perry, William Graves, date.
   Forms of intellectual and ethical development in the college years : a scheme /
William G. Perry, Jr.—1st ed.
      p.   cm.—(Jossey-Bass higher and adult education series)
   Includes bibliographical references and indexes.
   ISBN 0-7879-4118-2 (pbk.)
   1. College students—Psychology.   2. Mental discipline.   3. Emotional
maturity.   I. Title.   II. Series.
LB3609.P4   1998
378.1'98—dc21   98-33543

FIRST EDITION
PB Printing   10 9 8 7 6 5 4 3

The Jossey-Bass

Higher and Adult Education Series

Contents

~~~ Introduction

L. Lee Knefelkamp

It is ironic that an individual who taught so many of us to listen to college students would himself have endured a lifelong hearing impairment. But then, as Bill Perry was so fond of saying, "irony is all we've got."

It is also ironic that the reissuing of his landmark book, *Forms of Intellectual Development in the College Years: A Scheme,* which will literally bring his work to life again, should happen in the year of his death. He knew it would be reissued and was pleased, and I believe he would have had a wry appreciation for all the ironies involved.

William G. Perry, Jr., is unique in his influence on those individuals who teach, study, and work with America's college and university students. His work—and by that I mean his entire career and the manner in which he lived it—has influenced generations of faculty members, administrators, and those who themselves have created theories of college student development and instruction. In this introduction, I hope to capture something of his presence in our lives. He always answered the phone with "Bill Perry, here!"—and hearing these words, you knew he would listen, not just to your words, but to thoughts and feelings you hadn't yet expressed even to yourself. I remember the man with the double hearing aids saying, "I may not be able to hear you, but I can listen."[1] And listen he did, to thousands of students and colleagues over the years, reading between our lines as we struggled to articulate what we meant, what we thought, what we believed. His recognition of all of us made it possible—made it necessary—for us to find ways to listen to and encourage our own students and colleagues. Some of us found new ways of assessing student needs, some created new models through which to understand students, some discovered new approaches to teaching. Some became better therapists, and most of us even became better people and friends. And for all our differences in role and perspective, we came to share his view that "students are our common purpose." His belief in students and their courage was a certainty in the tentative world of teaching and learning. He wrote, "A fundamental belief in students is more important than anything else. This fundamental belief is not a sentimental matter: it is a very demanding matter of realistically conceiving the student where he or she is, and at the same time never losing sight of where he or she can be."[2]

In addition to the very specific contributions of the Scheme itself, Perry's thinking contributed significant and fundamental notions to our understanding of the nature of students and the nature of developmental models. The Scheme became a grand metaphor that allowed us to listen to students with a sense of obligation to be responsive and to approach the study of other models with respect and expectation. It provided a context for listening to students and a context for learning about students through the perspectives of others.

The first significant contribution was Perry's use of the concept of *positions*. His sense of the positionality of students as they approached learning certainly anticipated the rise of standpoint theory that began a decade and a half after the book was first published.[3] This emphasis on standpoint—the perspectives acquired from one's lived life—has been a major foundation of much of the social identity theory of the past two decades. Our ability to take into account the influences of gender, race, ethnicity, and socioeconomic class as well as other aspects of identity has been greatly influenced by the concept of positionality, literally one's stance with respect to knowing, making meaning, and making commitments. Perry stressed the student's ability to construct meanings and to shift or change those constructions or standpoints to developmentally accommodate uncertainty, paradox, and the demands of greater complexity in knowledge and learning. He even suggested that students could be in several different positions at the same time with respect to different subjects or experiences. Thus he created a developmental model that both conformed to traditional hierarchical notions and, at the same time, broke free of them. Just as he always saw the student as more complex than any theory, he heard in their thinking more complexity than any benchmark along the way of his model.

Perry's understanding of positionality was deeply related to his understanding of *developmental transitions*. Again, he anticipated later models of adult transition when he strongly emphasized our need to understand students in motion and to not imprison them in stages.[4] He once wrote, "Perhaps development is all transition, and 'stages' are only resting points along the way" (Henderson, 1998). This notion of students-in-transition required that those of us who work with them think about what would be optimal conditions of growth. The very process of thinking about the complexities of students living in the in-between demands that we consider the specific conditions of challenge and support that will encourage their growth. Bill knew that as students' thinking changed, so did their self-concept, their roles, their ways of interpreting the world around them. For this reason, he wanted us to keep the dynamic view of students at the center of our thinking and to always link the needs of students to our notions of pedagogy.

His *recognition* of the students' *courage* brought with it the reciprocal demand that we *encourage* them. He was adamantly against any notion of trying to force growth or development (the notion of force being an antidevelopmental concept). Students were not potted plants to be watered in some academic hothouse, nor were they to be subjects of academic experiments. They were simply to be seen as courageous human beings who needed company and understanding along the way. He often said that faculty make the mistake of thinking that they have only two options when grading papers or working with students: praise and blame. But Bill constantly reminded us that there is a third, more powerful and necessary option: recognition. For when the student is recognized, the conditions of respect and encouragement that make risk possible and the pain of growth endurable are present. He often said, "If my pain has not lived, I cannot let go to move on." One of his most popular essays, "Sharing in the Costs of Growth," explores the mutuality of the relationship of recognition and encouragement.[5] He gently reminds us that students offer us both recognition and encouragement—and the possibility of wisdom that comes from the experience of loss. We are needful of each other in order to make meaning in our classrooms and in our lives. And he took such *joy* in students. He wrote: "A counselor's reward is the experience of wonder. When I counsel I don't hear problems, I hear courage in action" (Henderson, 1998).

Bill's capacity for joy and wonder filled so many areas of his life. He was an accomplished horseman, cabinetmaker, architect, sailor, teacher, counselor. He had a great gift for friendship and generosity. And he took extraordinary joy in his extended family—most of all in the relationship with his wife, Mary, who played a significant role in the development and refinement of the Scheme. He was a complex man, full of his own paradoxes and sorrows, but his capacity for joy and wonder influenced us all deeply.

That ability to be awed, to hear with new and wondrous ears, enabled Perry to emphasize the uniqueness of each student's *voice,* for the Scheme was created through listening to student voices. And it has been expanded and extended in the past thirty years by our listening to an ever-diverse student population. The heart of the model has always been the voice of the students. That is perhaps one of the reasons why so many faculty have found the model helpful over the years. Bill always suggested that faculty development really began with student development—and that our understanding of student development began with their voices, their experiences, their meanings. So many of the theorists who were influenced both by Perry the person and by his model have clearly acknowledged that among the many influences, the uniqueness of the student voice was central.

Perry was always fascinated by the *forms* that the students' voices would take. And he was therefore interested in the forms that counseling or instruction or coaching would take. Ever the master architect, I think that he was always wary lest the forms conform not to the nature of the student, but to the agenda of the authority figure. He and I engaged in many discussions about this over the years, and he only became comfortable with the pedagogical models Carol Widick and I had created when he understood them as ways of designing environments in order to encourage students in their growth. He became a great proponent of the "Developmental Instruction" approach when he saw that the pedagogical form was designed to match the student and not to form the student to match the pedagogy.[6] His love for nature and the very forms of nature surely influenced his philosophical stance with respect to this issue. He once had a wall and window completely redone—just after it had been finished—because the initial effort had "got it all wrong" and didn't allow the eye to line up to view the pond and the sky and the sunsets. He was right. The correction was right. Nature was served. This belief reminds me of Donald Browning's notion of generativity and care. "Care," he wrote, "is to be guided by the nature of that which is to be cared for."[7] In that sense, the form of pedagogy is to be guided by the nature of the students in the class.

Bill was an unselfish theorist. He always believed that "to understand what's going on, you need at least three theories." Just as he saw the nature of college students as complex and full of possibilities, he saw the need for multiple models of student development to be used in conjunction with one another—to, as he wryly put it, "see the student least worst." He was particularly intrigued by the possibilities of combining developmental stage theory with learning styles theory. Such a combination allowed the instructor to design a learning environment that facilitated both cognitive growth and the expansion of learning skills and capacities. It was also a way of responding to the wide range of diversity represented in college and university classes. Because Bill saw students as beings in developmental transitions, he was eager to study new models and always curious about their data collection methods and theoretical underpinnings. He did require that the models have integrity, and that the authors set forth the previous influences on their work, as there were debates over the years—there are debates still—about "copycat" models.

CHANGES IN THE MODEL

In the thirty years since the publication of the first study report of Perry's research (the book was published two years later), there have been significant elaborations on the original model. As more and more data were collected on an ever-diverse student population, we were able to expand and deepen our understanding of the various positions and transitions involved in the developmental scheme. While the model remains essentially the same in structure and scope, we simply know more about the characteristics of both the models and the students whose words inform the model. Prior to reading Perry's work in its original form, it is important to keep in mind several significant elaborations of our knowledge that have come from extensive data collection over the past three decades.

The issue that often arises is the issue of the *original sample of students* from which the model was shaped. The Harvard and Radcliffe students of the late 50s and early 60s are not generalizable to "the American college student" population for many reasons (many more men than women in the sample, socioeconomic class, the sociological characteristics of the era, likely educational background, age, and certainly race and ethnicity). However, it must be remembered that the assessment procedures that have been developed (especially by Knefelkamp and Widick, and by Moore) have facilitated the measurement of tens of thousands of students at all types of American colleges and universities. Careful records have been kept that indicate that the model is useful with a wide range of diverse students. Its efficacy remains strong, and there continue to be studies that extend the range of students for whom the general characteristics of intellectual development are accurate and valid. After careful consideration, this should come as no surprise to those of us who work in higher education. We are well aware of the socializing effects of school systems, and that many (perhaps even most) students are educated in environments that Freire would characterize as "banking models," with their emphasis on authority, information exchange, and the quest for right answers.[8]

The second major issue has to do with *assessment of student characteristics* through the filter of the model. The original longitudinal studies utilized typed transcripts of student interviews. The procedures are described by Perry; generally, they involve the elaborate (and expensive) task of transcribing the interviews and then having individuals (faculty, counselors) who are familiar with college students and their characteristics provide a "judgment" of the relative positionality of the transcripted material. This basic method is used in theory building as it allows a fairly comprehensive view of the student over time. When Carol Widick and I first began to do research with the model, we realized that faculty needed a more heuristic method to assess students. The "Perry Interview" method that we developed based on the original studies would be used by researchers. But faculty who were interested in designing more effective learning environments would likely need something less labor intensive, but still valid and reliable. Over a period of several years, Carol and I developed the Measure of Intellectual Development (MID—sometimes referred to as the KneWi in the early research literature).[9] This method requires that the students respond to a series of essays concerning their perspectives on good learning environments, disquieting decisions, career development concerns, and specific academic subjects or disciplines. This first instrument and the rating system developed with it are still widely used and have influenced the procedures of other methods of intellectual development that have been developed on the basis of the assessment work done in the late 70s and early 80s. The MID requires trained raters who read the essays for statements, phrases, or perspectives that are associated with each position and make a judgment of the position represented. The rating scheme is designed to allow developmental transitions to be documented. A student rarely thinks in only one position along the model; most student data are evaluated as in transition from one position to another. The MID is popular with faculty because it is a production task that makes sense to students ("tell me about your preferences for learning environments so we can design this class more effectively") and because it can be easily collected in a class period. While not as extensive as the interview method, this approach provides accurate data with respect to general intellectual development and more specific data with respect to particular academic subjects or pedagogical methods. (M. Mentkowski, director of research at Alverno College, has written a manual that codifies the process and criteria that Knefelkamp taught in her role as consultant to the student outcomes project. It remains the most complete description of the Knefelkamp-Widick criteria and of Alverno's use of the MID essays in a longitudinal assessment project.)[10]

Bill Moore remains a pioneer with respect to the development of essays that are tailored to the needs of a particular academic class.[11] He is also the developer of the most widely used "paper and pencil" measure of the Perry Scheme, the Learning Environments Preference instrument (LEP). This recognition task instrument asks students to select from a list the items that most reflect their thinking about learning, the role of the instructor, evaluation, the role of peers, and the nature of knowledge. The items from which they select their preferences have all been compiled from the original rating cues developed by Knefelkamp and Widick and have been researched extensively. The LEP is widely used in research and is the only successful paper-and-pencil measure developed to measure student characteristics along the Perry Scheme. The student responses are "scored" using a rating formula, and results are provided that indicate both position and transition. A review of the research done in the past decade shows that most researchers use a combination of two of the three basic approaches: Perry Interview, MID, and LEP.

The work with assessment has allowed a *greater elaboration of the characteristics of students* that are associated with each position. During the 70s and early 80s, Knefelkamp developed an extensive rating manual for work with interviews and the MID. Those positional cues were both cognitive and affective. For example, a student who is experiencing the transition from Position 2 to Position 3 often remarks about the fact that there is more to learn, that learning seems both more challenging and more interesting than it previously did, and that there is a feeling of uncertainty and doubt that has entered his or her experience of negotiating learning assignments. At the same time, learning is more varied and more fun—and this is expressed as well. The research on assessment always had at least an equal number of female and male students; many of the affective cues came from the female students, although not exclusively. We consistently found that men and women had similar Perry position patterns, but that they often used different cognitive and affective cues within the positions.

Knefelkamp and Cornfeld developed an elaborated chart detailing the characteristics of students in Positions 2 through 5.[12] In this chart the reader can trace how eight crucial variables change as the student becomes more intellectually complex (view of knowledge and learning, role of the instructor, role of the student, role of peers in the learning process, intellectual tasks that are understood, evaluation issues, sources of developmental disequilibrium or challenge, and sources of support). This more elaborated set of characteristics is the result of twenty-five years of investigations into how students think and how they make meaning of the learning process within the perspective of the Perry Scheme.

An additional finding in the research reveals that there are at least three distinct but related uses of the Scheme as metaphor: 1) "General Perry"—that general overview of an individual's intellectual development that is derived from the analysis of several interviews about the topics of ways of knowing and the nature of knowledge and education; 2) "Contextual Perry"—the particular way of thinking associated with a particular context such as an academic discipline, a religious belief system, or a specific course (students can vary in position in different courses in the same academic term); and 3) "Functional Regression"—the phenomenon seen when adult learners undertake new learning in a new learning environment and "functionally" regress to multiplistic thinking until they feel comfortable in the new environment (we first observed this with graduate students).

An additional issue with respect to assessment is the question of how *cultural perspectives and values* affect the student data and the rating or evaluation methods. This is, of course, an increasingly important issue in American society as well as in our colleges and universities. The original model is Western in nature; it reflects the perspective that a more mature student moves through levels of thinking complexity and is able to develop "independence" of thought and judgment. The model was developed during a period before the new scholarship of gender, race, and class questioned the assumptions of "independence" as a maturity characteristic. Serious questions, then, arise—about gender, about various domestic diversity cultures within the United States, and about international students. We have been carefully studying what are now called "culture cues" that are present in the data. (For example, first-generation Asian American students often indicate a complexity of thought consistent with contextual relativism and at the same time use phrases of respect and adherence to learned authorities that have been associated with more dualistic or early multiplistic forms of thinking. In this case, such students are not dualistic, but are reflecting appropriate cultural perspectives.)

This work is particularly important as it allows us to monitor the efficacy of the model and determine its limits. Neither Perry nor anyone deeply associated with the model assumed universality of its characteristics or its applications. And certainly no one assumed that the model would be the *only* one used to assess student needs. In addition to the combination of intellectual development with learning styles, a very powerful combination is of the Perry model with the theoretical work reflected in *Women's Ways of Knowing.*[13] One can argue persuasively that there are significant parallels of insight that come from overlaying the two models. Both models trace students' increased abilities to become active generators of learning and to learn with and from their peers. Both stress the constructed and contested nature of knowledge, and both, using very different language, describe the students' move from silence into agency and voice. I have found, for example, that the *WWK* concept of *subjective knowing* allows my own students to have a deeper understanding of the characteristics of *early multiplicity* and to have a greater appreciation for one of the major characteristics of that position: namely the realization that one can and should bring one's own experiences to bear on the interpretation of knowledge and not just be expected to "apply" what one learns in the classroom to other aspects of one's life. This notion of reciprocity is first experienced as subjective, and then develops into an expectation of what the *community of scholars* should be about.[14]

One of the most important lessons of working with the model has to do with *terminology.* There has been considerable confusion with respect to Positions 4 and 5 (later multiplicity and relativism). People have confused the "do your own thing" aspect of late multiplicity with relativism. This criticism comes particularly from those who feel that the academy has lost its standards and academic values. Perry was particularly vexed over this misunderstanding. "Relativism," he would say, "means relative to *what—to something—it implies comparison, criteria, and judgment!"* Part of the confusion came from the pullout diagram of the model in the original text (which seemed to divide the Scheme into three parts with three positions each). This was partially corrected in the diagram used in Perry's chapter on the Scheme in *The Modern American College* (pp. 79–80; see Note 6). When there was still confusion, even after the writing of that chapter, Perry and I felt that the deliberate use of the phrase *contextual relativism* whenever referring to Position 5 would help to make the point that contextual relativism, far from being anchorless, was in fact a position that required a great deal of cognitive complexity and intellectual moral courage to investigate and compare things and to make judgments about adequacy or inadequacy, appropriateness or inappropriateness.

Another way of looking at the model appears in Figure I.1.

This diagram attempts to show clearly that the first four stages are elaborations on dualism; that contextual relativism is a qualitatively different way of thinking than the earlier stages; and that the later stages are the anticipations, decisions, and experiences of the consequences of commitments. Thus, it is primarily Positions 2 through 5 that are significant in the context of student learning. By the time students have entered college, they are not likely to be in Position 1 (where difference is granted so little importance and reality that little dissonance results). And the *post-contextual positions* are more likely to be reflected in value questions and decision dilemmas than in a particular approach to learning. The work of Slepitza and Knefelkamp explored the later positions and found that Position 8 was actually quite elongated in time, as it reflected not just the experience of the consequences of the initial commitment made in Position 7 but now

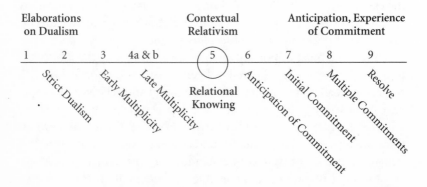

Figure I.1.

the multiple commitments—and the consequences when some of them are competing or even contradictory to one another.[15] Since commitments are made after doubt, in the context of other legitimate alternatives, and as a statement of self or identity, this experience of competing and contradictory commitments is a major aspect of adult life. We found that Position 9 was a resolve to continue with these competing and interlocking aspects of one's self and one's life—not a resolution of the conflicts. Nine is an active existential stance.

Perry's elaboration of the *alternatives to growth* has been one of the most important contributions of the model. A study of his concept of *retreat* allows us greater insight into the difference between the naive dualism of the new learner and the pernicious dualism of the angry bigot in retreat from complexity. His perspectives are most helpful in analyzing the angry backlash at the issues of affirmative action and multicultural curriculum transformation. Perhaps the concept of *temporizing* does need modification. When the original study was done, one year's "delay" was considered an alternative to growth. However, when we consider Piaget's concepts of vertical and horizontal decalogue (increased complexity of structures and the use of those structures in different aspects of one's life), what may have seemed a delay was actually a reflection of horizontal decalogue.

MAJOR INFLUENCES ON OTHER THEORETICAL MODELS

Bill Perry was trained in English Literature. His first book was a well-reviewed and enduring translation of the Iliad. He was the director of the Bureau of Study Counsel at Harvard University. And he was an extraordinary professor of undergraduate reading classes and graduate classes in counseling and the therapeutic process. Several years ago he was given a special award for his lifelong achievements in psychology from the Massachusetts Psychological Association. His wide range of interests and areas of study gave him the intellectual depth which formed his work and his teaching. He created the sacred hour (actually hours) at the Bureau—weekly meetings during which all counselors and staff would listen to each others' counseling tapes to learn more about students and to help each other become better therapists. In all these things he had an uncommon attention to story and to structure. He was passionately interested in stories (and he was a great story-teller!) and the structures or forms through which we tell them. He saw his own model as symbolic of the student's story of the journey

to identity. Just as he enabled so many thousands of students to become more mature, he was a great mentor and colleague to a significant number of individuals who have developed theoretical and
pedagogical models that have been, at least in part, inspired by him.
And his work also influenced many who did not know him. Only in
the scope of a biography could one attempt to do justice to the many
mutual influences within his own generation (Margaret Mead, Larry
Frank, Mary Frank, Gardner Murphy, Larry Kohlberg, and Erik and
Joan Erikson come to mind). Yet it is important to mention several of
the individuals still writing whose work could not have been possible
or as richly textured without Bill's influence. While he was certainly
not the sole intellectual influence on these researchers, his concepts
have clearly been used. The authors of *Women's Ways of Knowing* dedicated their new book *Knowledge, Difference, and Power* (Goldberger,
Tarule, Clinchy, and Belenky, 1996) to Bill Perry and Carol Gilligan
"who led the way."[16] This is especially gratifying since *Women's Ways
of Knowing* was often misinterpreted to be the only way women
thought and Perry's model as the only way men thought. Such a false
dichotomy was not reflected in actual research (both men and women
have a wide range of ways of knowing, as these particular models
demonstrate). Indeed, a careful comparison of the two models will reveal significant similarities as well as nuances that are particular to
each body of research (the research was conducted decades apart; the
subjects in *WWK* were nontraditional, female adult learners; the range
of questions was different; and the educational environments were
very distinct from a traditional, four-year undergraduate campus).

Two other models that owe a great deal to Perry's work are King
and Kitchener's model of Reflective Judgment (additional and acknowledged influences are Popper, Harvey, Hunt and Schroder, Loevinger, and Dewey) and Baxter-Magolda's Epistemological Reflection
Model (additional and often unacknowledged influences are the
authors of *WWK* and William Moore). Each of these models has a
well-established system of measurement and evaluation. King and
Kitchener's work is widely used and continues to form the basis of rigorous research. Baxter-Magolda's work pays particular attention to
women's modes of thinking. A careful reading of all the models will
reveal strong similarities in these cognitive-constructivist models. It
will also reveal a mutual influence in the "naming" of the different development positions or stages.

A new book, *Student Development in College* (Evans, Forney, and
Guido-DiBrito, 1998), offers an excellent, though brief, analysis of the

Perry influence on what the authors call "later cognitive-structural theories."[17] Basseches's work *Dialectical Thinking and Adult Development* is another cognitive-structural model which bears Perry's influence. Robert Kegan acknowledges his influence in *The Evolving Self* and uses the famous spiral diagram Perry originated to illustrate the evolving model. (This spiral is also used by David Kolb in his work on learning styles.) Milton Bennett's widely used model of intercultural sensitivity ("Towards Ethnorelativism: A Developmental Model of Intercultural Sensitivity") has Perry as a strong foundation. This model was the first to actually focus on the interaction of the Perry thinking positions with the experience of cultural diversity. As such, it will likely gain a significant following on college campuses in years to come.

Other writers who have strongly indicated their debt to Perry include Larry Dalos, Carol Gilligan, Sharon Parks, David Kolb, and Arthur Chickering. Each of these individuals has worked to create a theory of human development; some of the models are more directly derivative than others. It is important to note that a significant number of these individuals worked with or were taught by Bill Perry and also know each other. A brief bit of history will illustrate. In the early 70s, Clyde Parker, a counseling psychology professor and leading interpreter of college students, had returned from a Fulbright year in India. He hired two graduate students (Carol Widick and Lee Knefelkamp) to read everything they could on student development theory and to meet with him once a week to go over that material. (These discussions became, in part, the monograph *Applying New Developmental Findings*.) Carol was the first to read Perry; soon the Perry work became a significant focus of the weekly discussions. Carol and Lee created the pedagogical model based on Perry's work, Developmental Instruction, and created the MID assessment measure and rating protocols. After they graduated, Karen Kitchener and Patricia King continued the weekly seminars with Parker, now officially named the "Perry Seminars." Both of the graduate students became faculty members and their students continued much of the work in this area. A study of the individuals who knew and worked together at Harvard and at the Bureau would reveal similar patterns of intellectual work and friendship—all with Bill Perry in common.

MODELS OF INSTRUCTION

During the year 1974–75, Widick and Knefelkamp began the task of translating Perry's model into one that was usable for the classroom and in other educational settings.[18] Our goal was to understand the underlying characteristics of the student-as-learner so that we could design instructional environments that were characterized by a balance of intellectual challenges and supports. We wanted to facilitate student learning and intellectual development. Another goal was to develop and vary instructional variables so that we would, in Bill's words, "find ways to encourage" our students. We also believed that students who became more complex in their thinking in the classroom could apply that thinking to the complexities of citizenship in American life. (Bill was often asked if development was better, to which he replied that he thought it was a more adequate way of coping with a complex world.) We identified four variables that seemed to underlie the developmental model: 1) the student's experience of and response to diversity; 2) the amount of authority-provided structure for the learning environment; 3) the nature of experiential learning that was experienced as part of the class; and 4) the degree to which the class could be characterized as respectful, collaborative, and able to relate the subject matter to the context of the students' lives (personalism). Each of the variables exists on a continuum that represents greater or lesser presence of the variable in the pedagogical design. Students who are in earlier positions of the Perry model are in need of greater amounts of structure and experiential learning as they move into the uncertainty of knowledge and learning. Students who are in the later positions along the model often value experiential learning, but do not need as much instructor-guided structure in order to work with the concepts of the class. Research with the Developmental Instruction model has been widespread for the past twenty-five years in a wide range of academic and professional school disciplines. It has also been used as a basis for career development and academic advising. Early pedagogical work was also done by Larry Copes in mathematics and by Craig Nelson in the sciences.

CONCLUSIONS

For a period of a decade (from 1975 through 1986), Bill and Mary Perry and I traveled around the country speaking to national conferences and to hundreds of colleges and universities. Most of the work was done with both faculty and student affairs staffs. Bill would present his developmental scheme—the "Pilgrim's Progress" of their movement to intellectual maturity. I would work with assessment techniques and the developmental instruction model. Mary would facilitate evening discussions about the importance of listening to students. We also worked together at the Bureau of Study Counsel. It was an exciting time. What I have kept with me from that time is our enduring friendship, memories of dinners with students at the conferences, flying in very small planes which made us all nervous, having a sense of being a part of something worthwhile and lasting. But most of all I remember the response to Bill and his presentation of the model. Faculty who cared about teaching but despaired of doing it better found new encouragement. It was as if they rediscovered their students and the joy that teaching can bring. People remembered their own undergraduate years and their own ways of making meaning. Wonderful, moving, funny stories would be told in the evening discussions. When Bill would say, "Every student in my class had a completely different teacher," or "Teaching evaluations don't hurt your vanity. They wound your sanity," we all felt understood—known—recognized—and confirmed. We all became better teachers because of Bill and Mary. And we recognized that though it was a work of love, it was hard on him. Bill's head would echo with noises of the room when his hearing aids caused difficulties. (He even had a disarming sense of humor about that—he would say, "If you can't hear me in the back of the room, raise your hand and I'll turn my hearing aid up.") He never rushed a question-and-answer period. We would stay and respond to issues and queries until there were no more. It pleases me so very much that his book is being reissued at this time. He was a great man and the current and future generations of students and faculty have great need of his work. I look forward to students again taking the time to read the work carefully and to asking themselves what their reciprocal obligation is now that they know these things. Bill used to say, "I don't love you all. I love you each one. But that takes a long time." We loved him back. And now we have his book back for a long, long time.

Notes

1. I am indebted to Ann Fleck Henderson for collecting "Perry-isms" at Bill's 80th birthday party and for reproducing them. We all wrote down our favorite Bill Perry sayings. Most of the quotes in this chapter are from that collection. Ann is chairperson of the Department of Social Work at

Simmons College. For fourteen years she was the associate director of the Bureau of Study Counsel working closely with Bill.

2. This quotation is found on page 215 of the original text of *Forms of Intellectual and Ethical Development in the College Years*. That section of Perry's text calls for a reciprocity of obligation between faculty and students and inspired Knefelkamp's "Faculty and Student Development in the '80s: Renewing the Community of Scholars," which is a call for the renewal of the academic community through greater understanding of our students. While other theories are discussed, Perry's model forms the heart of the article. The article was first delivered as a speech to the AAHE National Convention (Perry had spoken to the body the year before) and was followed by a workshop conducted by Perry and myself. The period of 1975 through 1986 was the time that the higher education community had discovered Perry's theory and had taken to it with enthusiasm. Also, much research on the model and its applications was being conducted during this time. FIPSE had funded a large number of grants that used the Perry model as a focus for studying intellectual development. Alverno College used the model as a significant aspect of their longitudinal study of their students' experience with their competency-based curriculum.

3. We associate constructivist models and standpoint theory with a wide number of individuals whose thinking is transforming their disciplines: Elizabeth Karmack Minnich, Sara Ruddick, and Lorraine Code (philosophy), Patricia Hill Collins (sociology), James Banks (multicultural studies), Michelle Fine (education), Katie Canon (theology). Perry's use of the concept of "position" to describe the perspective of the student assumed that each student's position would be influenced by the totality of his or her life experience and the socialization received in school. Standpoint theorists emphasize that theory is built from our daily "lived lives," and that too often our educational institutions ignore the life experiences of the majority of their students, especially women, the poor, and racial and ethnic minorities. They most particularly suggest that the structures of our universities, curriculum, and pedagogies should take this into account.

4. I have found it very useful to use Nancy K. Schlossberg's model of adult transitions when considering how students become more complex in their thinking and what some of the effects of those changes are in their worldviews, roles (especially their roles as students and the degree to which they are constructing knowledge), and self-concepts. Schlossberg also proposed a theory of marginality and mattering that is related to the adult experience of transitions. Use of these two concepts in combination helps the educator think about the design of learning environments that enable the student to

make intellectual transitions in an environment in which they feel they matter.

5. "Sharing in the Costs of Growth" appears as the last chapter in Clyde Parker's *Encouraging Development in College Students* (1978). This book was based on a conference held in May of 1976. Organized by Parker, the conference brought together for the first time many of the major student development theorists (Perry, Douglas Heath, Roy Heath, Peter Madison, David Hunt) whose role at the conference was to comment on a series of presentations by individuals who had used the models in practice (most of the practical applications of theory were based on Perry and Chickering's work). The conference had been charged with tension; deliberate design of educational practices using developmental theory was not a universally popular movement. While the theorists were kind to the application presenters, many in the audience were not. Perry's speech at the end of the conference enabled us all to come together in our "common purpose," the education of our students. The conference echoed the 1975 APA symposium in which many of the same presenters first made public their research in using Perry's work in curriculum design, career development, and faith development. This was the first time Bill had known of this research and he was invited to the symposium to critique the work. The papers presented at the symposium can be found in the *Counseling Psychologist,* 6(3), 1976. The presenters at the APA symposium were all connected to the developmental work that first went on at the University of Minnesota. This was the first time that the researchers met Bill and Mary Perry.

6. Perry has a lengthy review of Developmental Instruction and other instructional applications in his chapter "Cognitive and Ethical Growth: The Making of Meaning" in Arthur Chickering's *The Modern American College* (1981). Perry presents his developmental theory in a thorough yet concise manner and provides what was then a complete review of the research that was being conducted using his scheme.

7. Donald Browning's book, *Generative Man* (1973), is, unfortunately, out of print. It is a collection of essays on Erikson's concept of generativity. He provides an excellent analysis of the relationship of generativity and care to teaching.

8. Paulo Freire's powerful critique of the "banking model" echoes the pedagogical approaches that support Perry's concept of dualism and the *Women's Ways of Knowing* concept of received knowledge. See especially Freire's *Education for Critical Consciousness* (1973).

9. The Measure of Intellectual Development (MID) was first developed in 1974. Current MID research involves collecting data on students' views of

multicultural diversity in the curriculum and in campus life. The essays are evaluated using criteria developed over the years by trained raters. Most of the work with the MID is coordinated by William Moore and Kathe Taylor. They are the individuals who are most aware of the national trends with respect to Perry data collection. See also note 11.

10. Marcia Mentkowski is director of research and evaluation at Alverno College. In the mid-70s she went to Alverno to create the office that would be responsible for studying the development of the Alverno students and the evaluation procedures associated with the competency-based curriculum. Mentkowski has an unusual depth of understanding of student development, assessment, learning evaluation, and the conducting of research on students and college outcomes. In the early 80s she brought Lee Knefelkamp to Alverno over a period of several years to train the research staff in the administration and evaluation of the MID. Marcia and two of her staff members (Moeser and Strait) wrote an exhaustive two-volume workbook that contains their work with the essays and the rating cues. The workbook, *Using the Perry Scheme of Intellectual and Ethical Development as a College Outcomes Measure: A Process and Criteria for Judging Student Performance* (1983), is the most comprehensive explanation of the MID measurement process to date. It should be studied carefully by anyone conducting research on the Perry Scheme.

11. William Moore is director of assessment for the Community College System in the state of Washington. Bill is also the director of the Center for Developmental Instruction and the Perry Network and acts as a research consultant to individuals conducting "Perry" research and as the director of all the scoring of the MID and the LEP. He is particularly adept at helping faculty members who wish to work with the model in the context of their teaching.

12. The chart by Knefelkamp and Cornfeld represents the elaborations and extensions of the Perry model over the past several decades. It was originally presented in a paper, "Combining Student Stage and Style in the Design of Learning Environments" (Knefelkamp and Cornfeld, 1979), and has been updated regularly since that time. See Table I.1. after the Notes section.

13. I have found that the names and descriptions of student characteristics of each of the developmental phases of the *Women's Ways of Knowing* model (silence, received knowledge, subjective knowledge, procedural knowledge, and constructed knowledge) provide us with additional insights to the first five positions of the Perry model. The *WWK* terms are readily accessible (whereas "multiplicity pre-subordinant" is not) and provide additional in-

sight into the ways of making meaning that are described in the Perry Scheme. *Women's Ways of Knowing* is a "second generation" theoretical model (much like Reflective Judgement or Epistemological Reflection) that benefits from the earlier Perry work and also extends and deepens our understanding of student characteristics in the context of learning.

14. In these times of virtual reality universities and the extension of distant learning models, the concept of a community of scholars needs review. All the student development models provide a basis for that review. Yet Perry's work is the most specific in its call for collaboration in learning and for a mutual reciprocity between faculty and students. Perhaps because he worked with students in a variety of contexts—counseling, study skills, and instruction—he is clear that the outcomes of learning should result in greater self-efficacy and self-understanding as well as in an understanding of the subject studied. His own understanding of liberal learning always combined the affective with the cognitive. He saw learning as an "ego-threatening task" (for both the student and the teacher) and saw that basic understanding as the foundation for creating a community of learners.

15. Ron Slepitza and I worked over a period of years to adapt Perry's model to the area of career development. Students who responded to the MID essay asking them to describe difficult decision-making areas of their life often wrote about the dilemmas of choosing a major or a career. Ron developed a career-development essay which we used extensively to study students' perspectives about careers and career decision making. The career-development model that evolved from this research can be found in the *Counseling Psychologist* (see note 5) and in Parker's *Encouraging Development in College Students* (see note 5). Over the years we began to study the upper stages of the adapted model and found the characteristics mentioned in the chapter text. The experience of competing and contradictory commitments is an especially significant finding as it helps us understand the tensions brought about by having deep commitments. Perry's reminder that commitment has three distinct characteristics is helpful to understanding those tensions: Commitment is made in the face of other legitimate alternatives, it is made after doubting that to which one commits, and it is an affirming statement of self and identity. As we look at the interlocking nature of the multiple parts of our selves (gender, race, ethnicity, sexual orientation, socioeconomic class, and so on) we are aware of the tensions that arise from these committed parts of ourselves that are often competing for our sense of identity. The adaptation of Perry's model that is reflected in the career-development research is helpful to understanding these issues of identity development.

16. One of the most anti-intellectual experiences of the past two decades has been the dualistic manner in which many compared Carol Gilligan and Lawrence Kolhberg's work and the work of Bill Perry and Mary Belenky and others (of *Women's Ways of Knowing*). In each of these pairs one will find similarities between the models and distinct emphases and differences. Each of the pairings can be studied collaboratively to increase our understanding of human development. It is also true that there were feelings of bad faith and the concern that sufficient credit had not been given to the earlier models. However one thinks about the debates and discussions, the simple fact is that we now have complementary models that deepen our experience of intellectual and ethical development; we should study each model for its distinctive contributions and also seek the integrative insights that come from the use of the models complementarily.

17. *Student Development in College,* by Nancy J. Evans, Deanna S. Forney, and Florence Guido-DiBrito (1998), also has an excellent discussion of the Developmental Instruction model. I recommend this comprehensive and well-written book as a basic text in graduate classes and as a reader for faculty who are interested in studying student development theory in the context of improving their teaching and their understanding of students.

18. See Table I.2 for a chart defining each of the Developmental Instruction variables.

	Dualism (Position 2)	Early Multiplicity (Position 3)	Late Multiplicity (Position 4)	Contextual Relativism (Position 5)
View of Knowledge	All Knowledge Is Known There is a certainty that *Right* and *Wrong* answers exist for everything. Knowledge is collection of information.	Most Knowledge Is Known *All is knowable* (first view of learning as a *process* that the student can learn). Certainty that there exists a *Right Way* to find the Right Answers. Realization that some knowledge domains are "fuzzy."	In Some Areas We Still Have Certainty About Knowledge. In Most Areas We Really Don't Know Anything for Sure Certainty that there is *No Certainty* (except in a few specialized areas). Hence "do your own thing"—all opinions can be just as valid or invalid as all others.	All Knowledge Is Contextual All knowledge is disconnected from any concept of *Absolute Truth*. However, right and wrong, adequate and inadequate, appropriate and inappropriate can exist within a specific context and are judged by "rules of adequacy" that are determined by expertise good thought processes.
View of the Role of the Instructor	Source of Knowledge Role is to give the knowledge to student. Good Instructor equals Absolute Authority and Knower of Truth.	Source of Right Way to Find Knowledge, of How to Learn. Role is to model "the way" or process.	Source of the Process of Thinking Modeling the use of supportive evidence—modeling "the way they want us to think"—modeling good methods of scholarship. Instructor can also be completely discounted.	Source of Expertise Role of expert-guide-consultant within the framework of "rules of adequacy" and within context. Mutuality of learning is sought. One earns authority through having expertise.
View of the Role of the Student	Role is to receive the information or knowledge and to demonstrate having learned the right answers.	Role is to learn how to learn, how to do the processes called for, to apply oneself, and to work hard.	Role is to learn to think for oneself and to learn to use supportive evidence. Independence of thought is valued.	Role is to exercise the use of the intellect, to shift from context to context, and to apply rules of adequacy to information, concepts, perspectives, judgments.

Table I.1. Analysis of the Learner Characteristics of Students Implied by the Perry Scheme.

Cornfeld, J. L., and Knefelkamp, L. L. Copyright © 1979 by L. Lee Knefelkamp.

Table I.1. Analysis of the Learner Characteristics of Students Implied by the Perry Scheme *(continued)*.

	Dualism (Position 2)	Early Multiplicity (Position 3)	Late Multiplicity (Position 4)	Contextual Relativism (Position 5)
View of Peers in the Learning Process	Peers are not a legitimate source of knowledge or learning.	Peers are now more legitimate, often with respect to processes like small group discussions. Interest in variety of perspectives of peers, but still see the instructor as the Final Authority.	Peers are quite legitimate. In a "new dualism," they may replace others. But peers (and others) may not really be listened to, as everyone's opinion is just as good (or bad) as everyone else's.	Peers are legitimate sources of learning if they use appropriate rules of adequacy and contextual presentation of perspectives. Seek out diversity of opinions and experiences of others. Position alone does not determine legitimacy; process does.
Evaluation Issues	Evaluation directly related to sense of self. Bad-Wrong answer equals Bad-Wrong person. Evaluation should be clear-cut, because questions asked and answers should be clear-cut. Is real concern if teacher and content and evaluation format are fuzzy.	Evaluation is The Primary Issue. Often related to amount of time, hard work, "style," and *quantity* focus. Primary question: How are my answers judged? *Fairness* is issue: fairness in judging, in assignments, in amount of work. A fair evaluation rewards the effort of the student.	"New Truth"—independent thought should get good grades. Can play evaluation game of "give them what they want" no matter what you think. Learning to accept qualitative criteria as legitimate in evaluation. Value the courage of independence.	Evaluation of work done can be separated from evaluation of the self. Understand that a good critique has positives and negatives. See evaluation as opportunity for feedback, improvement, and new learning. See evaluation as legitimate process or part of learning.
Primary Intellectual Tasks	Learning basic information and definitions of words and concepts. Learning to identify parts of the whole. Beginning to be able to compare and contrast things. Learning to provide explanation of why they answered as they did.	Can do compare-and-contrast tasks. Can see multiples—perspectives, parts, opinions, evaluations. Do basic analytic tasks. Use supportive evidence. First understanding of *Process* as a concept. See difference between process and content for the first time.	Good at analysis. Can do some synthesis. Can do critique with positives and negatives. Use supportive evidence well. Can relate learning to other issues in other classes or to issues in "real life"—if they will apply themselves to that task. Learning to think in abstractions.	Relate learning in one context to learning in another with some ease. Look for relationships in the learning. See complexity. Can evaluate, conclude, support own analysis. Can synthesize. Can adapt, modify, and expand concepts because they understand the concepts. Fluidity of thought and analysis. Good with abstraction.

Cornfeld, J. L., and Knefelkamp, L. L. Copyright © 1979 by L. Lee Knefelkamp.

	Dualism (Position 2)	Early Multiplicity (Position 3)	Late Multiplicity (Position 4)	Contextual Relativism (Position 5)
Sources of Challenge	Ambiguity, diffuseness or its appearance, multiple perspectives on something, uncertainty (especially by an Authority), any disagreement between two respected Authorities, concept of independent thought, request for the interpretation of the student.	View that uncertainty isn't just temporary. Complexity—initially seen as quantity, not quality. Evaluation causes great concern. Learning processes as opposed to facts. Trying to determine "which of the multiples is *really* right." Quantity is challenge—amount of work and effort required.	Demand to use evidence to support opinion. Learning to sort out which are good sources and which are not. Learning to accept responsibility in the learning process. For some, learning to listen to Authority again. For others, learning to think independently.	Requirement of choice or commitment. How to choose between equally good alternatives? Highly challenged to intellectual excellence. Good role modeling of scholarship that is still beyond their capabilities. New context.
Sources of Support	High degree of structure. Concrete examples and experiential learning. Joy in the opening of the world of knowledge. Careful sequencing and timing of presentation of diversity. Safe learning environment where people are respected and treated kindly. Modeling on part of instructor. Chance to practice skills and evaluation tasks.	Still need structure to help as they move into more and more diversity and ambiguity. Clarity of evaluation procedures and assignment instructions. Enjoy new freedom in the learning. Peers are big source of support. Comfort still in the thought that someday we will know it all. Comfort that we know the right answer and the right process is out there waiting to be found.	Enjoy diversity. Tend to balk at structure—seek independence. Seek class atmosphere that is free and independent. Comfort with different formats, although may clearly prefer one. Can play the intellectual "game" fairly well. Enjoy some of the thinking tasks.	Truly enjoy all the diversity and options until they become a new form of the old Position 3 confusion. Feel comfortable moving across contexts and have the intellectual tools to do so. Feeling of intellectual mastery. Comfortable seeking aid of appropriate authority or expert.

Table I.1. Analysis of the Learner Characteristics of Students Implied by the Perry Scheme (*continued*).

Cornfeld, J. L., and Knefelkamp, L. L. Copyright © 1979 by L. Lee Knefelkamp.

Table I.2. The Four Developmental Instruction Variables.

Structure

The amount of framework and direction provided. It is a continuum that moves from a high to a low degree of structure.

Some ways of providing structure:

A. Provide a context for the course, including how the course fits into a curriculum sequence and what the particular course will involve.

B. Provide basic definitions of terms used in the course.

C. Sequence the presentation of material with attention to issues of increasing complexity.

D. Allow opportunities for students to rehearse evaluation tasks.

E. Provide written material such as outlines, directions, assignments, and evaluation procedures in as detailed a manner as possible.

F. Provide guidelines for each new learning task.

G. Provide opportunities for processing or cementing the learning.

H. Use specific examples that relate to issues in the students' experience.

Experiential Learning

The amount of involvement, directness, and concreteness involved in an activity. Experiential learning varies on activities where involvement is vicarious. All students can benefit from direct learning opportunities, but students at the lower levels of cognitive complexity tend to *need* such experiences in order to really cement their learning. Most college teaching is vicarious in nature (reading, writing, talking about ideas) and students often have a difficult time making connections between their learning and their own lives (the old "real world" versus the "ivory tower" problem).

Some ways of providing experiential learning opportunities:

Much of the concrete learning options can be done outside the class—provided that students have sufficient guidelines and instructions and that the experiences be processed in the classroom. Case studies, role playing, simulation exercises, interviewing projects, service learning, projects done in teams, design projects that have pragmatic use, data collection, assignments designed to have students record events and then reflect on them—all tend to facilitate the student's being able to make personal connections with the subject matter.

Diversity

The number of alternatives or perspectives that are encouraged or presented in the material. Diversity involves both quantity (the student often experiences process as involving learning *more* material) and quality (the student comes to perceive hierarchical differences with respect to complexity of material and learning tasks). Diversity is a double continuum of low to high with respect to amount and complexity.

Complexity (High)

A few highly complex concepts or tasks

Many highly complex concepts or tasks

(Low) ——— Quantity ——— (High)

A few fairly simple pieces of information

Many fairly simple pieces of information

(Low)

Some ways of providing diversity:
Most subject matter/college courses have a richness of diversity that needs to be sequenced so that students can come to understand the diversity that is there. Diversity is provided by variety in readings, points of view, assignments and methods of learning. It is also provided when a student is taught the hierarchical process tasks that are needed in order to perform the evaluation tasks in the course.

Personalism

The classroom is a community of scholars where it is safe to learn, where risk-taking is encouraged, where students learn rational dialogue and objective discussion, and where they learn to listen to one another and to evaluate ideas and concepts. Personalism includes the amount of interaction in the classroom, the amount of legitimacy given to helping students make connections between the subject matter, and the ways they are thinking about out-of-class issues. It does *not* include inappropriate self-disclosure. It varies from moderate to high on the continuum. (Sanford considers impersonal environments to be nondevelopmental.)

Some ways to foster personalism:
Discussions, assignments that help students make connections, availability of the instructor, comprehensive feedback, nonpunishing environment, environment characterized by objectivity, and by enthusiasm for learning and for the subject matter.

Copyright 1981 by L. Lee Knefelkamp.

Bibliography for Introduction

Banks, J. *Multiethnic Education: Theory and Practice* (3rd ed.). Boston: Allyn and Bacon, 1994.

Basseches, M. *Dialectical Thinking and Adult Development.* Norwood: Ablex Publishing Corporation, 1984.

Baxter-Magolda, M. B. *Knowing and Reasoning in College: Gender-Related Patterns in Students' Intellectual Development.* San Francisco: Jossey-Bass, 1992.

Belenky, M. F., Clinchy, B. M., Goldberger, N. R., and Tarule, J. M. *Women's Ways of Knowing: The Development of Self, Voice, and Mind.* New York: Basic Books, 1986.

Bennett, M. "Towards Ethnorelativism: A Developmental Model of Intercultural Sensitivity." In R. M. Page (ed.), *Cross Cultural Orientation: New Conceptualizations and Applications.* Lanham, MD: University Press of America, 1986.

Browning, D. *Generative Man: Psychoanalytic Perspectives.* New York: Dell Publishing, 1973.

Canon, K. *Katie's Canon: Womanism and the Soul of the Black Community.* New York: Continuum, 1995.

Chickering, A., and Associates. *The Modern American College: Responding to the New Realities of Diverse Students and a Changing Society.* San Francisco: Jossey-Bass, 1981.

Code, L. *What Can She Know? Feminist Theory and the Construction of Knowledge.* Ithaca: Cornell University Press, 1986.

Collins, P. H. *Black Feminist Thought.* New York: Routledge, 1990.

Daloz, L. *Effective Teaching and Mentoring: Realizing the Transformative Power of Adult Learning Experiences.* San Francisco: Jossey-Bass, 1986.

Evans, J. E., Forney, D. S., and Guido-DiBrito, F. *Student Development in College.* San Francisco: Jossey-Bass, 1998.

Fine, M. *Framing Dropouts: Notes on the Politics of an Urban Public High School.* Albany: SUNY Press, 1991.

Freire, P. *Education for Critical Consciousness.* New York: Continuum, 1973.

Gilligan, C. *In a Different Voice: Psychological Theory and Women's Development.* Cambridge: Harvard University Press, 1993. (Original work published in 1982.)

Goldberger, N., Tarule, J., Clinchy, B., and Belenky, M. *Knowledge, Difference, and Power: Essays Inspired by Women's Ways of Knowing.* New York: Basic Books, 1996.

Henderson, A. *Perry-isms.* Personal Manuscript, 1998.

Kegan, R. *The Evolving Self.* Cambridge: Harvard University Press, 1982.

King, P. M., and Kitchener, K. S. *Developing Reflective Judgment: Understanding and Promoting Intellectual Growth and Critical Thinking in Adolescents and Adults.* San Francisco: Jossey-Bass, 1994.

Knefelkamp, L. L. *Developmental Instruction: Fostering Intellectual and Personal Growth in College Students.* Unpublished Doctoral Dissertation, University of Minnesota, Minneapolis, 1974.

Knefelkamp, L. L. "Faculty and Student Development in the '80s: Renewing the Community of Scholars." In *Current Issues.* Washington, DC: The American Association of Higher Education, 1980. Also in: H. F. Owens, D. H. Witten, and W. R. Bailey (eds.), *College Student Personnel Administration: An Anthology.* Springfield, IL: Thomas, 1982, 371–391.

Knefelkamp, L. L., and Cornfeld, J. L. "Combining Student Stage and Style in the Design of Learning Environments." Paper presented at the annual meeting of the American College Personnel Association, Los Angeles, 1979.

Knefelkamp, L. L., and Slepitza, R. "A Cognitive-Developmental Model of Career Development: An Adaptation of the Perry Scheme." *Counseling Psychologist,* 1976, *6*(3), 53–58. Also in: C. A. Parker (ed.), *Encouraging Development in College Students.* Minneapolis: University of Minnesota Press, 1978.

Knefelkamp, L. L., Widick, C., and Parker, C. A. *Applying New Developmental Findings.* New Directions for Student Services, no. 4. San Francisco: Jossey-Bass, 1978.

Kolb, D. A. *Experiential Learning: Experience as the Source of Learning and Development.* Englewood Cliffs, NJ: Prentice Hall, 1981.

Mentkowski, M., Moeser, M., and Strait, M. J. *Using the Perry Scheme of Intellectual and Ethical Development as a College Outcomes Measure: A Process and Criteria for Judging Student Performance.* 2 vols. Milwaukee, WI: Alverno College Productions, 1983.

Minnich, E. K. *Transforming Knowledge.* Philadelphia: Temple University Press, 1990.

Moore, W. S. "The Learning Environment Preferences: Exploring the Construct Validity of an Objective Measure of the Perry Scheme of Intellectual Development." *Journal of College Student Development,* 1989, *30,* 504–514.

Parker, C. A. (ed.). *Encouraging Development in College Students.* Minneapolis: University of Minnesota Press, 1978.

Parks, S. *The Critical Years: The Young Adults Search for a Faith to Live By.* New York: HarperCollins, 1986.

Perry, W. G., Jr. *Forms of Intellectual and Ethical Development in the College Years: A Scheme.* New York: Holt, Rinehart, & Winston, 1970.

Perry, W. G., Jr. "Sharing in the Costs of Growth." In C. A. Parker (ed.), *Encouraging Development in College Students.* Minneapolis: University of Minnesota Press, 1978, 267–273.

Perry, W. G., Jr. "Cognitive and Ethical Growth: The Making of Meaning." In A. W. Chickering and Associates, *The Modern American College: Responding to the New Realities of Diverse Students and a Changing Society.* San Francisco: Jossey-Bass, 1981, 76–116.

Ruddick, S. *Maternal Thinking: Toward a Politics of Peace.* Boston: Beacon Press, 1995. (Original work published in 1989.)

Schlossberg, N. K. "Marginality and Mattering: Key Issues in Building Community." In D. C. Roberts (ed.), *Designing Campus Activities to Foster a Sense of Community* (New Directions for Student Services, no. 48). San Francisco: Jossey-Bass, 1989, 5–15.

Schlossberg, N. K., Waters, E. B., and Goodman, J. *Counseling Adults in Transition: Linking Practice with Theory.* (2nd ed.) New York: Springer Publishing Company, 1995.

Widick, C. *An Evaluation of Developmental Instruction in a University Setting.* Unpublished Doctoral Dissertation, University of Minnesota, Minneapolis, 1975.

Widick, C., Knefelkamp, L. L., and Parker, C. A. "The Counselor as a Developmental Instructor." *Counselor Education and Supervision,* 1975, *14,* 286–296.

Widick, C., and Simpson, D. "Developmental Concepts in College Instruction." In C. A. Parker (ed.), *Encouraging Development in College Students.* Minneapolis: University of Minnesota Press, 1978.

━ᴧᴧ━ Foreword

by Robert W. White

College teachers who believe they know their business, and developmental psychologists who believe they know theirs, both stand to learn more about their business from the research described in this book. The college years have been plentifully studied with respect to social and emotional development, but they have not, oddly enough, received basic research as a stage of intellectual growth. Does anything happen in the mind between the ages of 17 and 22 beyond a large intake of information, an enrichment of content? Is there any substance to the familiar claim that a liberal education means learning how to think? Is there during the college years any fundamental evolution of intellectual process comparable to the childhood stages described by Piaget or the levels of cognitive representation brought to light by Bruner and his associates? Perry shows us that there is indeed a basic progression in ways of thinking—in the forms of thought—during the course of the college experience. So important is this pattern of change that the teacher who hopes to nurture it must practice his art with responsive versatility. What is a freshman's meat may be a senior's poison.

This discovery runs counter to recently prevailing opinion. Research with intelligence tests suggested that the maturing of intellectual power was finished by the time a student entered college; never again would capacity be higher. Studies conducted by means of questionnaires seemed to signify that four years on campus produced little change in outlook, attitudes, and values. In spite of these dampening findings college enrollments shot upward and degrees became an obsession, but this popularity appeared to be a tribute less to the concept of liberal education than to the hope of processing young people to succeed in the upgraded occupations of a booming technological economy. None of these influences encouraged consideration of the college years as a period of inner personal growth. None suggested that there might be a true evolution in the forms of thought and in the related processes of valuation and commitment. Nor did any of these influences encourage the use of research methods capable of disclosing such developments.

Perry's method of investigation is so straightforward that its scientific virtue can easily be overlooked. It is based on the principle that if you want to study *how* people think, you must first get them to think. This is not easy; it sets an exacting specification which is poorly met by intelligence tests and not met at all by the ubiquitous questionnaire. Intelligence tests require thought, but generally in little spurts and restricted operations that are incapable of revealing its larger outlines. Questionnaires prohibit thought by setting up precast alternatives and forbidding the respondent to say how he would frame the question and qualify the answer. If college students were not so good-natured about taking psychological tests, they would probably reflect the evolution Perry describes by a progressive refusal to participate in the sloppy mental processes required by questionnaires. Perry rejects all shortcuts and time-saving devices in procuring his observations. He invites the students to think, taking their own time, doing it in their own way, choosing their own topics. And he listens. A tape recorder that is also listening guarantees that nothing will be forgotten.

The material collected in this way is subsequently analyzed, as the reader will discover, in great detail, using independent judges to protect the findings from observer bias. But this is familiar procedure; what is most unusual here is the sterling quality of the observations themselves. When psychologists fail as scientists, it is usually not because of what they have done with their data, but because they have skimped on the first step in scientific method—scrupulous observation—and are simply working with bad data. To obtain specimens of thinking, it is essential to create conditions favorable to that operation. The student subjects in this research felt that their thoughts about themselves and their world were of absorbing interest to the listener, that he became deeply involved in following them, that he would listen forever as they fumbled and backtracked and slowly discovered what they wanted to say, that he took them seriously and viewed them with respect. In this atmosphere they were moved to take themselves seriously and to think at their best. Perry's observations of thinking are thus of the real thing—not a laboratory model, not a disjointed set of elicited responses, but an involved, serious attempt to formulate and convey one's personal reflections. Obviously the conducive atmosphere could not have been artificially contrived. If the observations were repeated by an experimenter who assumed the role of a person showing absorbed interest, deep involvement, patience, and respect, his research could not be accepted as a replication. The sincerity of what the students said, which is obvious in the protocols, was possible only because of the sincerity of the listener. This book, therefore, in addition to its major findings with respect to intellectual development, teaches an enduring lesson in scientific observation when the thing to be observed is part of the deeply personal life of another human being.

Cambridge, Massachusetts
January 1970

—⁓— Preface

In this book we trace a path from adolescence into adulthood. We map this journey from the accounts of college students, and we illustrate its unfolding views of the world in the words of the students themselves. We assume that the discoveries and struggles they recount are relevant outside the boundaries of the college experience. Could it be that in a changing, pluralistic culture in which man's very knowledge and values are seen to be relative, the sequential challenges of this journey are essential steps in a person's maturation? We think so, and offer the question for the reader's judgment.

The development we trace takes place in the *forms* in which a person perceives his world rather than in the particulars or "content" of his attitudes and concerns. The advantage in mapping development in the *forms* of seeing, knowing, and caring lies precisely in their transcendence over content. It takes a long time to make and repeat a longitudinal study, even within the four college years. By the time it is complete, the times have changed. The particulars of content that were important to people when the study was made have been supplanted in vitality of interest by other matters. Yet the general pattern of personal development at the level of forms may be more enduring, manifesting itself through many generations of particulars. Indeed, the sequence of forms of personal development in a diverse culture may have its own logic and necessity.

We discovered the scheme of development presented in this book in the accounts of college students of the so-called "Silent Generation"—undergraduates during the fifties and early sixties. The question of the scheme's general relevance may therefore be directed toward the specific present: Is the development portrayed in this study still relevant to experience in these most unsilent times of activism, protest, reform, involvement, and confrontation—both peaceful and violent? We are frequently asked this question and we ask it of ourselves.

The question may arise from immediate urgency: Does this study help to "explain" the present unrest or help us understand what's going on and how to address it? Even in this topical focus of the question our answer is that we do think the findings of this study help us understand much of what people are saying and doing now. The times seem to have made only more vivid the distinction we found in our students' reports between commitment in an all-or-none world of moral absolutes and that more difficult and considered commitment in a relative world of contingent ethics. Self and integrity in these two worlds are very different, and an awareness of how the differences work is surely helpful in sensing how different people see the issues of today and invest their care in them.

Urgent as present relevance may be, it is nonetheless but part of that broader question: Can this scheme be considered a relatively enduring outline of major vicissitudes in human experience from adolescence into adulthood in a pluralistic culture? Does it help us understand the way that "modern man" finds to address his predicament in a relativistic world?

To this big question a solid answer could be derived only from repeated studies in diverse settings. It is a huge jump from one generation of students in Harvard and Radcliffe colleges to such universals.

And yet the question will be in the reader's mind as he explores this book—as it has been in ours. To whatever generation the reader feels he belongs, he will surely find that the students' experience we portray echoes his own life. I shall point, too, to striking parallels in studies made in settings very different from ours. And finally the scheme of development itself may carry its own plausibility. Indeed, its essentials may on occasion seem to reveal only the inevitability of the obvious, in the sense of "How could life be otherwise?" These feelings of recognition and plausibility must be honored; in most of life they are all one has to go on. But these feelings can be seductive of belief; they require the check of explicit limit and the balance of generous skepticism.

In speaking for all of us who took part in this study, I have therefore made its limits explicit in the first chapter, and thereafter I have attempted to convey the degree to which I feel myself to be reporting from within these limits or speculating beyond them. Skepticism and generosity remain in the purview of the reader.

The work reported in this monograph was supported by gifts from Sally Higginson Begley of New York and Irving Edison of St. Louis, and furthered by grants from the Laboratory of Social Relations of Harvard University.

For assistance in the evolution of this study, my colleagues and I acknowledge the generous advice of Robert W. White and the late Samuel A. Stouffer.

WILLIAM G. PERRY, JR.

⁓ The Author

William G. Perry, Jr., graduated from Harvard in 1935 with a B.A. degree in English and Greek, earned his Master's degree in English there five years later, and became a Harvard faculty member in 1947. That same year, he founded the Bureau of Study Counsel, a center for counseling and tutoring at Harvard College, where he and his staff counseled approximately four hundred students per year over the next thirty years. Perry became a full professor of education in the Harvard Graduate School of Education in 1965.

Through his work, Perry developed methods of mapping the cognitive and moral development of students that led to the original publication of *Forms of Intellectual and Ethical Development in the College Years: A Scheme* in 1970. He published a translation of Homer's *Iliad* with A. H. Chase in 1950, as well as numerous articles and essays over the years; one, "Examsmanship and the Liberal Arts," was included in the *Norton Anthology of American Literature.*

Mr. Perry passed away in January 1998.

CHAPTER ONE

Introduction and Résumé

We describe in this monograph an evolution in students' interpretation of their lives evident in their accounts of their experience during four years in a liberal arts college. The evolution consists of a progression in certain forms in which the students construe their experience as they recount it in voluntary interviews at the end of each year. These "forms" characterize the structures which the students explicitly or implicitly impute to the world, especially those structures in which they construe the nature and origins of knowledge, of value, and of responsibility.

"Form" and "structure," even when used at concrete visual levels, refer to concepts notoriously difficult to define. What we mean by "forms in which the students construe their experience" will become clear as the reader proceeds. However, both the abstract level of the "forms" and their relation to concrete "experience" may be suggested here by an illustration in which I shall assume the risk of caricature in the service of brevity:

> Let us suppose that a lecturer announces that today he will consider three theories explanatory of _____ (whatever his topic may

be). Student A has always taken it for granted that knowledge consists of correct answers, that there is one right answer per problem, and that teachers explain these answers for students to learn. He therefore listens for the lecturer to state which theory he is to learn.

Student B makes the same general assumptions but with an elaboration to the effect that teachers sometimes present problems and procedures, rather than answers, "so that we can learn to find the right answer on our own." He therefore perceives the lecture as a kind of guessing game in which he is to "figure out" which theory is correct, a game that is fair enough if the lecturer does not carry it so far as to hide things too obscurely.

Student C assumes that an answer can be called "right" only in the light of its context, and that contexts or "frames of reference" differ. He assumes that several interpretations of a poem, explanations of a historical development, or even theories of a class of events in physics may be legitimate "depending on how you look at it." Though he feels a little uneasy in such a kaleidoscopic world, he nonetheless supposes that the lecturer may be about to present three legitimate theories which can be examined for their internal coherence, their scope, their fit with various data, their predictive power, etc.

Whatever the lecturer then proceeds to do (in terms of his own assumptions and intent), these three students will make meaning of the experience in different ways which will involve different assessments of their own choices and responsibilities.

If, for the purposes at hand, this hypothetical lecture is allowed to represent a variety of human experiences, and if students A, B, and C are allowed to represent one and the same person at three stages of his life, the illustration will suggest what we mean by a "progression of forms in which a person construes his experience." Furthermore, such words as "progression," "evolution," or "development" (as distinct from the more generic "difference" or "change") would then refer to the fact that, as I have arranged them in the illustration, the three sets of assumptions are in the order of increasing scope. That is:

B's assumptions are of a form which includes the form of A's; and C's assumptions include, in a different and broader form, the forms of both A's and B's. This is evident in the different predicament of each student in the event that what the lecturer proceeds to do conforms to the expectations of one of the other students. For instance, student C, faced with the lecture expected by either A or B, would have little difficulty in interpreting the experience accurately without revising his basic assumptions about the nature of knowledge. His assumptions logically extend to the possibility that a given lecturer might "have the point of view that" there was but one correct answer. Student A, however, faced with the kind of lecture expected by B or by C, must either revise his basic assumptions or interpret the experience in some such way as, "The lecturer is talking all over the place" or "This just doesn't have anything to do with the course."

A person moving from the assumptions of student A to those of B to those of C may therefore be said to be involved in a development, not simply because his assumptions become "better" or more "true"—which is another question—but because the forms of his later assumptions subtend those of his earlier assumptions in a coherent manner, as cannot be said in reverse.

Of course a person will use a variety of forms in construing different areas of his experience at any given time. However, we made the assumption in this study that within this variety it is possible to identify a dominant form (or central tendency among the forms) in which the person is currently interpreting his experience. The outcome of the experiments which we included in the study support the validity of this assumption, especially in regard to those forms in which a person addresses knowing, valuing, and responsibility.

Since the sequence of these forms in our students' reports appears to us to manifest a logical order—an order in which one form leads to another through differentiations and reorganizations required for the meaningful interpretation of increasingly complex experience— our description itself takes its own second-order form as a pattern or scheme of development. In its full range the scheme begins with those simplistic forms in which a person construes his world in unqualified polar terms of absolute right-wrong, good-bad; it ends with those complex forms through which he undertakes to affirm his own commitments in a world of contingent knowledge and relative values. The intervening forms and transitions in the scheme outline the major steps through which the person, as evidenced in our students' reports, appears to extend his power to make meaning in successive confrontations with diversity.

The young person's discovery of diversity in other people's points of view is of course part of the folklore of adolescence and of "growing up" in the college years. It would seem, too, to be occurring earlier and earlier in life. The impact of this discovery has been directly and indirectly considered in many of the studies we cite in this report or list in its bibliography. The present study focuses on the vicissitudes of the experience over time, and finds in the shapes and sequences of these vicissitudes a major theme of personal growth.

Although we are necessarily limited to the college setting in both our data and the validation of our findings—and to the setting of a single college at that—we proffer our scheme of development for its more general implications. We presume its relevance to the understanding of the intellectual and ethical development of late adolescence in a pluralistic culture.

ORIGIN OF THE STUDY

In 1953 the staff of the Bureau of Study Counsel at Harvard College undertook to document the experience of undergraduates in Harvard and Radcliffe over their four years of college. In our daily counseling with students whose presenting concerns centered on their academic work, we had been impressed with the variety of the ways in which the students responded to the relativism which permeates the intellectual and social atmosphere of a pluralistic university. Among the students who consulted us, a few seemed to find the notion of multiple frames of reference wholly unintelligible.[1] Others responded with violent shock to their confrontation in dormitory bull sessions, or in their academic work, or both. Others experienced a joyful sense of liberation. There were also students, apparently increasing in number in the years following World War II, who seemed to come to college already habituated to a notion of man's knowledge as relative and who seemed to be in full exploration of the modes of thinking and of valuing consequent on this outlook.

---

[1]For example, in response to such an assignment as "compare the concepts of the tragic heroine exemplified by Antigone and Cordelia," these students would fail to perceive the direct object of the verb "compare" and would write comparisons of Antigone and Cordelia, as persons, against the background of a single, implicit frame of reference. We came to feel that persistent misperception of the form of such intellectual tasks, even after repeated explanations of them, could not be ascribed to intellective factors alone.

This variety in the way students first experienced their pluralistic environment seemed to us to be followed by an equally wide variety in the ways in which students went on to assimilate that experience. Although an occasional student would retreat, defeated, and some would detach themselves through a cynical exploitation of intellectual gamesmanship and moral opportunism, most seemed to go on to develop a personal style of commitment in both their thinking and their care.

We could hardly suppose that these issues were peculiar to the experience of students who came to consult us. Nor indeed did we suppose that these were parochial phenomena limited to the environs of Harvard University. We did suppose that the pervasiveness and inescapability of the impact of relativism on college students might well be a development of the twentieth century, and we have since documented the supposition. Our documentation is limited to Harvard College, but the implications for other colleges with a diverse student body and a pluralistic intellectual outlook seem obvious.

The change in the outlook of the faculty is evident in the character of the intellectual tasks set for students on final examinations. The graph shown in Figure 1 is based on the final examinations for courses in History, Government, English Literature, and Foreign Literatures enrolling the largest number of freshmen in Harvard College at intervals from 1900 to 1960. The assumption made is that the kind of operation called for by an examination question expresses the examiner's conception of knowledge of his subject. Analysis was performed by sorting questions into categories, with appropriate tests of reliability. The graph presents the percentage of weight on each examination given to questions requiring considerations in more than one frame of reference, that is, relativism.

Figure 1 documents a revolution in the very definition of knowledge confronted by freshmen in a college of liberal arts in this century. The new relativism of knowledge has inevitably been accompanied by a relative address to values. In Henry Adams's words: "The movement from unity to multiplicity, between 1200 and 1900, was unbroken in sequence and rapid in acceleration. Prolonged one generation longer, it would require a new social mind" (Adams, 1931). The rate of acceleration has been greater than perhaps even Adams foresaw, and not one but two generations have passed.

For the college student, the confrontation with pluralism of values has become inescapable, not only in his courses but in his daily life with his peers. Cultural diversity in the student body has become a deliberate policy of selection in nonsectarian colleges of liberal arts.

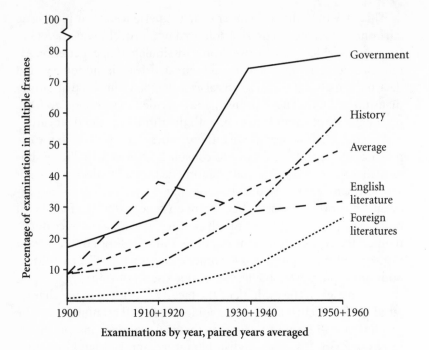

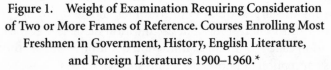

Examinations by year, paired years averaged

Figure 1.   Weight of Examination Requiring Consideration
of Two or More Frames of Reference. Courses Enrolling Most
Freshmen in Government, History, English Literature,
and Foreign Literatures 1900–1960.*

In the instance of Harvard College, the freshman class in 1900 consisted of 537 students drawn from 175 schools. In 1960 the freshman class of 1,082 was drawn from 499 schools. In 1900, 45 percent of entering students came from outside Massachusetts; in 1960, 72 percent. It could hardly be said any longer, as Adams had said of his classmates in the 1850s, that the students had nothing to give each other because they had been "brought up together under like conditions" (Adams, 1931). The same movement toward diversity is evident in most insti-

---

*Since these categories of courses deliberately ignore major changes in curriculum, especially the introduction of the program in General Education in the mid-forties, the graph portrays the minimum of the range of the change. With the large courses in General Education included, the average of relativistic questions confronting freshmen in 1950–60 is estimated at 75 to 80 percent.

tutions of higher learning in the country, and extends to socioeconomic as well as geographical criteria.

Such diversity, as faced by a student in a college of liberal arts, would seem to be unique in Western society today only in its concentration and intensity. The increased mobility of the population at large, together with the new mass media, make the impact of pluralism part of experience in the society as a whole. The growing person's response to pluralism in thought and values, and indeed his capacity to generate pluralism himself, are therefore critical to the destiny of a democracy. Whether he responds productively rather than destructively may be up to him in the end, but society may surely nourish the prospect of a productive outcome through an understanding of the learning and the courage the development entails.

This understanding must derive from systematic descriptions of the experience through time—descriptions of its characteristic stages and its major points of choice between fragmentation and integration, alienation and involvement. Several such descriptions will be required, because no one system can encompass the complexities. The several extant systems of conceptualizing child development have shed light on the early years, and even on adolescence. The extension of inquiry into the transition from youth to maturity has only recently begun. However much personal development in the later years may depend on the vicissitudes of earlier experience, it may still be examined in its own right for its normative characteristics. The college years provide an advantageous setting for the initial sweeps of such exploration.

It was in the light of these considerations regarding present-day liberal education and personal development that we set out to learn about the experience of students other than those who came to us for counsel. Our initial intention was purely descriptive, and not even systematically so. We planned simply to collect accounts of the experience of 20 or 30 students as they might tell us about it in open interviews at the end of each of their four years in college. We hoped to be able to reduce these documents to brief, readable portraits expressive of the variety we saw in students' educational experience. We thought that such documents might be interesting in their own right and also suggestive of issues relevant for more systematic research.

PROCEDURE

We started out, then, to illustrate the variety in students' response to the impact of intellectual and moral relativism. Wishing to secure this variety in a small sample of students, we felt it best to obtain the largest possible range between those freshmen bringing with them a strong preference for dualistic, right-wrong thinking and those bringing with them a strong affinity for more qualified, relativistic, and contingent thinking. We considered such differences as a manifestation of differences in "personality" (in keeping with much psychological thinking of the time). It had not yet occurred to us that it might be more fruitful, at least for our purpose, to consider such differences primarily as expressions of stages in the very developments we were setting out to explore.

Starting, then, from the research on the authoritarian personality (Adorno et al., 1950) and G. G. Stern's work at Chicago using the *Inventory of Beliefs* (Stern, 1953), we devised a measure called *A Checklist of Educational Views* (CLEV). In preliminary trials in 1953 to 1954, the measure promised to identify students along the dimension we desired.

We administered CLEV to a random sample of 313 freshmen in the fall of 1954 and to the same students in the spring of 1955. On the basis of their scores on the measure, we then sent invitations to 55 students, 31 of whom volunteered to tell us in interviews about their college experience. Among these freshmen were some who had scored at the extreme of dualistic thinking, some at the extreme of contingent thinking, some from the mean, and some who had changed their scores markedly from fall to spring.

Our interviews with these students in late May and June of each of their college years resulted in 98 tape-recorded interviews, including 17 complete four-year records. We conducted the interviews themselves in as open-ended a way as possible so as to avoid dictating the structure of a student's thought by the structure of our questions. That is, we asked only for what seemed salient in the student's own experience, beginning interviews with an invitation of the form: "Would you like to say what has stood out for you during the year?" After the student's general statements, we then asked: "As you speak of that, do any particular instances come to mind?" (See pp. 19 ff.)

Perhaps as a consequence of these procedures, the variety in the form and content of the students' reports appeared at first to exceed our expectations and to exclude any possibility of orderly comparison. However, *we gradually came to feel that we could detect behind the individuality of the reports a common sequence of challenges to which each student addressed himself in his own particular way.* For most of the students, their address to these challenges as they experienced them in their academic work, in the social life of the college, and in their extracurricular activities or employment seemed to represent a coherent development in the forms in which they functioned intellectually, in the forms in which they experienced values, and in the forms in which they construed their world. The reports of those few students who did not evidence this development seemed meaningful as descriptions of deflection from some challenge in the sequence. In this sequence, tendencies toward dualistic thinking and tendencies toward contingent thinking now appeared less as the personal styles we had originally conceived them to be and more saliently as characteristics of stages in the developmental process itself.[2]

At this point we radically extended the purpose of our study and committed ourselves to experimental as well as descriptive procedures. We undertook (1) to obtain a larger sample of students' reports of their experience over their four years of college, (2) to spell out the sequence we had detected in the students' reports to form an articulated developmental scheme, and finally (3) to submit this scheme to tests of validity.

To obtain a second and enlarged sample, we sent invitations to 50 freshmen from the Class of '62 and 104 freshmen from the Class of '63. These freshmen were drawn from a random third of their classmates who had filled out a revised form of the *Checklist of Educational Views* in fall and spring. In this instance, however, we ignored their scores on this instrument and selected those we would invite through a random procedure. A total of 109 students responded, resulting later, in June of 1963, in 366 interviews, including 67 complete four-year reports.

As we were assembling this second set of volunteers, we undertook to describe more precisely the evolving sequence of challenges which we had discerned as the common theme in the accounts of our first informants. We first spelled out the development in first-person phenomenological terms—that is, in the words that might be used by an imaginary "modal" student moving along the center line of that generalized sequence of challenges and resolutions which we thought we

---

[2]The developmental aspect of these tendencies was observed by other researchers of the period (Loevinger, 1959), (Sanford, 1956, 1962), (Harvey, Hunt, & Schroder, 1961).

saw behind all the variegated reports of our individual volunteers (see description, Chapter 3). We then described in abstract terms, from the outside, the structure of each of the major stages (i.e., the more enduring or stable forms in which the students construed the world). At the same time, we attempted to explicate those transitional steps (i.e., the more conflicted and unstable forms) which articulate the development from stage to stage, transforming one structure to the next. With the main theme roughed out, we then traced around it the major variations which our data suggested to us, or which our scheme suggested through its own logic. Among these variations were included those deflections and regressions which we had interpreted as "opting out," or alienation from the course of maturation presumed in the scheme.

This full description of the scheme appears in Chapter 5, illustrated by excerpts from the students' reports. The following brief outline suggests its nature.

MAIN LINE OF DEVELOPMENT

Position 1:   The student sees the world in polar terms of we-right-good vs. other-wrong-bad. Right Answers for everything exist in the Absolute, known to Authority[3] whose role is to mediate (teach) them. Knowledge and goodness are perceived as quantitative accretions of discrete rightnesses to be collected by hard work and obedience (paradigm: a spelling test).

Position 2:   The student perceives diversity of opinion, and uncertainty, and accounts for them as unwarranted confusion in poorly qualified Authorities or as mere exercises set by Authority "so we can learn to find The Answer for ourselves."

Position 3:   The student accepts diversity and uncertainty as legitimate but still *temporary* in areas where Authority "hasn't found The Answer yet." He supposes Authority grades him in these areas on "good expression" but remains puzzled as to standards.

---

[3]The implication of upper-case initials is probably clear enough in context here. Their particular denotations throughout this monograph, especially when paired against lower-case initials (e.g., Authority vis-à-vis authority), are defined in the Glossary prior to the foldout Chart of Development at the end of this book.

Position 4: (*a*) The student perceives legitimate uncertainty (and therefore diversity of opinion) to be extensive and raises it to the status of an unstructured epistemological realm of its own in which "anyone has a right to his own opinion," a realm which he sets over against Authority's realm where right–wrong still prevails, or (*b*) the student discovers qualitative contextual relativistic reasoning as a special case of "what They want" within Authority's realm.

Position 5: The student perceives all knowledge and values (including authority's) as contextual and relativistic and subordinates dualistic right–wrong functions to the status of a special case, in context.

Position 6: The student apprehends the necessity of orienting himself in a relativistic world through some form of personal Commitment (as distinct from unquestioned or unconsidered commitment to simple belief in certainty).

Position 7: The student makes an initial Commitment in some area.

Position 8: The student experiences the implications of Commitment, and explores the subjective and stylistic issues of responsibility.

Position 9: The student experiences the affirmation of identity among multiple responsibilities and realizes Commitment as an ongoing, unfolding activity through which he expresses his life style.

CONDITIONS OF DELAY, DEFLECTION, AND REGRESSION

Temporizing: The student delays in some Position for a year, exploring its implications or explicitly hesitating to take the next step.

Escape: The student exploits the opportunity for detachment offered by the structures of Positions 4 and 5 to deny responsibility through passive or opportunistic alienation.

Retreat: The student entrenches in the dualistic, absolutistic structures of Position 2 or 3.

Although such a brief outline cannot express the articulation or coherence of the development traced by the scheme, it does suggest the level of generality of those forms in which we thought we saw a coherent evolution in the students' reports. In their free interviews the students had of course rarely spoken explicitly at such an abstract level. The distance was necessarily considerable between such general philosophical forms and the variegated, concrete details of the students' talk (e.g., a student's account of a conversation with his adviser or another's description of his experience in an extracurricular activity). We could bridge this distance, in respect to most of our data, only by inference. Any such inferential construct as our scheme, drawn from such varied data, faces the question of being no more than the observer's way of seeing an order where it does not exist. We therefore endeavored to reduce our scheme from its broadly discursive expression into a representation sufficiently condensed, rigorous and denotative to be susceptible to a test of reliable use by independent observers. The results of these efforts were (*a*) a glossary of twenty words to which we assigned specific meanings, and (*b*) a two-dimensional map or chart delineating and coding sequential forms of the developmental scheme itself. (This Glossary and Chart of Development appear at the end of this book.)

We were then ready to present independent observers with random samples of students' reports and to ask them to identify that point on the developmental scheme which they felt best represented the dominating or modal form among the structurings of the world evident in each report. The extent to which the several observers' placements or "ratings" might agree with one another, beyond the level of chance, would then be the measure of the validity of "existence" of our scheme in the students' accounts of their experience.

Such a test would at best certify the relevance of our scheme in respect to the accounts of students from which we had derived it. However, the investment required to carry out this limited assessment promised to involve our full resources, and we postponed any testing of our conviction that the relevance of the scheme of development extended into the experience of people in this general age group in wide areas of the society.

The study up to this point of actual test constitutes the subject of this monograph: Chapter 2 will summarize our sampling procedures and describe in full the kind of interview in which the students gave their reports; Chapter 3 will describe the experience of the development through an informal essay; Chapter 4 will describe our solutions to the problems involved in conceptualizing the development as a scheme; Chapter 5 will present and illustrate the scheme itself; and Chapter 6 will consider its significance for issues in education. As for the subsequent tests, a summary of their nature and outcome appears directly below. These tests were supported by Cooperative Research

Contract SAE–8973, Project No. 5–0825. Their full details and the statistical procedures used in their analysis are reported in the Final Report for that Project.[4]

For the tests, we assembled in the fall of 1963 a group of six judges—graduate students in English and in Comparative Literature. We first gave these judges a copy of the Chart of Development, a sample interview protocol, and a manual. The manual contained a general, nontechnical essay describing the study (see Chapter 3 of this book, pp. 33 ff.), the Glossary of twenty terms to which we ascribed special definitions, observations on the task of rating interviews in relation to the Chart, and a sample rating form. After the judges had studied these materials, we met with them for one hour of discussion. We then assigned them in the subsequent months a series of tasks. The tasks and their results were as follows:

RATING OF FOUR-YEAR PROTOCOLS

We first presented the judges with complete, unedited transcripts of four-year sequences of the interviews with 20 students, one student's set at a time. Ten of the students were selected at random from the sample of the Class of '58, ten from the sample of the Classes of '62 and '63. Each judge made his ratings independently of the other judges and rated all of the four interviews in a set. After rating each set, the judges met with us to hand in their rating sheets and then to discuss their experience. These discussions helped to sharpen definitions of terms, but we made no attempt to develop a consensus through revision of the independent ratings previously made.

Assuming that our scheme of development had no validity at all, our null hypothesis read: "The judges will agree in matching interviews with Positions on the Chart at a level of agreement not exceeding that attributable to chance."

---

[4]W. G. Perry, Jr., *Patterns of Development in Thought and Values of Students in a Liberal Arts College: A Validation of a Scheme* (U.S. Dept. of Health, Education, and Welfare, Office of Education, Bureau of Research, Final Report, Project No. 5–0825, Contract No. SAE–8973, April 1968). The Report includes also a detailed analysis of the student samples and a study of the *Checklist of Educational Views.*

In the test of this hypothesis, the mean estimated reliability of the mean rating for individual interviews for each of the four years was found to be, respectively, +0.966, +0.875, +0.872, and 0.916. The probability of these levels of agreement occurring by chance is less than .0005 for the lowest.

The range of the reliabilities of the mean ratings of the four interviews of individual students was between .815 and .978. The narrowness of this range warrants the conclusion that the judges were able to agree reliably in relating the scheme to the report of *all* students in the sample.

RATING OF SINGLE INTERVIEWS

Since the agreement among the judges exceeded our expectations for the rating of such complex materials, we wondered if the judges' knowledge of the student's year in college was affecting their estimate of his degree of development. This possibility was contradicted by the range in the Positions agreed upon for different students in any one college year, but we nonetheless undertook the test of giving the judges single interviews from which we had deleted cues which might identify the student's college year. Though the judges proved unable to guess, beyond the level of chance, which college year a given interview represented, their agreement about the student's Position on the Chart remained at the level reached with four-year sequences.

RATING OF EXCERPTS

We then examined the kinds of statements in the interviews which had been noted by the judges as contributing most significantly to their rating of interviews. One judge and the chief investigator then excerpted from other interviews 40 statements which seemed similar in character to those which the judges had noted. These excerpts ran from one sentence to a page in length. The rating agreed upon for each excerpt by the one judge and the chief investigator was then entered as the rating of a single judge, and the remaining judges were asked to rate each excerpt independently. Agreement remained at its customary level.

This finding confirmed our notions about some of the evidence through which the judges developed their ratings in complete interviews. However, its immediate usefulness was in validating the use of excerpts in communicating to others the nature of the developmental scheme itself. Alone, the abstract conceptualization of the scheme fails to communicate because it is disembodied of phenomenal experience. Complete records of students' experience are uneconomical for communication because of their particularity and their sheer mass. The illustrative excerpt is therefore the most efficient rhetorical vehicle, but it is properly suspect of all the sins of selective citation.

The full exposition of the scheme in this report (Chapter 5) will rely heavily upon excerpts. The agreement of the judges in rating excerpts, though it cannot guarantee the integrity of such exposition, does demonstrate that the various structurings constituting the scheme can be illustrated in excerpts which are, by consensus, representative.

RATING OF CONDENSED FOUR-YEAR REPORTS

In another test of means of communication, we examined the validity of reducing full-length transcripts to relatively short, readable portraits.

To test the integrity of such condensed reports, three judges rated the complete form and three rated the condensed form of four students' four-year reports. The results indicated that the condensed version gave a faithful portrayal for the purposes of rating, with the exception of the tendency of the edited form to exaggerate the simplicity of the impression conveyed of a student's outlook in his freshman year. These results encouraged our hope that such condensed, readable reports would make useful public documents—a hope with which we had begun our study ten years before.

LIMITS OF THE FINDINGS

These experimental validations apply only within the most stringent limits of our study. The major limits are dictated by the following conditions:

1. The subjects were student volunteers in a single college during the years 1954 to 1963.

2. The investigators abstracted the developmental scheme from oral reports given by the students during annual interviews with the investigators themselves.[5]

3. In testing the validity of the scheme the judges performed operations in relation to the data from which the scheme was derived.

SIGNIFICANCE OF THE STUDY

Within its own strictest limits the study demonstrates the possibility of assessing, in developmental terms, abstract structural aspects of knowing and valuing in intelligent late-adolescents. Substantively the study confirms the validity of one scheme of such development, showing it to be reliably evident as a theme common to all students' reports sampled. The developments traced in the scheme are of construal rather than of content, of contextual configuration rather than of linear increment, and involve what might be called the growth of conceptual hierarchies. Of special interest with respect to the advanced levels of the scheme is the assessment of the evolution of personal commitments, again in terms of structuring activity and style rather than simply of content.

The findings confirm also the feasibility of illustrating such developments, at the level of the data itself, through excerpts and highly condensed student reports.

Since our experiments demonstrate only the coherence between our scheme and our own data, any consideration of the further "significance" of the scheme requires that we move from demonstration to new hypothesis, that is, from the context of science to the context of judgment. Here the possibilities are vast. In education, such a developmental scheme would promise relevance to procedures of selection, curriculum design, classroom teaching and advising. Such considerations are fair game only when the reader has the basis for his own judgment, and I shall address the matter in the final chapter.

---

[5]The question of the degree of interviewer influence may be partially answered by the fact that we developed the first outlines of our scheme *after* completing our interviews of the sample from the Class of '58 and *before* interviewing the sample from the Classes of '62 and '63. No difference appeared in the reliability of the rating of interviews from the two samples. (For a discussion of interviewing procedures and interviewer influences, see pp. 19 ff.)

CHAPTER TWO

Context of Students' Reports

THE STUDENTS

The *First Sample* of students consisted of 31 from the Class of '58, 27 from Harvard, 4 from Radcliffe. The *Second Sample* of students consisted of 30 from the Class of '62 and 79 from the Class of '63, 85 from Harvard, 24 from Radcliffe. Interviewing of these students resulted in 464 interviews and 84 complete four-year sequences.

With the few exceptions which will be noted, the illustrations and validation in this study will draw on the reports of the men. However, we did include two complete four-year reports by women in the judges' experiments. After rating these reports the judges engaged in a lively discussion of the differences between men and women, especially in the experience of Commitment. They concluded, however, that for the purposes of the study these differences were evident in the content and manner of the students' reports rather than in those structurings of experience relevant to the developmental scheme. The sample is of course very small, but the actual ratings provide no reason to question the judges' statement that they experienced no significant difference in locating men's and women's reports on the Chart of Development.

As noted in the Introduction, the invitations to the First Sample of volunteers were sent out on the basis of their scores on the *Checklist of Educational Views,* whereas invitations for the Second Sample were sent out randomly. However, both samples appear, on conventional criteria, to be reasonably representative of their populations. Exceptions in the First Sample consisted of a somewhat larger proportion of commuting students and a slightly lower average grade prediction as compared to the class as a whole.[1] The rate of volunteering in response to invitation was 56 percent in the First Sample, 71 percent in the Second. It was impossible to investigate directly the relevant correlates of an unwillingness to volunteer. We did give our judges, without identification, single interviews from the reports of "volunteers *manqué*"—students who did not complete their four-year sequence. The judges rated these interviews against the scheme with the same reliability as those from students completing their four-year reports. Though this test itself does not provide a firm inference that the judges would have found reports of nonvolunteers equally relevant to the scheme, it does add to the confidence we derive from our counseling and informal talks with many nonvolunteers. For us the crucial question is whether nonvolunteers would have revealed more instances of alienation. Alienated students were found by the judges to be rare in our sample; however, these few seemed quite as ready to talk with us as the rest who were fully involved in growth. Perhaps they were not so deeply alienated but that they felt it important to have their experience on record. In any case, even if we suppose the students in our sample to represent only that proportion of students who would volunteer for such a study as ours, their reports stand in remarkable contrast to current notions, national and local, about the alienation of youth in these decades. (See discussion of Commitment, pp. 38 ff. and 149 ff.)

The invitation asking students to volunteer ran as follows for the First Sample:

Dear Mr. _____
    You will remember having helped us by filling out our "Checklist of Educational Views"[2] in September and again in May. We are much

---

[1]Detailed analysis of the samples appears in Perry, *op. cit.*

[2]The Second Sample had filled out CLEV as simply one part of a quite unconventional test of reading skill (*Harvard University Reading Test,* Bureau of Study Counsel, unpublished) taken by all freshmen in September. The invitations to the Second Sample read accordingly.

in need of your help again and hope that out of an interest in education here you will feel it worthwhile to assist.

Now that the year is almost over, we would like to talk with a number of students about their experience at college. We feel that students with different views about education may experience their years in college in very different ways and that it is vital to know about the different paths of this experience. We are writing to you because we feel that you can contribute to this understanding. Would you come to the Bureau to talk with us?

(There followed a paragraph about making an appointment.)

INTERVIEWING

Our address to the students when they first came to us, and our ways of talking with them thereafter, defined for them the context to which they spoke. An understanding of our procedures is therefore crucial to an assessment of the data the students gave.

Our original purpose in the study—to obtain from students their own reports of their college experience, in their own terms—demanded that we leave the student as free as possible to speak from his own ways of perceiving himself and his world. We did suppose that in even the most "open" interview the students would speak to some extent in such areas and forms as they expected to be of interest to researchers in an office called the Bureau of Study Counsel. However, exploratory trials with students from the Class of '57 had suggested that if we addressed the students appropriately in the early minutes of interview, almost all of them would abandon stereotyped expectations about our expectations in favor of a candid exploration of what was important to them in their own experience.[3]

The procedure we finally adopted made the beginning moments of an interview socially awkward. We found, however, that if we openly

---

[3]The students' expectations about our interests must have been shaped to some extent by their impressions of the purpose of the *Checklist of Educational Views* (or, for the Second Sample, Part V of the Reading Test), which they had filled out under our auspices. So far as we could judge, however, these impressions were diverse, and their effects in actual interview quite transient.

acknowledged this stress and asked the students' cooperation in bearing with it, the experience appeared to contribute an advantage, not only to the study but to the students as well. We feel that our way of addressing the issues at stake in these moments, beyond being crucial to the data of this study, may have general relevance for the conduct of any inquiry in which the primary purpose is to allow the respondent freedom to speak from his own ways of finding meaning in his life.

The researcher who wishes to conduct "open" interviews with subjects whom he has asked to contribute their time must confront at the outset the subjects' sensible expectation that a researcher knows what he wants to know. The subject presents himself and expects to be asked reasonably precise questions. The social initiative is therefore with the researcher, who finds himself under considerable pressure to specify the topics to be considered, to indicate the order of their importance, and to suggest, at least as a takeoff point, the terms and forms in which his respondent may most profitably discuss them. In research where the primary concern is the respondent's own style of giving meaning to his experience, these are the very matters the researcher most wishes to leave unbiased by the forms imposed by his own initiatives. The dilemma is similar to that of the "client-centered" therapist or counselor to whom a troubled person comes expecting to be asked expert diagnostic questions in accordance with ordinary medical (and educational) convention. The researcher's difficulties are compounded, however, because his respondent usually is possessed of no strong motive, such as personal distress, for abandoning his expectations and undertaking the initiatives of conversation himself.

In our own trial efforts we therefore first experimented with questions we hoped would be adequate for the students and sufficiently general to minimize the imposition of structures—for example: "What do you think has influenced you most during the year?" or "Do you think you have changed in any way?" "Are there ways in which you look at things differently than you did a year ago?" We discovered, however, that some students found it an effort to fit their thinking into even such general structures as those implied by concepts like "influence" or "change" and that their replies seemed wooden and trite. One student seemed unable to produce even a stereotyped answer. We pressed him: "For instance, when you go home, do you think your parents will notice any difference in you?" After a long pause, he replied, "Well, . . . maybe I have put on a little weight."

For us this particular defeat was final, especially in the light of the richness of what this very student had to say when he finally broke free to speak in his own way of perceiving his experience. We settled thereafter on a single form of opening: we first welcomed the student, restated our interest in hearing from students about their own experience, and asked permission (with assurance of anonymity) to record. We then said, in the general form developed by Merton (Merton, Fiske, & Kendall, 1952): "Why don't you start with whatever stands out for you about the year?"

"Stands out" does imply a structure, that of salience, or figure against ground. Klein, Gardner, and others have shown that people differ in the degree of salience with which they perceive and remember, some tending to heighten saliences, others to level them (Klein, 1951, 1958, 1960; Gardner, 1953, 1962; Gardner et al., 1959; Gardner, Jackson, & Messick, 1960; Witkin, 1953, 1958; Witkin et al., 1962). Nevertheless we felt it safe to assume some sort of figure-ground structure as a universal in human perception (cf. Rubin, 1958). Indeed, even those students whose first reaction was of the kind, "Well I don't know that anything stands out particularly," came in time to think of experiences which they felt to be important to them, or more important than others.

It was proffering the students time to get started that caused the social stress. We would steadfastly refuse their requests for more specific questions, acknowledging that our refusal made it hard work for them, but that anything else would substitute our guesses for their sense of what was relevant in their experience. "It would be better for us both to feel a bit awkward and just to take our time, if we can bear it together!"

With only one student out of all our volunteers did we feel that humanity required the abandonment of this position. For the rest, the sheer surprise of the experience seemed to convey, better than anything we could have said, the genuineness of our interest in hearing from them in their own terms. This very interest then seemed to compensate them for the effort required in taking the lead. Thereafter, our recognition of what they were saying usually provided all the resonance they needed to support their thinking in its natural flow. Occasionally, in a pause after some general statement, we could ask, "As you mentioned that, were you thinking of some specific incidents, or do any examples come to mind?" (cf. Merton, Fiske, & Kendall, 1952). Once again, "thinking of" and "come to mind" seemed to function as recognizable universals with a minimum of structural bias. Then, when a given vein had run dry, we could ask again: "Well, now, do any other things stand out for you?"

To illustrate this kind of conversation in its formative minutes, I have taken the following transcript of a freshman interview quite at random from the file of those rated by the judges in their experiments. It may be considered representative, except that the initial moments are less awkward than usual, perhaps because the interview provided the student with a legitimate opportunity to talk with someone about what had been for him a rather painful year. In any case, the interviewer's willingness to share in the awkwardness of getting started did not require a statement beyond that communicated by his manner. The transcript endeavors to express something of the rhythms of the conversation as well as content: words in slashes, for example, /Yeah, yeah/, are those of one participant speaking in the background of the major speaker's voice; a series of three dots, thus, . . . , represents a pause, suspension, or break in thought somewhat greater than that expressed by a comma, but less pronounced than that designated explicitly by "(*pause*)":

I.   You let me know if you mind if I record, O.K.? Sit down? /Thanks/ Well, as you gathered, I guess, from the letter, we thought maybe you'd be willing to come in and sort of look back, and /Yeah/ tell us how the year went, and how you feel about it . . .

S.   Uhhm. Well, it's a subject I'd like to talk on, actually. I suppose that every freshman wants to shoot off about their freshman year! . . . Good things, bad things, I guess. /Yes/ I don't know, I . . . I really don't know where to start. (*Pause*)

I.   Well, wherever, I think, sort of-ah, looking back over what sorts of things sort of *stood out*, in one way or another as you . . . ah . . . (*Pause*)

S.   Well, I know that-ah it was sort-ah . . . of unwise for me to make any decisions about classes or courses to take before I came here. Actually-ah I had a tentative list of courses, and the second day I was here, everything was completely changed. I, my ideas, values, everything was *completely* changed the minute I started talking to roommates and other people in the dorm, and so forth.

I.   Sort of right away, some sort of a change?

S.   Well, it's just that you hear other people talking about how everyone is going to take Hum. 3 or Hum. 4, or whatever it is, so, but-ah . . . your values change because other people are doing other things, and you sort of like to follow along. But you're not sure exactly what *will* be best. /Sure, sure/ And-ah, well that, that's the first thing actually, it's really-ah . . . oh, I don't know . . . not necessarily *unwise* to make-ah decisions before you come here, at least to sort of leave your mind wide open.

I.   You find this sort of true in . . . courses?

S.   Yes-ah . . . primarily in courses, I should say. I mean, those are the big decisions to make, right off the bat . . . ah, I think-ah . . . at . . . at the beginning of the year, you have sort of a, a feeling of . . . oh, I don't know . . . hopelessness, I think, because-ah, you get the first, the first assignments-ah, homework assignments, that is-ah you get a five-hour assignment in every course for the week, and you just don't know *when* you're going to do it all. But-ah . . . I think, the, after the first month or so, you, you just, you just don't worry about it any more, and-ah everything seems to work out mir-, miraculously, most of the time. Ah . . . I found, I found that in the beginning of the year-ah . . . it was, everything was continually oppressing you—"When am I going to get this done, and when that done?" /Yeah/ But-ah . . . after a while—ah you just don't . . . feel that way. I just let things come as they come, /Yeah/ and, if you don't get an assignment done on time, you don't worry about it, 'cause you know you'll make it up sooner or later, and if you have to work a little extra hard over a weekend, that takes care of it /Uhuh/ . . . But-ah . . . I think, I don't know-ah, really, in the beginning of the year there is quite a feeling of hopelessness . . . ah . . .

I.   Sort of snowed to start out with . . . ?

S.   Yes, exactly. Ah (*long pause*) I was, I just wondered if there was some, some way of pub-, having some sort of pamphlet published for freshmen. I don't know, just little bits of advice, because . . . (*Pause*)

I.   What sort of specific things come to mind on that? I mean, the, the, what if, if-ah . . . say, let's say, arbitrarily that we have such a thing in mind /Uhuh/, what sorts of things would come to your mind, as the sort of things that would help on that?

S.   Well, this *Crimson Confi Guide* on courses is sort of a lifesaver at the beginning of the year. I mean, you don't know anything about courses, or just what some other people comment /Sure/ on what they're taking. /(*I. offers cigarette*) Join?/ No thank you. Ah, and that really helps out quite a bit. . . . I think-ah study procedures especially might be good-ah, I still don't think I've found the, the key in studying for my Hum. course . . . I find it rather difficult.

I.   That one has hit pretty hard, somehow?

S.   Yeah, I, I think that I've got everything else up pretty good. I, I just, I have a set pattern for going about study for the course, tak-ing notes, and so forth, but I *still* don't know how to, how to hit this course . . . and I thought perhaps that-ah there might be . . . ah, some sort of study guides, or just a topical list, say. I mean, everyone knows what you're supposed to do: you're supposed to study with good light, /Yeah/ you're supposed to study quiet, and so forth, and . . . ah, ask yourself questions, while you're reading. /Yeah/ But . . . if someone *says* it to you, it, it seems to have greater emphasis, and you take greater stock in it than . . . if it was just sort of implicit in your mind. (*Pause*)

I.   Uhuh. Sort of, some sort of a handle there, you feel that-ah, it looked a lot in the beginning as if-ah it was just big and no handle . . . ?

S.   Exactly. /Uhuh/ Ah, I don't think that it feels that way right now, but I *still* don't know how to go about this one course, see. /Uhuh/ Ah . . . it might be significant that I'm not getting a very good mark in this course, and my other marks are fairly good.[4] (*Pause*)

I.   The others are up, and this, in this course, you, you don't feel as though you've found the handle, more or less, that you have spotted in others?

S.   Well-ah, I think this, this course is really a good course, that's the bad part of it. . . . I, I think the reading list is probably the best that I've had /Uhuh/, the lectures are good, and so forth. But I, I, if you don't get a good mark every now and then, it sort of sours the

---

[4]His other courses are those elementary sciences required in a pre-medical program.

course for you (*Chuckle*) /Yeah/ I think that's the prime thing-ah
... (*Pause*) Oh, I don't know, the other thing I can remember is
that-ah ... (*suddenly raises voice*) *I think that pre-meds are the-ah,
the greatest group of cut-throats I've ever met in my life.*

I.   You sort of found that here, too?

S.   Definitely. The spirit of competition is-ah ... (*he goes on to
illustrate*).

In these opening moments the student has named the major foci
of experience on which he will expand for the remainder of the interview: his feeling of need for more authoritative guidance, his impression of assignments in terms of sheer quantity, his difficulties in
Humanities (as opposed to elementary science), his feeling of desperate competition in his field, and his relief in having survived periods
of hopelessness.

It is in the remainder of the hour that he suggests the meaningful
relationships among these experiences—their sensible connections
within the structures through which he construed the world. He appeared to assume that the ultimate reference in all matters of knowledge and conduct lay in a set of right answers. He saw these answers
as the possession of authorities, to be dispensed by them through explicit exposition or detailed advice. A student's responsibility, in turn,
was to acquire these answers (and to compete for authority's approval)
through honest hard work. Honest hard work (in keeping with the assumption that knowledge is an aggregate of substantive facts and procedures) consisted of a literal, step-by-step accretion of each detail in
each assignment. College assignments, however, often seemed too extensive to be mastered in the time available. In his Humanities course,
moreover, the authorities did not seem to be clear either about the
right answers or about how one was to go about one's work in obtaining them. In the struggle among students for authority's rewards,
which was bad enough in the sciences where one knew when one had
finished one's work, the Humanities seemed to leave the door open
for unfair competition; those who did little work, or even neglected
it, might influence authorities through mere glibness of tongue, or
perhaps by "using their personalities." Thus the moral order of the
world was threatened, and the student had fought many anguished
battles against intimations of rage and helplessness.

Here, then, the student portrayed in his implicit epistemology, in his procedures of study, in his views of social relationships, and in his system of moral values a coherent structure through which he construed his experience. The judges found this structure congruent with that of one of the more simplistic of the stages or "positions" in our developmental scheme, a position earlier in the development than that characteristic of most freshmen. It seems probable that whatever "truth" there may have been in the student's perceptions, his suffering may have derived in large part from the discrepancy between his assumptions and those held by his instructors and his peers.[5] Indeed when he finally broke out of these assumptions in a burst of maturation in his junior and senior years, he looked back in relief from a broadened view of the world and remarked soberly, "Maybe *I* was the cut-throat." Then, realizing that within the assumptions he had carried with him from his particular schooling he could have had no likely alternative, he was willing to accord himself a certain forgiveness.

This, then, was the general form of our interview and the general way in which the students responded to it as an opportunity to describe their experience in their own ways of finding meaning in their lives. When this general form seemed well accepted by the student— usually after the first half hour—we found that we could on occasion risk some specific question—questions raised for us by what the student had said and phrased in the terms he himself had used. On some such occasions also, we ventured to offer some new vantage point: "If you had a cousin, say, who was coming here next year, and asked you what to expect and so on, how do you think you might answer?" Then, near the very end of each freshman interview we asked each student if he would like to look over the *Checklist of Educational Views* as he had filled it out in the fall and spring. On receiving the regular statement of interest, we would put the papers before him and ask his comments on whatever items most interested him or which he had addressed differently in fall and spring. Frequently these discussions would remind a student of experiences which expanded or deepened his earlier thoughts. The nature of such planned departures from our

---

[5]This particular student applied for and received two hours of counseling from our staff in his sophomore year. The proportion of students in our sample receiving counseling was the same as that for the student body at large, approximately 15 percent.

strictest forms will be evident in the excerpts given as illustrations of the data in Chapter 5.

Although we were attempting through the overall discipline of our procedures to minimize the degree to which we might distort a student's report by the introduction of concepts and structures which might not be characteristically his, the records reveal that our best efforts were occasionally insufficient to counterbalance our frailties. We made mistakes. Nonetheless, the sheer variety in the ways in which students expressed their perceptions suggested in itself that they spoke primarily from themselves rather than for us, in both their vocabulary and their manner of construing their experience.

We remained concerned, however, about more subtle ways in which we might be influencing the students in their reports. Supposing that we did not actually introduce into the conversation those structures pertinent to our emerging interests, might we not still influence their salience or importance once the student had introduced them himself? This possibility concerned us most particularly in our interviewing of the Second Sample, since our very purpose was to check the generality of that sequence of structures we had abstracted from the interviews of the First Sample. Since we now knew what we were looking for, we felt it probable that subliminal, "Ouija-board" clues in our behavior might be steering the students into expanding on our interests at the expense of theirs. Conceivably we might even induce by our interest the very developments we were attempting to test.

Simple awareness of this possibility seemed to provide us with no insurance against it. We could not suppose that we could suppress all signs of the interests we now possessed, and most people appear to be responsive, even unconsciously, to "selective reinforcement" from their listeners (Greenspoon, 1951; Cohen, Kalish, Thurston, & Cohen, 1954; Hildum & Brown, 1956). We knew, too, that our students could be counted on to be both perceptive and, within the limits of their integrity, cooperative. Most students, to be sure, showed by their occasional questions that they had derived no conscious sense of any special interests we might hold. One, however, a member of the First Sample, revealed that he was even ahead of us. In his senior year, he began his interview by pondering out loud: "Now let's see where am I along the lines you're most interested in?" He then proceeded to tell us.

We concluded that efforts to be completely "deadpan" would be not only unpleasant but ineffective. Rather than concentrating on restraint, we settled for a more positive discipline. This was the obvious subjective discipline of asking ourselves periodically what our *ultimate* interests really were. Either we were most interested in "proving" notions of our own that might not be true, or we were most interested in discovering what really concerned the students in their own lives. We felt that within human limits the choice was ours to make. To the degree that we really preferred the second alternative, we could allow full expression to our interest in the students' own experience and truths and in doing so provide the students a relatively greater freedom that we could create by self-conscious attention to particular restraints.

We cannot believe that we were completely successful. However, certain results of the judges' experiments suggest that whatever the degree of our influence it was counterbalanced by the strength of the students' integrity. It will be remembered that our developmental scheme emerged for us from the reports of the students of the First Sample and took its full form in our minds only after our interviews with them were completed. If our special interest in this development significantly heightened its salience in the reports of the Second Sample, the judges should have found these later interviews easier to rate reliably against the scheme than those of the First Sample. In rating 20 complete four-year protocols, the judges first rated 5 from the First Sample, then 5 from the Second Sample, then 5 from the First Sample and 5 again from the Second. Even though the figures suggest that the judges needed the practice afforded in the first 5 ratings to reach maximum levels of agreement, there was in the end no overall difference in the reliability with which they rated protocols from the two samples. The same was true in their rating of single interviews without knowledge of the student's year in college or of the sample of which he was a member. We read these results at least as a negative. That is, the degrees of agreement reached by the judges offer no evidence that our having formulated our notions of student development at the end of our interviewing of the First Sample caused us to elicit more defined evidence for such a development in interviewing the Second Sample.

There remains, however, the question of the effect of holding such interviews at all, quite regardless of any bias in the interviewer. I remarked earlier that the social stress consequent on our initial procedures in interview seemed to be more than counterbalanced by its positive results, not only for the study but for the students themselves.

I have described what we feel to be the gain for the study. Our readiness to carry our share of the discomfort seemed to convey a sense of our care for the integrity of the students' own reports, freeing most of the students from questioning us as to what we were "trying to get at," and enabling them to search their experience for themselves. At the same time that the students gave us less biased data, therefore, their own gain seemed to emerge from discovery, recognition, and confirmation of the meaning of their experience. In taking their leave of the interviewer the students regularly stated their interest and satisfaction. In a minority, including especially those who did not return in later years, this expression had the feel of a conventional "good-bye." For most students, however, its meaningfulness was attested by their candid acknowledgment of surprise. It is relevant to any evaluation of the study that the students expressed surprise at something more than the interview's being more enjoyable than they had expected. Their surprise focused sharply on what they themselves had learned: "I didn't know all these things had happened. I mean, I wouldn't have realized . . . put them together and seen them all so clearly. But there they are."

In subsequent years' interviews, furthermore, most students would report having "looked forward" to the occasion, saying that they had noted this experience or that during the year as important to tell us about. At the end of his senior year, one student said, "I don't know what *you've* learned from all this research, but *I've* learned that the most important thing that could happen around here is that every student should have an interview like this at the end of every year. . . ."

We take it that the act of observation always influences the events observed. If this proposition holds for the physical sciences (Kuhn, 1962; Heisenberg, 1952; Polanyi, 1958), it surely holds for the social sciences (Erikson, 1964; Kaplan, 1964). In previous studies analogous to our own, some startling effects have been documented. In one (Heath, R., 1964), the investigator "followed" a representative sample of 31 college students through their four years, meeting with them individually and in groups every week or so. Of these students, 13 graduated with honors, as did only 5 of their matched controls. That the study had effects in addition to that upon academic performance seems probable.

The effects the four interviews our students held with us in our more limited study have seemed beyond our means to ascertain. Sample attrition and other variables made systematic inquiry seem impracticable. That some effect occurred we have no doubt. We cannot seriously suppose, however, that our influence went so far as to create outright the very phenomena we thought we were observing. We can acknowledge such a possibility in theory, but to examine it as a probability would be to step outside the limits within which we feel responsible for the exercise of skepticism. Supposing that there were students for whom the interviews had significant effects, we believe these students made use of the occasion simply to strengthen or hasten, in some degree, the natural course of their growth—a growth in which we, for our part, were endeavoring to trace not a rate of movement but a coherent sequence of forms.

CHAPTER THREE

The Students' Experience

T his chapter outlines in essay form the phenomenology of the experience reported by our students. The informality of an essay allows this generalized summary of the developmental sequence to be presented as if through the eyes of some "normative student" going through the experience. It was from the emerging patterns which seemed evident in this phenomenology that we abstracted our developmental scheme.

In addition to providing the reader with an experiential context for the abstract terms in which the developmental scheme is to be presented, the essay will document the manner in which we introduced our judges to their undertaking. The *Judge's Manual,* with which we provided them, opened with an introductory section describing the educational concerns summarized in the opening pages of this monograph.

It then continued with the essay presented here. The remaining sections of the *Manual* are included for examination at appropriate places in this report.

A preliminary note is in order. The essay was not originally written specifically for the judges, but derived from a draft of a book about the study intended for the general reader. It appears here, without revision, as printed in the *Judge's Manual*. For the reader's purposes in this report I should mention one explication I would now make in this draft.

The first paragraphs of the essay portray the simplistic structure through which a person presumably finds meaning in experience in earliest childhood. The essay then uses this portrait as an analogue descriptive of the starting point, in adolescence, of that revolution in a person's address to the nature of knowledge and the origin of values which is traced in our developmental scheme. The assumptions behind this analogy or metaphor seem to me to require more explicit acknowledgment, even in a deliberately impressionistic exposition.

That the forms of early development at levels of concrete experience appear to be recapitulated in later developments at levels of more abstract experience is an observation which the reader will recognize as originating with Jean Piaget. In Piaget's formulation, a person moving from a level of relatively concrete functioning to a level of more abstract functioning appears to repeat at the new level, from its beginning, a sequence of developments analogous to that which he had completed at the earlier level.[1] This recapitulated development, recurring on each level, consists of a movement from an egocentric, undifferentiated position to one of more objective and differentiated relations with the environmental aspects of the particular level of function. Our own developmental scheme portrays this kind of movement on the level at which a person undertakes the development of his "philosophical assumptions" about his world, beginning with those primitive forms characteristic of the beginnings of each of his previous developments at more concrete levels from infancy on. Although our conceptualizations depart radically from those of Piaget in ways which will be considered in the critique of our scheme in Chapter 6, it is this similar assumption of recapitulated development that underlies the metaphor from childhood with which this essay opens.

After reading the *Manual*, the judges inquired into this assumption, since they did not find it sufficiently explicit in the essay as it stands.

---

[1]See Flavell's treatment of Piaget's concept of vertical *décalage* (Flavell, 1963, pp. 22–23) and also the concept of "saccadic development" presented by Harvey, Hunt, & Schroder (1961, pp. 18, 85, 96, 110).

THE GENERAL EXPERIENCE[2]

In a child's first awareness of his world, what are the "terms," meaningful to him, through which he interprets his experience? It seems probable that they are the basic dual terms of his sense of well-being and dis-ease: comfort and irritation, desire and aversion, light and dark, safe and frightening. These are the terms from which he coordinates his first "purposeful" actions in his own behalf: physical movement of toward and away, social communication of appeal and rejection. Most importantly for our concerns, the child will use the simple either-orness of good and bad, permitted and not permitted, as a foundation for his first realization of himself among the people of his moral world. His imperative concern must be to know if he is to be patted or punished, praised or scolded. Is he good or is he bad?

This is not to say that in the neutrality of the play-pen children do not reveal the early development of a more complicated awareness. A child soon discovers for his own purposes that two quite different sights are nonetheless the same toy viewed from different sides. Jean Piaget has traced how the child expands this discovery into the realization of later years that the same thing can look differently to different people, a structure of thought central to our concerns.

This development, however, seems to be delayed in the sphere of values and morals, perhaps because the child must be preoccupied with the demands of social discipline. The child must know of every act whether it will fall in the category of the approved or the disapproved, the allowable or the forbidden, the right or the wrong. Shades of gray in the moral world are so unsettling that even in adolescence the young will pressure adults into maintaining the pretense that the oversimple, dual distinctions apply to all acts. "Never mind the flimflam—do you approve or don't you? Can I or can't I? Do I pass or don't I?"

This view of the world feels perfectly coherent from the inside. I go as a child to my parent or my teacher with my little offering for judgment—my wish to go play with my neighbor, my spelling word, my arithmetic example—is it right, or wrong? The large beings before me survey my offering and compare it with some model, some absolute unchanging platonic idea of rightness known to them, or perhaps engraved on some tablet in the sky, and inform me, "Yes, it is right," or

---

[2]From the *Judge's Manual.*

"No, it does not conform." In such a world, divided down the middle, it behooves me to stay as much as possible on the side of right. In school, instances on the side of right and wrong, correct and incorrect, are all recorded, added algebraically, and the result used to indicate the degree to which I have been right or wrong, good or bad. In this total I am periodically compared with my classmates above and below me, on a single scale of goodness—of success and of failure.

This picture of the world receives, of course, some severe jolts. Mother may say "Yes" and Father "No." In high school, I find that English teachers disagree about the value and even the meaning of certain poems. At first, disillusion makes me suspect the competence of my particular teachers, but I find that others are no better. Perhaps the tablets of truth about poems are at too high an altitude for anyone to discern, or the sky over English teachers is particularly cloudy. If so, then at least I am free. I suddenly see that the world is not as I first thought, divided between right and wrong. No, it is divided between those things about which opinions can be determined to be right or wrong and those things about which "anyone has a right to his own opinion."[3] That I continue to be graded on my opinions about poems, I ascribe to the unfairness of English teachers, an unfairness understandable in the light of their desire to hold up their heads in company with teachers of mathematics and physics, who, after all, can know what they're doing.

By this maneuver I have saved the clear dual nature of my world, the only world in which I can demand of authority that it state its rules precisely and abide by them. If English teachers cannot make these rules clear, I can then forget the material, "find out what they like," and give it to them. This is less than high-minded, of course, but they started it.

I still have no real doubts that "right answers" themselves are a matter of morals, not of utility. I see evidence of this everywhere. It is not enough that an answer works; to be really right it must be properly arrived at, that is, by hard work. The same answers come upon by unconventional means, "guesswork," or other cleverness are counterfeit. Sammy, who is known to work very hard for the few answers he gets, is never scolded. Alex, who is discovered to have been exploiting a

---

[3]This concept of pluralism will be referred to in these researches as "Multiplicity."

knack for getting all the answers without cracking a book, is taken aside and talked to for not making the most of his opportunities. The Right still reigns.

The crisis may be harder to postpone in college. In college I am older and stronger and at the same time I am severely shaken by the absence of solidarity among my peers. It may be that other students are in the same predicament, but for the first time I see that they differ from me radically in regard to the things they assign to right or wrong, and to the determinable or the indeterminable. In school the reiteration of the "right" and of authority's limits was the affirmation of friendship's bonds. In the college dormitory it appears that I must cease to reject the "wrong" if I am to have any friends at all.

Worse than this, I can no longer maintain the illusion that virtue alone determines rewards in the intellectual world. It is all too clear now that Sammy's efforts may fail to gain him honors and that Alex, who only reads Sammy's notes after sleeping through class, may receive an A. I get discouraged by my hours of labor over themes, which bring me only C; I procrastinate; I guiltily dash off a midnight scrawl—and receive B+. The foundations are crumbling.

A heavy burden now falls on my teachers to justify themselves, and the breakthrough may come in my battle with them. At first the old story repeats itself. I came to college with a new faith in my teachers—perhaps now my Humanities instructor will not be so ignorant of the graven tablets of the truth. Or if the tablets are not visible, he will at least recognize "everyone's right to his own opinion." My hopes are raised when he adjures the class not to write a mere summary of the author's views but to state our own ideas, our own opinions. I do so, my opinion being largely of the form that I like the book or I don't. I receive a D. Alas, my teacher is not to be trusted after all, and is revealed as a mere section man, wrapped up in his own efforts toward a Ph.D., and hypocritically subservient to those prejudices necessary to minions. The next section meetings will be devoted to elaborate efforts to bait him into the revelation of these prejudices.

As part of this maneuver, I take my paper to him for his comments, to find out "what he wants." He informs me that I state too many generalities with too little data. Suppressing my retort, "But sir, you said . . . ," I leave to fill my next paper with data with a vengeance. The D on this paper is attributed to my lack of ideas. "Look," says the section man, and for a moment we face each other, even across my resentment, "You must learn to show how the facts relate to each other to generate your ideas, to support them. The ideas and the facts must go together, and you must not let them fly in the face of the implication of some other fact to which you do not refer. And furthermore," he says as he sees me to the door, "the privilege of having your ideas respected depends on your presenting them for what they are, not the truth, but interpretations which you prefer among other interpretations. You may not have to spell other interpretations out but you must let your reader know that you are aware that they exist as relevant qualifications of what you have to say."

Something has happened, but it is a matter of pride not to admit it. I trudge off saying, "All right, if *that's* what they want, I'll give it to them." And I sit down with my next paper to "relate" facts and ideas. Perhaps it is at such a moment as this that I become thoroughly involved and after two hours' work suddenly look up to say, "Holy cats, they *do* relate." I can then put forward my interpretation with pride in its integrity. It is this confidence that allows me to afford the realization that the same data might appear in a different light to others and that we must still all stand judgment. Here I can experience my proper conviction that my ideas are in a new sense "right," and still speak with humility.

I am fortunately too involved in the "point" I am trying to make in my paper to notice the full implications of the new world I have recognized. But the implications will present themselves to me one by one, forcing their reiterated choice between courage and despair—unless I find some way to shut my eyes. It will be easy enough to see at the outset that interpretations of a book may lie on a range, with those demonstrating the greatest integrity near the center, and others grading off to either side toward the relatively untenable.[4] Next it would be clear why very different interpretations, from either side, might be assigned the same value.

Soon I may begin to miss those tablets in the sky. If this defines the truth for term papers, how about people? Principalities? Powers? How about the Deity Himself? And if this can be true of my image of the Deity, who then will cleanse my soul? And my enemies? Are they not *wholly* in the wrong?

I apprehend all too poignantly now that in the most fateful decisions of my life I will be the only person with a first-hand view of the

---

[4]The concept of pluralism appearing in these paragraphs will be referred to in the study as "Relativism."

really relevant data, and only part of it at that. Who will save me then from that "wrong decision" I have been told not to make lest I "regret-it-all-my-life"? Will no one tell me if I am right? Can I never be sure? Am I alone?

It is not for nothing that the undergraduate turns metaphysician.

Not all students are "sophomores," in this sense, in their sophomore year. Some come to college as "juniors" or even "seniors." Some go all the way through college and somehow manage to remain schoolboys to the end. In the sense in which we are speaking, indeed, many people achieve the consequences of a college education without ever going to college at all. The function of a college, however, is to present to the students' attention in concentrated form all the questions that the sophomore in man has raised for himself through the ages and which he has then spent the rest of his history trying to resolve, rephrase, or learn to live with.

We need not stop to analyze the motives that bring man to metaphysics. It seems evident enough that the higher animals gained their relative freedom and mastery through developing the ability to form concepts—that is, to think. Man has gone on to his own greater freedom—and bewilderment—by learning to conceptualize about concepts, to think about his thoughts. Man is distinguished from the ape not by his reason, at which the ape is often no slouch, but by his meta-reason, which is a blessing with which the ape is presumably uncursed. The characteristic of the liberal arts education of today, as we have pointed out, is its demand for a sophistication about one's own line of reasoning as contrasted with other possible lines of reasoning. In short, it demands meta-thinking.

William James would hold that there is nothing useful or good about a meta-thought unless it has useful consequences for a thought that has useful consequences for an action. We agree, and so do most of our students. It is when an intellectual community idealizes its own techniques for their own sake that it forgets action. Meta-meta-thoughts become "higher" than meta-thoughts, and meta-meta-meta-thoughts higher yet, *per astra ad absurdum.*

It is not this tendency that causes the sophomore his pain, even though, when first the floodgates let go, he gets lost in just this way. The issue at hand, we think our records show, is responsibility. If all I have been taught up to now is open to question, especially to *my* question, then my sense of who is responsible shifts radically from outside to me. But I see too that my questions and my answers are likewise open to question. Yet if I am not to spend my life in questions about questions and am to act, choose, decide, and live, on what basis am I to do it? I even see now that I have but one life to live.

This then is the issue of individual personal commitment in a relative world, the next step beyond the questions of the "sophomore." Its central burden, and joy, is responsibility. If one quails before it, there are many well-trodden paths to postponement, escape, or even retreat. We shall mention these as they appear in our records later. They can be seen most clearly against the experience of those who take up the challenge.

The commitment we are talking about is of a special form. We have called it personal commitment in a relative world. By this we mean to distinguish it from commitments which have been taken for granted to the extent that they have never been questioned, never compared to alternatives which could be "thinkable" to the self. All of us operate on many habitual never-questioned commitments. For some they constitute the entirety of life—that is, the unexamined life. Socrates said such a life was not worth living. Surely this statement is extreme and reveals the snobbery of consciousness. People with unexamined lives have been known to fight for their lives very well indeed. Of course they could not tell you why and remain people with unexamined lives.

Unexamined commitments can exist in all areas of life. One of our students, diligently "committed" to his goal of medicine ever since he could remember, never asked himself whether he really wanted to be a doctor until he was admitted to medical school. At this point the question hit him like an earthquake. When he had weathered the crisis and decided to go on, his commitment was of the form to which we particularly refer.

In religious life the distinction has long been familiar as the difference between simple belief and faith. Belief may come from one's culture, one's parents, one's habit; faith is an affirmation by the person. Faith can exist only after the realization of the possibility of doubt. We shall have more to say about the relation of religion to the intellectual and emotional growth of our students. We are concerned now with their experience of commitment as we have defined it.

Our students experience all such commitments as affirmations of themselves. Many of our students use the terms of existential philosophy in describing them, though most do so apologetically, knowing the ease with which the jargon can take over. The feeling they describe is one of some decision, some choice among actions, values, or meaning which comes from themselves and defines them as individuals. Not that they feel self-created, as if they could choose all their values without reference to their past. On the contrary their commitments seem always to be made in acceptance of their past. Even when a student is breaking with the tradition of his upbringing, he seems first to have to accept the fact of it, that this happened to him, that he lived in it, and that now he must take a stand over against it, knowing that a part of himself must pay the cost.

More usually commitments follow lines similar to those laid down in the unexamined past, but the act of affirmation brings a new and different feel to it. The student who finally "decided" to become a doctor was not unmindful that his long efforts carried weight and momentum into his choice. Yet he did not feel trapped or resigned or passive. He knew he might be fooling himself, but had to take this chance also. He had to decide for himself even about the degree to which he could feel that he had really "decided."

What is required is a capacity for detachment. One must be able to stand back from oneself, have a look, and *then* go back in with a new sense of responsibility.

The act of standing back is forced in a liberal arts college by the impact of pluralism of values and points of view. The shock may be intentional on the part of individual professors, as it is most frequently, though not always, in courses in General Education, or it may be simply the by-product of the clash of different professors, each one of whom is sure he teaches "the" truth. Only in the smallest and most carefully guarded faculties can this diversity be avoided.

We gather from what our students have told us that the educational impact of diversity can be at its best when it is deliberate. When a teacher asks his students to read conflicting authorities and then asks them to assess the nature and meaning of the conflict, he is in a strong position to assist them to go beyond simple diversity into the disciplines of relativity of thought through which specific instances of diversity can be productively exploited. He can teach the relation, the relativism, of one system of thought to another. In short, he can teach disciplined independence of mind.

This is the commonplace of good teaching of the liberal arts in college and in good schools of today. And the idea is older than Socrates. In more recent times Henry Adams said that if he were ever to do college lecturing again it would be in the company of an assistant professor whose sole duty would be to present to the students an opposite point of view.

We think we are describing, however, a new thing under the sun. Deliberate teaching of this sort seems to be no longer the exception but the rule—so much the rule that it becomes the very heart of liberal education as revealed in these records. We wonder if this event is not the product of a great educational revolution of the past fifty years.

Some evidence is at hand. [Here the Manual describes the evidence from examination questions presented on pp. 4 and 5 of this report and then continues as follows.] On this evidence, the faculty at Harvard appears to have revised its conception of the educated man in the past fifty years. The Harvard faculty may not, of course, be representative of institutions of higher learning in this country. But even in the face of notable instances of leadership by other colleges, we doubt that Harvard has ever been more than ten or fifteen years behind the times in its definition of knowledge in its students.

The faculty's emphasis on independence of thought in examinations coincides, then, with the students' concerns in these records. There is hardly any doubt that the faculty's deliberate effort is a good thing. One would have to be quite anti-rational to maintain that education consciously and thoughtfully considered is less to be desired than that which happens accidentally. But it is not without its pitfalls. Education for independence of mind is a tricky business, as these records show. Unlike the haphazard clash of dogmatic professors, it can double back on itself and undo its own good works.

The problem is not simply that a teacher's bias can sneak back into his efforts to be impartial and subvert his offer of freedom. It often does, but the students soon discover how to deal with it, even when it appears in forms subtle and unlovely. The problem, as these records occasionally document, is that, where independence of mind is demanded by authority, its forms can be mastered and "handed in" while the spirit remains obediently conformist. As a student said of his performance on an examination, "Well, I decided to be in favor of that book they asked about, but I did not forget to be balanced."

The "pros" and "cons," the glib presentation of "several points of view," the summary which judiciously selects one position to be in favor of, "all things considered"—these become the stock armamentarium of the gamesman who has "caught on" to "what they want" and is giving it to them in exchange for grades and a diploma.

From what our students have revealed to us in their candor we find it impossible to imagine an educational system that would be proof against a wish on their part to defeat its ends. They would always find ways of imitating, of holding before the tired eyes of the professor the image of his fondest hope, all done up in his favorite words and his pet references and treasured qualifications. While their souls . . .

Students' souls, we have learned from both these researches and our daily counseling, are safe even against being saved. We find this encouraging. Certainly we prefer to see gamesmanship played cynically, if it is to be played at all, rather than automatically and unconsciously. The cynic, at least, maintains a claim to independence.

Modern pluralistic education, with all its pros and cons on every subject, is criticized for not teaching commitment, indeed for leading students away from it. What we have been saying from our understanding of our records is that: (1) without a clear view of pluralism, commitment as we define it is impossible; and (2) commitment can be provided for and given recognition, but it can never be brought about or forced.

There are too many ways out. As in *Pilgrim's Progress* there are stopping places, Sloughs of Despond, paths that lead aside or back. The first crucial trial is in the student's initial confrontation with multiplicity—with pluralism, ambiguity, and contingency. One or two of our students would have none of it at all. Presumably, for them to have answers black and white, clear, known, available was so important emotionally that any other world was intolerable. These students either left college or retreated into a deep reaction. Another student stated in effect that this "many-points-of-view business" was O.K. for other people but not for him! A few others accepted the fact of multiplicity, in the loose sense that "everybody has a right to his own opinion," and struggled against the college's demand that they think further.

Perhaps the most critical point in most of the records comes at the moment where the student has indeed discovered how to think further, how to think relatively and contingently, and how to think about thinking. For here it is up to him in what crucial spirit he is to employ this discovery.

He appears to have a number of options. He may allow this form of thought to be simply "what they want" and assume no responsibility himself. He may put his mind in the service of this opportunism and become a cynical gamesman. He may isolate his discovery in the world of academics alone and never allow it to raise questions about his own life and purposes. Or he may see clearly enough what is now incumbent upon him and yet not feel up to it. He can feel not quite old enough or strong enough to make his commitments, and simply procrastinate.

Or he may go on. If he does so, his first commitment may well be to his major, his field of concentration. He has had enough of too much "breadth." He sees now the breadth of his ignorance; it is time to take the plunge, to know some one thing well. And so as a junior he works at his peak and looks forward to his thesis.

Not infrequently, he discovers later, the old hope for certainty has just gone underground, and in his senior year he has the whole job to do over again. "Knowing one thing well" turns out to have meant "Knowing something for sure," and when his thesis, that looked so narrow and specialized, opens out on him into the uncertainties of the whole universe again, he is taken aback.

We think this is the most crucial moment in higher education. Here the student *has* his tools; he has learned how to compare "models" of thought, how to relate data and frames of reference and points of ob-servation. But now differences of opinion among experts in his field appear even more irreconcilable than ever. No one can *ever* be sure. "It's all up to the individual in the end."

Well, indeed it is. But the tone of this statement too often implies "So why bother. If it's all a matter of opinion in the end, why not in the beginning? Why bother with all the intellectual effort?" This is a retreat to simple multiplicity, to "everyone has a right to his own opin-ion." It says that unexamined opinion is as good as examined opinion. It is the moral defeat of the "educated" man.

It was our wonder and delight, therefore, to hear most of our stu-dents survive this crisis also. Many would laugh when they came to the realization that a commitment must be made and remade in time and at deeper levels. They would see also that many areas remained where they had not yet begun to take their stands. But they would go on.

Perhaps the reader will find his reading of a few records more meaningful if we spell out briefly here what we think we have learned from the whole series of records about the anatomy of commitments and the way they go together to make a style of life.

Students seemed to think of their commitments in two ways, which we will call *area* and *style*. Area refers primarily to social content: decisions regarding major field, career, religion, tastes, morality, politics, finances, social concerns, friendships, and marriage.

The *stylistic* aspects of commitments concern balances both external and subjective. The external balances concern decisions of emphasis between studies and extracurricular activities, number and intensity of friendships, amounts of altruistic social service, degree of specialization vs. breadth, and so on. Issues among these external stylistic balances are closely interwoven with commitments in given areas, often determining them or affected by them.

A student's subjective style in regard to his commitments also appears to be both an important part of them and influenced by them. This subjective style involves certain inner commitments or affirmations or acceptances. In these records the students speak often of such inner balances as those between action and contemplation ("I've come to learn when to say to myself 'well, now, enough of this mulling and doubting, let's do something'"); permanence and flexibility ("Sometimes you have to go into something with the feeling you'll be in it forever even when you know you probably won't be" or "I used to think I had to finish anything I started or I'd be a quitter; now I see it's a nice point when to stop something that may be unprofitable and put the effort in more hopeful directions"); control vs. openness ("Well, you have to let experience teach you; it's good to have a plan, but if you insist on following it without a change ever—"); intensity vs. perspective ("That's the trick, I guess, you have to have detachment, or you get lost, you can't see yourself and your relation to what you're doing, and yet if you stay detached you never learn from total involvement, you never live; you just have to do it by waves, I guess").

It is the particular equilibrium that a student finds for himself among such subjective polarities that define him in his feeling of who he is as much as the concrete commitments he makes in different areas of his life. There are others too—a sense of continuity of self through mood and time in the face of the need to take one's immediate feelings seriously; and most particularly the realization that however much one wants to feel one has "found oneself" one wants more to keep growing all one's life ("I sometimes wonder how many times I'll be confronted").

With some moving, flowing equilibrium, some kind of style, among all these issues, the senior in our records tends to look more outward. His competence assured, he tends to be less preoccupied with the ingredients of self-hood, to accept himself as he is and grows, and to hanker for action. In a curious way he may startlingly resemble himself as a freshman. Here is the promising freshman-scientist who has established his competence, is accepted at graduate school and knows just where he's headed. Here is the once freshman-who-would-be-doctor and who next year will be called Doctor "on rounds." They look ahead and outward. They may find little to say in interviews except to allow in a quiet aside that they are getting married next week. Ironically enough some of these seniors have forced us to consider what the difference may be between their kind of outwardness and that of the most hard-shelled anti-intellectual. The difference defines a liberal education—not as an ideal, but as an actuality in real people.

The difference is surely not simply the "content" of so many courses in Chemistry or History. Anti-intellectuals have been known to master mountains of data and technology. The anti-intellectual cannot be passed off as one who refuses to think. Many think dangerously well. Similarly the liberally educated man cannot be caricatured as one who sees so many sides of a subject that he cannot act. Our records belie such stereotypes.

We have come to believe from all these hours of listening that the anti-intellectual, be he in or out of college, is definable not as "against thinking," but against thinking about one particular thing: thought. Most particularly his *own* thought.

In contrast, the liberally educated man, be he a graduate of college or not, is one who has learned to think about even his own thoughts, to examine the way he orders his data and the assumptions he is making, and to compare these with other thoughts that other men might have. If he has gone the whole way, as most of our students have done, he has realized that he thinks this way not because his teachers ask him to but because this is how the world "really is," this is man's present relation to the universe. From this position he can take responsibility for his own stand and negotiate—with respect—with other men.

(End of section from *Judge's Manual*)

CHAPTER FOUR

Concepts of the Scheme

It was in the general experience described in the previ-ous chapter that we felt we could discern a coherent evolution of forms. When we presented the description itself to a variety of students and adults, each one seemed to find it generally recognizable, familiar, or even "obvious." This was encouraging, but only to the extent of making our task seem worthy of a try. The task before us was to abstract from the experience the sequence of articulated structures that we supposed to function as its armature or skeleton.

We saw the requirements of such an abstraction to be (1) that it be economical and concise; (2) that its economy be obtained at minimum cost to its relevancy to significant aspects of the experience; (3) that it be of sufficient generality to encompass a maximum variety of individual variation; (4) that the inferences by which it is derived from the data be demonstrable, and (5) that it be open to validation by replicable operations to be performed with it.

The formulation of such an abstract scheme is subject to all the conceptual pitfalls, logical and psychological, inherent to symbolizing a complex organismic process in language. I shall acknowledge these difficulties in the critique of the scheme in Chapter 6. For the present

I shall move as directly as possible to the scheme itself by noting only the most central of the concepts and assumptions we found appropriate in its construction.

ASSUMPTIONS ABOUT THE GENERATION OF MEANING

People tend to "make sense," that is, to interpret experience meaningfully. The "meaning" of experience consists of some sort of orderliness found in it, and the nature of this orderliness in a given person's experience can often be deduced by others from the forms of his behavior, including, especially, what he himself has to say on the matter.

The meaning of a given moment in experience emerges from a highly complex and selective interaction of forms derived from two pools: (1) the pool of those forms or orderings a person brings with him to the moment as expectancies; (2) the pool of those forms humanly discernible as "inherent in the environment" of the experience (physical, social, internal, etc.). The meaning emerging from the interaction will bear varying degrees of congruence and incongruence with the forms of expectancies the person brought with him to the experience. The degree and nature of the incongruence will determine the work a person has to do to "make sense" of the experience. The work of making sense will consist of some balance between two processes: (1) *assimilation* of the emerging forms of the experience to the forms of the expectancies the person brought with him (by means of selection, simplification, or distortion), and (2) *accommodation* of the forms of the expectancies to the forms emerging in the experience (by means of recombinations and transformations which result in new forms of expectancy).[1]

Phenomenologically one is usually unaware of the act of assimilation. If one is accustomed to chairs, one sees a given chair simply "out there" as a chair and is unaware of one's attribution. One usually becomes aware of one's attributary assimilations only in retrospect after a mistake, for example, "I saw him as somewhat naive, but was I wrong!" In a person's verbal reports, such as those of our students, therefore, most assimilations are implicit rather than explicit and must

---

[1]These terms—*assimilation* and *accommodation*—will be used, as here, in the meanings given by Piaget (see Flavell, 1963, pp. 58–77).

be inferred from the classifications the speaker takes for granted. Accommodation, in contrast, is sometimes in awareness where it is sensed as a "realization." This is particularly likely in respect to an insight or reconstruction that suddenly reveals "the" meaning of some incongruity of experience we have been trying for some time to make sense of. For the purposes of this study, a student's verbal reports of such moments are especially valuable, as they may reveal, both implicitly and explicitly, (*a*) the structure of the earlier expectancies which had proved inadequate, (*b*) the structure of the new interpretation which resolved the incongruity, and (*c*) the transitional process by which the new structure was created.[2]

THE CONCEPT OF STRUCTURE

In this report the word "structure" will refer specifically to the formal properties of the assumptions and expectancies a person holds at a given time in regard to the nature and origins of knowledge and value. In our data, structures are sometimes made verbally explicit in such statements as "I used to think anything was either true or false, like on tests at school; now I see you have to consider the whole *context*, sort of, and there's lots more to it than either-or." Often such a structure may be inferred from a student's effort to account for some incongruity in his experience, as when a student complains that all his professors seem to him to have carried their efforts to make students practice "thinking for themselves" to the unfair point of "hiding things." At other times a structure may be inferred from a student's narrative report of overt action in which particular assumptions about a value and the means of realizing it seem clearly implied, as, for example, from his account of his ways of study, his talk with his adviser, or his recent argument with his parents.

Such structures in a person's assumptions about knowledge and values may be classified in accordance with their formal attributes, for example, "dualistic," "relativistic," and so forth. They can be further characterized by the quality relationships among content elements, for example, the "authoritarian" or "equalitarian" relations of teacher-learner, parent-child, society-individual. In these relations

---

[2]These are the birds we were hunting. An understanding of their life cycles would seem of central importance to all aspects of education.

among content elements a structure extends its logic and forms into the forms of action appropriate to it. For example, structurally different epistemological assumptions imply different forms of teaching and learning congruent with them. So also, structurally different assumptions about the origins of moral values dictate different forms for the expression of responsibility.[3] In sum, while the word "structure" in this report will refer in its narrowest uses to the form of an assumption about the nature of knowledge and the origin of value, its reference can appropriately extend beyond the purely cognitive assumption to those forms of action, thought, feeling, purpose, and care that are congruent with the assumption and incongruent with any other.[4]

THE CONCEPT OF DEVELOPMENT

The sequence of structures we observe in our data qualifies as a "developmental" pattern in the special sense originally derived from biology in that it consists of an orderly progress in which more complex forms are created by the differentiation and reintegration of earlier, simple forms (Werner, 1948; Witkin et al., 1962). The word "growth" will be used in the usual way to refer to progress in the development.

---

[3]Since these extensions of the structure of assumption about knowing and valuing will include differences in forms of control, both in interpersonal influence and in *self*-regulation, the structures can occasionally appear isomorphic with the "structure of personality."

This extension, however, seems warranted only in the case of extremely closed structures (cf. Adorno et al., *The Authoritarian Personality,* 1950), and even then it has its own rigidifying dangers. In a scheme tracing the development of a particular order of structure, it is best to assign "the structure of personality," whatever that may be, to some superordinate position, thus allowing for competing structures (of the order being considered) to coexist, differentiate, and integrate within the "personality." In the instances in our data where the isomorphism seems relevant, I shall remark on it.

[4]Cf. Piaget's *schema.* The implication that the forms of some motives are a function of the structure of cognitive assumptions rather than *vice-versa* will be allowed to stand, with the prior postulate that people are fundamentally motivated to form cognitive assumptions (cf. Bruner, 1957a, vis-à-vis Festinger, 1957a).

However, since the word "growth," when applied as a biological metaphor in psychological and social contexts, necessarily picks up assumptions about values, it is well to acknowledge them at the outset.

In any sphere of human development, perceptual, intellectual, social, emotional, and so forth, the word "growth" suggests that it is *better* to grow than to arrest growth or to regress. Where the development is laid out as a kind of scale on which a person's position and rate of progress can be measured, then a value becomes assigned to a person in an advanced position relative to others of his age. A similar value is assigned to a person with a relatively high rate of growth. Where progress in the development can be assumed to involve not only "natural" endowments but such "personal" attributes as will, effort, and courage, growth becomes a moral issue. An advanced person showing a high rate of growth becomes somehow a "better" person.

Since our developmental scheme concerns precisely a person's "moral" development, in the sense of his assumptions about values and responsibility, these implications require direct confrontation. For example, since each step in the development presents a challenge to a person's previous assumptions and requires that he redefine and extend his responsibilities in the midst of increased complexity and uncertainty, his growth does indeed involve his courage. In short, the development resembles what used to be called an adventure of the spirit. One psychologist dubbed it an "epistemological *Pilgrim's Progress.*"[5]

In our estimate these moral issues are inherent in any consideration of values in the context of human "development," especially normative development in a given cultural setting. It might be possible, of course, within the technical definition of development, to trace the differentiations and integrations in the development of a person dedicated to evil works; however, the use of the word "growth" for this progress would require rather strenuous contextual delimitation.

---

[5]Though the word "courage" seldom appears in psychological writing, even the clinical, it seems more precise here than such a word as "affects." "Affects" refers to emotional events themselves, commonly fear, anger, erotic response, etc. "Courage" (in the healthy sense as opposed to a "counter-phobic" defensive reaction against fear) seems to refer to a second-order emotional disposition characterizing an integrative address to first-order affects such as fear and anxiety, present or anticipated.

These very stresses suggest that the values implied by the word "growth" in our scheme are inescapable, and that they would be there even if some other word were used. In short, in any exposition of a presumably maturational development in the area of values, language intended to be purely descriptive will become value-laden. Efforts to avoid this tendency are likely to obscure its workings, and so to increase rather than decrease the possibility of bias. In our opinion the best course is explicit acceptance. This acceptance makes it possible to delimit the values involved and to objectify the implications of describing a person's development in terms of them.

The values built into our scheme are those we assume to be commonly held in significant areas of our culture, finding their most concentrated expression in such institutions as colleges of liberal arts, mental health movements, and the like. We happen to subscribe to them ourselves. We would argue, for example, that the final structures of our scheme express an optimally congruent and responsible address to the present state of man's predicament. These are statements of opinion. Even with the strength of convictions, they remain opinions and their explicit statement may relieve them of suspicion of pretension to the absolute. To the extent, then, that any "rating" of an individual person's maturation relative to our scheme carries with it a value judgment, that judgment must be conceived precisely as relative, that is, delimited by the context of the scheme.

Our judges found themselves deeply troubled by these issues in their initial efforts to rate students' reports. In instances where a student seemed to evidence no "growth," or even to show signs of "retreat," they felt a revulsion against implying in their rating that he was somehow a "bad" person, or at least "less good" than others. It was no comfort to them when we pointed out that they were making no judgments as to how the student happened to get that way. Nor were they reassured when we pointed out that since the scheme was derived from the students' own reports it could be considered a normative description rather than an arbitrary prescription. The judges experienced such rationalizations as weaseling.

What gave them their first relief was to stand back and observe that in their experiments it was not the students who were standing judgment but the very scheme itself. The problem of the whole study was to determine whether or not the scheme provided *a* useful ordering of the students' own reports of their intellectual and moral experience. With this issue clear, the judges went on to observe that the values inherent in the scheme seemed indeed to be shared by the students. The students quite evidently "rated" themselves, holding themselves accountable to a standard of progress.

Significantly, the satisfaction the students expressed when they felt they had gained was less one of self-"approval" than of measured gladness; and whenever they felt they had evaded an issue, or settled for some position which denied the responsibilities with which some realizations had confronted them, they expressed a discomfort which was less social guilt than personal shame. The standard, therefore, appeared to have less of the character of an "introjected" cultural demand and more that of an indigenous "humanistic conscience" (Fromm, 1965) which found a certain cultural nourishment.

I shall explore this standard further in connection with our notions of the students' motivation.

THE CONCEPT OF STAGES OR "POSITIONS"

The usual strategy for describing a developmental process (be it through words, drawings, photographs, etc.) consists of taking cross sections at chosen intervals along the course of development. Development is then described in terms of relevant characteristics of form and function salient in each cross section. Where the cross sections are taken at some regular interval of time, such as a day, a month, or a year, the analysis need not carry with it a prior assumption as to whether the development proceeds at a smooth rate or in spurts or in "stages."

However, the cross sections may be taken at irregular intervals, and may also be presented as "stages," e.g., oral, anal, genital (Freud); romance, precision, generalization (Whitehead). Here the prior assumption is made that the development is not smooth and that the points of cross section have been dictated by *a differential in stability* evident in the forms making up the development. "Stages" then refer to relatively stable forms, and those less stable forms which mediate between stages are said to characterize "transitions."

Since we have used this cross-sectional strategy in the construction of our scheme, it is well to look behind such a conventionally simple procedure. The outlines of any such scheme will obviously be a function of the relative stability of forms perceived by the investigator in his data. But what are his criteria of "stability"? If he means that a more stable form is one which is more enduring, the matter would seem fairly simple. However, the "stages" he observes may vary considerably in duration, and the extent of this variation suggests that some other criterion of stability has been at work. This criterion will be found to consist of the quality of coherence or "goodness of gestalt" of the forms. This is an almost aesthetic criterion, similar to that of "elegance" and "parsimony" in the evaluation of scientific theories. Its function in descriptions of development is seldom made explicit, presumably because enduring forms do usually appear to have coherence, to which indeed they may owe their longevity. Likewise a relative incoherence and internal conflict within a system commonly predispose the system to relative transience. But this coupling of coherence and endurance is by no means universal or necessary. In some developments there occur sharply delimited moments of remarkably coherent gestalt, as for instance in the sudden, brief flowering of some plants. The forms in such moments are so commanding that the observer will accord them the standing of a "stage" quite regardless of any time scale he may otherwise use in distinguishing between stages and transitions.

In abstracting stable forms from our students' reports, we focused primarily on this very criterion of *coherence*, without regard to endurance. The wide spacing of the reports gave us no objective way to measure the endurance of forms, and our impression was that the endurance of any particular form varied enormously in the development of different students. A student's report could tell us, however, about the coherence of the forms through which he was presently construing his experience. Similarly, his reminiscences, whatever they might say about timing, regularly portrayed the coherences and disjunctions in previous forms as he saw them in retrospect from the vantage point of present perception.

We therefore proceeded as follows:

1. We examined each student's report for the forms of those assumptions about knowledge and value with which he construed his experience in different areas of his life at different times. In this process certain forms emerged for us as internally coherent, "sensible," possessed of "good gestalt." We then found that these stable forms, which we labeled "structures," appeared to be recurrent in the data. That is, a given structure could be abstracted from the detail of a given report and, stated as a proposition about the world, could be found in the re-

ports of other students. Indeed the number of such "sensible" structurings which could be abstracted from the reports (and distinguished from one another on the basis of some significant formal property) seemed to be quite limited. When stated at a high level of abstraction, they seemed to number at most about six. When stated at the lowest level of abstraction that could still be called a student's *way* of interpreting his experience, they still seemed to number no more than thirty.[6]

2. We considered the order of appearance of these structures throughout the students' four-year reports and found this order to be remarkably regular. Although at any given time a student might express himself in a range of structures, both the range itself and the structure representing its central tendency appeared to progress along this broad general sequence from year to year.

3. After formulating these structures in general terms, we attempted to order them in the sequences evident in the students' reports. This arrangement soon began to reveal an internal logic, which in turn generated new perceptions as we looked back to the students' accounts. These perceptions further refined and extended the logic. This process generated new groupings and hierarchies among the structures. Two or three structures might appear as developmentally equivalent; in other instances one or more structures appeared to be simply variants or substructures properly subsumable under some other. These considerations resulted in an arrangement of the structures in a sequence of nine "positions" along a single dimension of development.[7]

The structures at each of these "positions" became in this way the progressive cross sections in terms of which we would describe the development. For our purposes the word "position" is preferable to "stage" for several reasons: (*a*) no assumption is made about duration; (*b*) to the extent that a student's report manifests a range of structures

---

[6]Nonetheless, with the exception of the structures of one or two Eastern philosophies, it is hard for us to see what internally coherent (and even minimally viable) interpretation the students missed.

[7]Certain other structures which appeared to express diversion from the development fell in "positions" related to the main line but apart from it. (See the foldout *Chart*.)

at a given time, a "position" can express the locus of a central tendency or dominance among these structures[8]; and (*c*) the notion of "position" is happily appropriate to the image of "point of outlook" or "position from which a person views his world."

ASSUMPTIONS ABOUT MOTIVATION

A student's movement from one Position[9] to another involves the reorganization of major personal investments. Even when such reorganizations appear "spontaneous," they express the work of considerable psychic energy. A student might report that he had one day simply realized that he had come to look at things differently, but in terms of energy he had just as surely been involved in the labors of unlearning and relearning as the students who reported long periods of conscious struggle.

---

[8]Since students often seemed to interpret different sectors of their experience through structures of different developmental status, the concept of a central tendency or dominant structure was essential to the judge's task of rating student reports as "overall" at a single position. We made only one test of the possibility that the judges rated each interview in three content-sectors (academic, extracurricular, student's experience). In rating the four interviews of one student's four-year report, the judges rated each interview in five content-sectors (academic, extracurricular, interpersonal, vocational, religious), and also "overall." The judges produced reliable ratings for each of the five sectors and these ratings revealed a considerable disparity in the student's development from sector to sector, especially in his outlook toward academic work and religion as compared to his outlook toward his career. Nonetheless, reliability was no greater in the rating of separate sectors than in the overall rating of the central tendency among them. Possibly the smaller amount of data available for any one sector counteracted the advantages of focus. Whatever the reason, the expense of rating by sectors appeared too great for our purposes, and we settled for the equally reliable overall judgment as a workable tool in the first test of our scheme. Clearly, however, the overall rating involves a second-order statement. It is a judgment integrating a range of developmentally disparate structures which themselves form subclusters in a student's interpretation of different sectors of his experience.

[9]In the remainder of this report the upper-case initial will be used to designate the special use of the term as defined above.

Since, then, the dynamic of each movement expressed the interaction of forces and countervailing forces, it would be impossible to describe the successive structures of our developmental scheme without making some sort of assumptions about the nature of the forces involved. Indeed, assumptions about the dynamics at work entered strongly into our earliest analyses of our students' reports, and their importance was dramatized for us in our every argument with one another about the nature of the students' development. What each of us saw in the reports, and how we formulated what we saw, seemed generated in some ultimate way from what he assumed the forces to be. Or to say it more accurately: from what he assumed these forces to be *like*. In complete accord with modern meta-theory regarding comparative psychologies of motivation, our debates tracked the issue to its lair in the metaphors of our assumptions.

For example, we could assume that our task was to trace the "impact" of the college "on" the students. This metaphor of forces taken as the lens through which to observe the students' reports would dictate by its particular internal structure what we could and could not see, and thus the meanings we could attribute to what we did see. Similarly, the structure of the metaphor underlying such a question as "how the students adjust to (or learn to conform to) their environment" would dictate an equally narrow but wholly different set of observations. The risks attendant on leaving such metaphors in their unexamined state are notorious.

A full consideration of the problems surrounding concepts of motivation being beyond the scope of this report, I shall simply present here the address to them which we found most appropriate to the study of our students' accounts. Then, in the next chapter, knowing the reader to be aware of our assumptions about the forces involved in our students' development, I shall be free to make salient the structure of the progressive forms through which the forces seemed to us to work out their destiny in our records.

We began by presuming that whatever our conception of our students' motivations, the conception would consist of some sort of metaphor. We presumed further that the structures implicit in this metaphor would demand a congruence in the meaning we saw in the students' reports. Indeed, since we claimed to be studying the ways in which the structures of the students' own assumptions influenced the meaning they attributed to their own experience, we could only acknowledge community with them in a predicament we had postulated as human.

Accepting this condition, we felt we should nonetheless make the best use of such freedom as was available to us within it. Folklore and theory provide a wide variety of metaphors for the conceptualizing of human motivation. With these resources we could (1) examine the students' accounts to assess which metaphors seemed to provide the most economical and congruent ordering for the largest arrays of data, and (2) select from these the metaphor that provided a conceptualization at the lowest level of generality which would still encompass the most striking differences among individual students' reports.[10]

Looked at with these purposes, the students' reports revealed a vivid configuration. Those students whom we saw as "progressing" made their own awareness of maturation clear, explicitly or implicitly, and conveyed a sense of satisfaction in it. Those whom we perceived as standing still, or stepping to one side, or reaching back, acknowledged that they were avoiding something or denying something or fighting something, and they regularly remarked on an uneasiness or dissatisfaction akin to shame. Some others referred to periods in which they felt they had "moved too fast" and had become alarmingly confused. In short, the students experienced quite consciously an urge toward maturation, congruent with that progression of forms we were learning to see in their reports.

The next question was whether this impetus was to be conceived as emanating from the environment, perhaps as a "press," or from the individual as a kind of "drive" or "need." Our records offer the obvious answer "both," but with qualifications far more suggestive than either the question or the answer.

First of all, many students did not experience the environment as imposing upon them a "press" to mature. A few even experienced "press" to remain immature. Most experienced the environment as offering not "press" but "opportunity," with the added remark that it was the peculiarity of this particular institution to leave the decision to use the opportunity "up to you." One said, "Of course it's always up to you really, but here, even those who care make it somehow awfully clear."

---

[10]This procedure is distinct from a synthetic eclecticism which attempts to combine the "best" concepts from theories based on metaphors which are logically incompatible. We believe in the complementarity of theories, in which different theories illuminate a concrete event through different facets. Here, the ordering of a general development called for a coherent dynamic which would shed the least distorting and most productive light.

Second, the students' remarks revealed that the urge was inseparable from a standard which they experienced as a sense of optimal rate of growth. This standard often varied from student to student, and also for the same student in accord with his circumstances. For example, one said: "Well, I've come a long way, and I've known for quite awhile what's next. I mean I can see it. I know that it is, all right . . . (*pointing to his head*) up here. But I'm not ready yet, somehow, and somehow that's all right. I mean, I'll get there. I trust myself and I'll do it when I get there. Right now, thank God, nothing's rushing me. I've got enough to do."

These two considerations suggested that our students experienced the energy of their development as primarily internal.[11] They did, of course, occasionally make comparisons which expressed awareness of both "press" from the environment and standards external to themselves. For example, one remarked, "Pretty soon now I've got to go out into the great big world and take up all kinds of responsibilities and stuff and it's going to be awful. I'm just not ready for it." Another observed that he sometimes felt less mature than his roommate but at other times just "less of a square." Furthermore, an increasingly differentiated appreciation of the varied expectations and standards in the environment formed a prominent part of the students' very development. From the point of view of motivation, however, all such perceptions seemed to find their ultimate relevance in some urge, yearning, and standard proper to the person himself.

Where a student was "on the move," he was usually so taken up with his discoveries that he took his motives for granted, and the ways he experienced the energies of his growth had to be inferred from the concerns and satisfactions which suffused his narrative. The impetus seemed compounded of many "motives": sheer curiosity; a striving for the competence that can emerge only from an understanding of one's relation to the environment; an urge to make order out of incongruities, dissonances, and anomalies of experience; a wish for a

---

[11]This observation, derived from the reports themselves, requires no resolution of the problems of the ontogenesis of the impetus, e.g., whether it is "innate" or "internalized," a primary or a secondary motive, etc. Our own presumption on such matters would be that in its origins the impetus is innate in the infant's tendency toward expansion of motoric autonomy. The impetus then finds sustenance and form in interaction with environmental support, implementation, and constraint.

community with men looked upon as mature; a wish for authenticity in personal relationships; a wish to develop and affirm an identity; and so on. It was the convergence of all such motives into an urge toward maturation that brought them under that encompassing inner standard to which each man held himself accountable.

If the motives making up this urge to progress were the only forces operative in the students' development, there would of course have been no problematic balance, no drama calling for courage, and no meaning in a standard. Maturation did indeed have its joys of discovery and expansion, but its moral significances derived from its challenge by countervailing forces. At every step, the movement required the students to "face up" to limits, uncertainties, and the dissolution of established beliefs, while simultaneously it demanded new decisions and the undertaking of new forms of responsibility.

This constellation of countervailing forces appeared to consist of such tendencies as the wish to retain earlier satisfactions or securities, the wish to maintain community in family or hometown values and ways of thinking, the reluctance to admit one has been in error, the doubt of one's competence to take on new uncertainties and responsibilities, and, most importantly, the wish to maintain a self one has felt oneself to be (Angyal, 1965). Pervading all such motives of conservation lay the apprehension that one change might lead to another in a rapidity which might result in catastrophic disorganization. Some students made this anxiety explicit in such statements as "A guy could really go to pieces around here, you really could." The compound of such forces has been called by various names, for example, the "need for stasis," the "need for continuity," and the like. We settled on the general term "urge to conserve."

A student's movement, or lack of movement, could therefore be conceived as the resultant of these opposing vectors: the urge to progress and the urge to conserve. These forces would be considered as primarily internal to the individual, each with its supports in the environment. This metaphor of opposing forces is a common one (Angyal, 1965; Freud, S., 1949; Lewin, 1935, 1951a,b). As a kind of shorthand, it proved adequate for our purposes.

As anything more than a shorthand, however, the metaphor's dichotomous structure of opposing linear forces would be an indignity to a fungus, let alone our students. In living organisms, only the most trivial or atomistic energies may be considered linear or opposing. A more proximate metaphor would be drawn from enormously complex self-regulatory systems of nonlinear "feedback" (Allport, F., 1955; Harvey, Hunt, & Schroder, 1961; Miller, Galanter, & Pribram, 1960). Indeed such concepts as "progress," "conservation," and also "regression" are themselves metaphors for no more than directional and formal properties abstracted from the observation of life's integrity.

If, then, our metaphor of opposing forces is understood as a shorthand referring to an infinitely complex function of organismic integrity, it conveys a sense of energy adequate for understanding our students' accounts. It provides a feeling for the students' moral struggles and a dramatic context for their courage. Most importantly to this study, it provides some sense of the alternatives open to a student at any given point in his development.

In our records, the balance of these forces is pervasively in favor of progress. Growth is so "normal" as to suggest that it is "natural." From this context the few instances in which the balance seemed to favor conservation emerged for us as exceptions requiring a second-level explanation. That is, we tended to assume that for these students too, the "normal" or "natural" state would be a balance in favor of growth, and that some kind of experience threatening to integrity had somehow strengthened the forces of conservation to a point where they frustrated the impetus to progress. Conceivably, however, this might not be the case at all. Such matters as the "urge to progress" or "courage" or the "urge to conserve" might be, like many human traits, "normally distributed" in the population, and our exceptions might simply represent quite "natural" instances from these distributions where the balance was in favor of conservation. What settled the matter in favor of our initial impression was the discovery that in every instance these students revealed in their accounts the special kinds of stress, and of distress, associated with internal denial and dissociation.

All the students experienced stress, of course, but for those who were advancing it was the stress of endeavoring to integrate the multiple and expanding aspects of their experience and being. They did not deny in themselves the feelings associated with the urge to conserve. On the other hand, those who seemed to stand still, or even to go into "reaction," seemed to be actively denying or fighting off within themselves awarenesses of their urge to progress. In short, they maintained their position at a cost to the integrity they were attempting to conserve.

Sometimes these students made their denials and dissociations explicit, always with acknowledgment of some dis-ease or even shame:

"It's all wrong, I guess, I mean *I* even think it's wrong, but that's how it is. Sometime I wonder if I'm maybe losing a lot, but I can't be bothered to change." In other instances, where a student was less candid, or perhaps less aware, the dissociation was forcibly suggested by such clinical signs as active avoidance, defensiveness, or highly selective apathy.

The issue seemed most explicit, and most poignant, where the balance was most unresolved. A senior, whose report the judges rated as expressive of "Temporizing at Position 6 (Commitment foreseen)," spoke as follows:

> Last year after I'd talked with you, I said to myself, "Next year I'm going to be further along. I'm going to be able to tell this guy that I've taken hold." I knew what my next job was, and I was determined. And for the first time I knew I *wanted* to move—I mean it wasn't just pressure or an "ought," sort of. But—well—sometimes I found reasons: like *this* wasn't right, or *that* wasn't certain, or usually it was just sort of—if I wait it will all settle *for* me. . . . Other times—well, I guess I didn't think at all. But one way and another I kept postponing. (*Pause*) Chicken. (*Pause*) So I haven't made it. It's the same with politics really, girls, even morals maybe. I mean I think I'm honest I guess, but I don't know if I've decided to be, or always would be. . . . And so I've felt pretty lousy—and I've even wondered sometimes—well, like, do I have what it takes. (*Pause*)
>
> So I'm going to graduate school all right—by default—like I said I *wouldn't*. (*Pause*) Maybe—maybe there's still time, even now—

The students' endeavor to orient themselves in the world through an understanding of the acts of knowing and valuing is therefore more than intellectual and philosophical. It is a moral endeavor in the most personal sense. As their words will show, their realizations confront them repeatedly with reworkings of the issues of competence, loneliness, community, and self-esteem. Their feelings in this endeavor are therefore the living flesh of their reports—feelings of discovering, resisting, claiming, rejecting, and especially those most personal weighings of doubt and hope, shame and self-respect, weakness and courage.

The next chapter makes salient the structural aspect of the students' development. But this portrayal of structures must be conceived as analogous to the projection of skeletal structures on an X-ray plate.

The skeleton is made salient, but its articulation is meaningful only within the context of the flesh and purposes of the living being.

LAYOUT OF THE SCHEME

The reader will now wish to have before him the outline of the scheme depicted in the foldout "Chart of Development." The Chart is designed to fold out at the end of this volume. The Chart appears in the form used by the judges in their experiments. Its general outline can be understood with the terms at hand; its detail is most easily approached in the next chapter through the discussion of each Position and the illustrative excerpts from the students' reports.

The main line of development extends from left to right as Position 1, Position 2, through Position 9. Above these headings, overlapping bands group these Positions by the most generalized characteristics of their structure: Simple Dualism, Complex Dualism, Relativism, and Commitment in Relativism. Each Position is then given its own descriptive title directly below its number. This is followed by a brief outline and diagrammatic representation of the major structure of the Position and its alternates or substructures.[12]

The alternatives and substructures of a given Position express the major variations of the central theme as we found them in the data. Or to use another metaphor, various linkages of these options offer alternate routes and byways through which the development can be achieved. What factors may dispose toward one path or another is precisely the order of question the scheme opens for investigation.[13]

---

[12]A *Glossary* of the special terms used, together with their codes, will be found on the page at the end of this volume immediately preceding the Chart. These terms will appear throughout the remainder of this report. They will be identified in most instances by the upper-case initial letter, e.g., Multiplicity, Relativism, Authority, Adherence, Opposition, etc. When a distinction depends on the use of lower-case vs. upper-case initial letters, e.g., authority vs. Authority, the point will be made explicit in context.

[13]Such investigations might require more closely spaced interviews, especially for the study of "short cuts." In this study, where the ratings of the second of two consecutive reports from a given student placed him two positions in advance of the first, the data did not always make clear how the advance was achieved. There were several instances in which it seemed quite possible that

Positions departing from the main line of development are represented in parallel to the development, below it on the Chart: Temporizing, Escape, and Retreat. The structures of these Positions may have
the form of any of the main Positions under which they are placed on
the Chart, but with some addition, subtraction, or alteration which
functions as a delay, detachment, or rejection of the movement expressed in the main line.

As we expected, no freshman in the study was found to express the
structure of Position 1 at the time of his interview in June. A few did
attempt to describe themselves as having arrived at college in just such
a frame of mind, but none could have remained in it and survived the
year. Position 1 is therefore an extrapolation generated by the logic of
the scheme. At the end of the year, freshmen normatively expressed
the outlooks of Positions of 3, 4, or 5. Most seniors were found to
function in Positions 6, 7, and 8. The Position at which a student was
rated as a freshman was not predictive of the Position at which he
would be rated in his senior year.

Position 9 expresses a maturity of outlook and function beyond
the level we expected the experience of a college senior to make possible for him, though he might have intimations of it. Like Position 1,
it is an extrapolation rounding out the limits of the scheme. On rare
occasions, however, one or another of our judges was so impressed
with some senior's report that he did rate the student at Position 9. In
discussion, the judge would reveal that the rating was a kind of tribute made in humble, and even somewhat envious, respect.

---

the student had resolved incongruities between his earlier structure and his
experience by transformations which landed him two positions along the
scale, without the use of structures characteristic of the intermediate position. This versatility is internally coherent in the scheme and appropriate to
the resources of intelligent college-age persons. Such persons would be expected to have at the disposal of their ingenuity a wide variety of forms and
of procedures of transformation developed in earlier levels of experience
(Flavell, 1963). On the other hand, the student might have actually passed
through the intermediate structure, perhaps in an act of thought too brief or
"obvious" to recall. For the moment, our widely spaced self-reports provide
uneven inferential evidence about such transitions, sufficient for speculative
description alone.

In the description of each Position in the following chapter, I shall consider not only the characteristics of the Position's major or general structure, but also its variants or particular substructures, and I shall discuss such transitional linkages as we felt we could discern in the data. The reader should keep in mind, however, that our validation applies only to the rating of Position. The judges rated each protocol numerically for Position and then coded their rating for the particular substructure. Our statistical treatments have demonstrated the reliability of the rating of Position alone. The reliability of the judges' agreement about substructures seems evident to the eye in the ratings, but the complexity of its analysis involved an expense beyond the limits of the study. Should subsequent analysis support the impression of reliability, a tracing of the most common linkages among substructures from Position to Position will then suggest further hypotheses about the transitional processes through which the development is achieved.

SYNTHESIS

The interpretation of life, at the level our students address, is a creative activity. Such concepts as motivation, structure, assimilation, accommodation, and "stages" are tools of analytic description only. So too is our developmental scheme itself. Our task is primarily analytic, and our standards logical; the students' task is primarily synthetic, its standards aesthetic. For example, in their address to incongruities, the students regularly transcended a mere effort to reduce all of them to pat logic; their concern was to assess a balance between what may be resolved and what must be borne. Ultimately, then, our scheme chronicles the course of an aesthetic yearning to apprehend a certain kind of truth: the truth of the limits of man's certainty. Persistence in this yearning is, if you will, an act of love—and humor.

CHAPTER FIVE

The Developmental Scheme

OVERVIEW

The foldout Chart at the end of this volume outlines the nine Positions of development of our scheme, and below these the three Positions of deflection: Temporizing, Escape, and Retreat. This chapter will consider the structures of each Position and illustrate them in our students' words.

Most broadly, the development may be conceived in two major parts centering on Position 5. The outlook of Position 5 is that in which a person perceives man's knowledge and values as relative, contingent, and contextual. The sequence of structures preceding this Position describes a person's development from a dualistic absolutism and toward this acceptance of generalized relativism. The sequence following this Position describes a person's subsequent development in orienting himself in a relativistic world through the activity of personal Commitment.

In a somewhat more detailed way of conceiving the scheme, it may be seen in three parts each consisting of three Positions. In Positions 1, 2, and 3, a person modifies an absolutistic right–wrong outlook to make room, in some minimal way, for that simple pluralism we have called Multiplicity. In Positions 4, 5, and 6, a person accords the diversity of human outlook its full problematic stature, next transmutes the simple pluralism of Multiplicity into contextual Relativism, and then comes to foresee the necessity of personal Commitment in a relativistic world. Positions 7, 8, and 9 then trace the development of Commitments in the person's actual experience.

The Positions of deflection (Temporizing, Escape, and Retreat) offer alternatives at critical points in the development. A person may have recourse to them whenever he feels unprepared, resentful, alienated, or overwhelmed to a degree which makes his urge to conserve dominant over his urge to progress. In the first three Positions in the development, the challenge is presented by the impact of Multiplicity, in the middle three Positions by the instability of self in a diffuse Relativism, and in the final Positions by the responsibilities of Commitment. This way of conceiving of the scheme is represented in the diagram shown in Figure 2, which sketches the main outline of the Chart of Development.

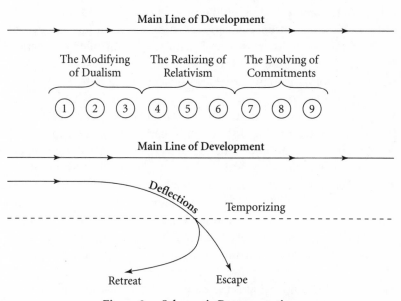

Figure 2. Schematic Representation.

—ᵕᵕ— Position 1:
Basic Duality

The structure we designate as Position 1 delineates the simplest set of assumptions about the nature of knowledge and values of which we found evidence in our records. The outlook is one in which the world of knowledge, conduct, and values is divided as the small child divides his world between the family and the vague inchoate outside. From this position, a person construes all issues of truth and morality in the terms of a sweeping and unconsidered differentiation between in-group vs. out-group. This division is between the familiar world of Authority-right-we, as against the alien world of illegitimate-wrong-others. In the familiar world, morality and personal responsibility consist of simple obedience. Even "learning to be independent," as Authority asks one to, consists of learning self-controlled obedience. In the educational aspect of this world, morality consists of committing to memory, through hard work, an array of discrete items—correct responses, answers, and procedures, as assigned by Authority. In this structure's most primitive form, Authority's omniscience is so taken-for-granted that no distinction is made between Authority and the Absolute. "Truth" and "what They say" function as tautological alternatives of expression, as do "right" and "what They want."

This set of assumptions may indeed be the simplest which a person in our culture may hold on epistemological and axiological matters and still be said to make any assumptions at all. The form of the assumptions appears to derive from childhood experience at more concrete levels of function and only emerges in consciousness at the abstract level we are considering when a person first asks himself "what is truth?" and "what is the nature of right and wrong?"

Since, at this abstract level, the structure recapitulates a childhood ascription of rightness to some sort of parental authority, there are doubtless persons in our society who have never developed such an outlook. However, a person who had never at any time thought of authority as "right" would be quite unlikely to appear in college or to concern himself, whether in college or out, with the issues traced in this study. The majority in our culture, and the college population in particular, we presume to have entertained such a notion at one time or another and to have looked upon matters of truth and morality within the framework to be outlined here.

Only three or four of our students seem to have come to college while still viewing the world from this Position's epistemological innocence. Furthermore its assumptions are so incompatible with the culture of a pluralistic university that none of these few could have maintained his innocence and survived to speak to us directly from it in the spring of his freshman year. Within the confines of our data, therefore, our portrayal of this Position involves inferences beyond those required for structures from which our students spoke directly. The inferences are derived in two ways: (1) by examination of students' efforts to describe the outlook in retrospect, and (2) by considering the outlook of students in slightly more advanced positions with the question: What would the world seem like to these students without what they describe as new discoveries?

Our construction from these inferences, however, finds confirmation outside of these data. In our counseling practice we have consulted with entering freshmen who have spoken directly from this structure in sharing with us their efforts to make sense of their new milieu. The outlook is also quite familiar in school settings where it sometimes receives explicit or implicit institutional support. Indeed, there is so little that is novel about it that it finds an almost full expression in the *Book of Genesis*.

It was, after all, the serpent who pointed out that the Absolute (the truth about good and evil) was distinct from the Deity and might therefore be known independently—without His mediation. The Fall consisted of man's taking upon himself, at the serpent's suggestion, the knowledge of values and therefore the potential of judgment.

In our records the serpent appears in the form of the university. While a student still views the world from Position 1, however, he does not perceive that the temptation is being offered by his instructors, for he views them as Authority itself and will misperceive their intentions (see Position 2). The unmistakable seduction will seem to come from his peers. A freshman looks back:

S.   When I went to my first lecture, what the man said was just like God's word, you know. I believed everything he said, because he was a professor, and he's a Harvard professor, and this was, this was a respected position. And-ah, ah, people said, "Well so what?" . . . And I began to-ah, realize.

In our records, however, innocence is not lost in a single moment of realization. Indeed the entire development may be looked upon as a drama in which a person apprehends, step by step, the extent of his loss and then learns how to affirm his own responsibilities in a world devoid of Eden.

The freshman's words "and I began to-ah, realize" announce, indeed, the undertaking of a longer and more complex journey than he could foresee—or than one might suppose, from the outside, was in store for him. On the face of it, there would seem to be no reason why the entire drama should not take the form of a simple confrontation between two opposing ways of looking at the world. That is, the student might simply learn from his peers and his instructors a relativistic epistemology and address to values. This then might directly displace, overthrow, or supersede the Authority-oriented structure he brought with him. However, this simple revolution or displacement does not appear in our records. Rather than being displaced, the dualistic Authority-oriented structure is first modified and loosened by a series of accommodations necessitated by its assimilation of the pluralism of both peer group and curriculum. These modifications then allow of the perception that Authority, as represented by the most respected elements of the faculty, is itself functioning relativistically and urging the students to do the same. Only then, at Position 5 in our scheme, does a real revolution of structures occur. And momentous as it is, this revolution is a particular and coherent transposition of part and whole: relativism, which up to the moment had been a subordinate function assimilated to the dualistic. Authority-oriented frame (in the form of "the way *They want* us to think") suddenly emerges as the frame itself, and dualistic structures are subordinated and assimilated to *it*. (See pp. 121 ff.)

The first half of the entire development, therefore, consists of the progressive modification of a dualistic Authority-oriented structure. Position 1 represents this structure in its "pure state" and reveals how the Tree of Knowledge at its center bears the seeds of its own dissolution.

As long as Authority and the Absolute (*The* Truth, the criterion of all knowledge) remain undifferentiated from each other, Authority remains omniscient, and the structure would appear to be a closed system. Even disobedience is impossible, since Authority's omniscience encompasses not only the Absolute but one's person as well. A freshman remembers his feeling at school:

> S.   It seems like they know just practically exactly how much you can put out and still get everything else done, but you have to work like a slave to do it. And I guess that's what they want you to do, work like a slave to get as much out of it as possible. It's very cold and cut, and you can't put anything over on the teacher at all. She knows just exactly how much time it takes to do so much work and how much effort. They, they don't usually give you too much, they give you *just* enough.

Another considers how he would advise an entering freshman:

> S.   Well, the only thing I could say to a prospective student is just say, if you come here and you do everything you're supposed to do you'll be all right. That's just about all.

A salient characteristic of this structure, and the source of its innocence, is its lack of any alternative or vantage point from which a person may observe it. Detachment is impossible, especially regarding one's own thought. A person cannot explicitly describe such an outlook while embedded in it.

This quality is evident in the difficulty our students experienced in trying to describe the state, even in retrospect. Most students who made the effort could shape only such brief summaries as, "Well, *then* I just wouldn't have thought at all," or, "These questions [of different points of view] just weren't there to worry over, sort of; I mean I guess everything seemed too settled. But I wouldn't have even thought of saying *that*."

The following excerpt is a senior's more extensive effort at retrospect. When considering other matters, he expressed himself with fluency and with an orderliness of syntax unusual in extemporaneous speech. His struggles in this passage, being peculiar to his subject, may be looked upon as descriptive in their own right.[1]

---

[1] I have therefore presented the excerpt in the most literal rendering which print can make of oral speech. In other excerpts I have attempted to ease the reader's burden by occasionally omitting redundancies and false starts where

I.   What would you say about yourself, as you've just been speaking, let us say, of yourself as a freshman? (*Pause*)

S.   Well, I-I don't know. It's pretty hard to—it's hard to say. As I-ah, as I came here for-ah, freshman. I, I, of course, the natural thing to say was that I was a pretty fundamentalist, pretty orthodox, and now I've been a complete movement to the more liberal point of view, but as on the other hand, I think it's—one could say that I perhaps just wasn't, wasn't very definite—didn't really *know;* I didn't have any answers, and now that I've been opened to all this, that I've sort of developed, so that I think it would be better to say that I was sort of, ah, *nominally* or just sort of wouldn't *accept* an orthodox view, but had never really *analyzed* it, so that-ah, so this is hard—it's really hard to say.

I mean, I couldn't—I'm trying to analyze myself as I—four years back which I don't know, but I, I tend to say that, really what you could say really say, really-ah that I would be sort of a *neutral,* sort of a, a "really-didn't-know" kind of position, sort of drifting, moving along. I mean, I never really analyzed these beliefs, but I never—I don't think I *really* accepted them. I mean, just sort of in a—in sort of the—I wouldn't say that I've—there's been a terrific-ah, real-ah in what I really mean, what I mean by these ideas, I mean-uh . . .

---

they do not seem relevant to meaning. We have experimented informally with this kind of editing in groups of our colleagues who have listened to the tape recordings while following a typed transcript. The literal, unedited transcript has invariably evoked criticism of the student as illiterate, while at the same time distracted attention from content. When the transcript has been minimally edited for a degree of smoothness and syntax, no such criticism emerges and no one appears to notice the difference between the typescript and "actuality." We conclude that the edited transcript represents a closer parallel to what people "actually" hear. That is, in oral conversation one tends to hear a degree of orderliness which one imputes to the speaker's intent and one only hears the speaker's "actual" wording when one's attention is forcibly drawn to it—as by slips of the tongue, significant confusion, or evasiveness. This phenomenon appears to be well understood by those who represent spoken dialogue in print, be they novelists or stenographic recorders (e.g., courtroom stenotypists).

I. Somehow I take it that you feel that, well you couldn't have talked like you've just been talking. You just didn't *know* anything?

S.   Yes, well, that's-ah—That would be it. Yeah. I certainly couldn't—before that I was, you know, I wouldn't ask. /Yeah./ That's the great . . . that's very interesting, as a matter of fact!

But I—I just couldn't. I wouldn't have—I wouldn't be able to *talk* on this subject at *all*. I mean, the-these four years have really sort of set this all up, because I never read any—well I've practically never read any philosophies or theologies before, so that what I have is just—well, was *there* you know.

The impossibility of objectivity from within this structure is well illustrated by his comments: "I wouldn't have—wouldn't be able to *talk* on this subject at *all.* . . . " In addition, the student's wavering into the present tense on two occasions may reflect the sense of the time-lessness pervasive of experience in the unconsidered "always" of an eternal, unchanging background.

The extraordinary stability of this structure—expressed by the student's remark "I wouldn't *ask*"—results from the consignment of all that might contradict Authority to the outer-darkness of the illegitimate-wrong-other. This dualism leaves the world of Authority free of conflict. All differences from Authority's word, being lumped together with error and evil, have no potential for legitimacy. As illegitimate, they complement and confirm the rightness of Authority instead of calling it into question.

In this dualism, any proposition or act must be either right or wrong. It cannot be better or worse. That is, when a person is considering the truth of propositions or the moral value of acts from this structure, he will never use the terms "better" and "worse" to refer to qualitative discriminations—as indeed he may have learned to do, in respect to friends or flavors of ice cream when, as a child, he had progressed beyond the dualism of "favorite vs. all others." If he uses "better" and "worse" at all in the context of correctness or virtue, he will use them only to compare summations of discrete right-wrongs (as in the grades of spelling tests) or summations of discrete good-bads (as in the assessment of "how good I've been this week"). In short, he will be found to refer to quantity, not quality. A genuinely qualitative meaning of "better and worse" in respect to a variety of propositions or values would necessitate a potential of legitimacy in otherness, a potential incompatible with this basic structure and inconceivable from within its pure state.

Similarly, no opinions or acts could be intrinsically neutral, but only "all right" or "not wrong," that is, approved or condoned by Authority. A category for the intrinsically neutral, which opens a domain into which Authority has "no right" to intrude, is a later development (see Multiplicity in Position 4). Here, at the outset, "all right" means "permitted," and though the category opens some area of freedom and diversity, as for play, it remains strictly within Authority's domain.

The degree to which this structure is a closed system was brought forcibly to our attention by a freshman whose responses to our *Checklist* contained a striking anomaly. In September he had checked most items in a way which expressed a strong belief in absolutes and, by implication, a strong rejection of pluralism, relativistic thought, and ambiguity. In May, most of his responses bespoke movement toward some openness to doubt and some acceptance of contingent thinking. For one item, however, this tendency seemed radically reversed. The item read, "There's nothing more annoying than a question that may have more than one answer." In September, he had checked "Disagree," a response quite incongruous with all his others; in May he checked "Strongly agree," a response which would have been expected of him in the fall, and which presented no great anomaly in his current attitudes. When we inquired of him about these matters in his interview in June, he replied:

> Oh! Well, when I came here I didn't think any question could have more than one answer—so why be annoyed?[2]

In the study of those of our records which referred to Position 1, the question before us was how such a closed system did in fact develop its openings in the students' confrontations with incongruent experience. The reader will recall the prolonged suffering of the student whose initial statements were contained in the illustration of our

---

[2]We had designed the *Checklist* to differentiate students along a polarized diversion of "personality tendency." Looked at developmentally in the context of our scheme, it might reflect very crudely the polar differences between Position 2 and Position 5 on, but this student's comment revealed that Position 1 was simply outside the limits of our scale, dramatically so for this item.

manner of interviewing (Ch. 2). In his case it seemed to be his anxieties about competition that made him intolerant of any relativism that might alter the rules of the game and threaten the morality of hard work and its rewards. We have known some students, in our work as counselors, who indeed found the impact of diversity so disruptive and unassimilable that they left college. In the section on Retreat in this report (pp. 204 ff.) I shall speak of others who somehow survived, but only at the cost of a bitter, uncomprehending entrenchment. Others, however, found the loss of Eden by no means so intolerable and spoke even of its liberating compensations.

Indeed, the student's remark that when he came to college he didn't suppose there was such a thing as a question that had more than one answer suggests that the parochialism of Position 1 may not bespeak "intolerance" in the reactive or pejorative sense. It may express no more than the outcome of a culturally homogeneous or narrow environment. Intolerance, in the pejorative sense, and hatred of "otherness," is certainly congruent with the structure; but the judgment of intolerance cannot be made until the person is confronted with the occasion for change. Even then, the occasion must be of a certain kind. Where the pressure comes from sources the person can perceive only as "other," his tightening of his boundaries in rejection or combat will be the same whether he is acting from "intolerance" or simple integrity. The issue will be clear only where the pressure for change comes from a source perceivable as within his own community, or where his resistance to the pressure would itself involve him in activities contrary to the values he already shares in that community.[3]

In our records, the students appear to bring with them the expectation of identification with the college community. Students who arrive looking at the world from Position 1 simply transpose to the college the same sense they have developed in the community from which they come. The pressure for change therefore emerges for them as anomalies of experience from within the boundaries of this community. If they do not react so violently as to reperceive the entire community as "other," divorcing themselves from it, they must assimilate the anomalous experience in ways that will force adaptations in the structure of their assumptions, opening the closed system to the progression of changes traced in this report.

---

[3]The nature of such intolerance will be considered in the section on Retreat.

In parallel with the structure of the Garden of Eden, Position 1, as it appears in our records, already contains a differentiation which makes the new experience more readily assimilable. For not even the Garden was a completely closed system. It contained a flaw: knowledge. Most dangerously, this knowledge, in addition to being accorded an existence of its own as separate in some degree from Authority, included specifically the understanding of good and evil, that is, of value. It was, of course, conceived as absolute and as the perquisite of divinity, but the distinction between the Absolute and Authority made possible man's escape from innocence.

This very distinction appears in our records, with little evidence to tell us how it got there. Perhaps Authorities themselves convey the notion to the young through their tendency to justify their pronouncements by "reasons" and other references to truths or principles existing outside themselves and compelling even for them. In any case the existence of the Absolute in its own right provides Established Order with an existence which is no longer completely dependent on Authority's omniscience.

The presumed existence of Absolute truth or knowledge in its own right (as if in a Platonic world of ideas) modifies the perception of Authority's role, most particularly in an educational institution. Since the student is there to learn, he looks to Authority as a mediator between him and the truth. Whatever higher attributes Authority may possess, it is also supposed to help him learn, and since Authority consists of many different instructors of varying ages and experiences, it is now possible to differentiate between those who mediate well and those who mediate badly—to separate those who really know and those who don't—true Authority and fraudulent Authority. This differentiation, though it does not throw the foundations of the system itself into question, does open possibilities for later assimilation of potentially revolutionary notions. A freshman reports a nicely controlled beginning of this differentiation:

> S.   I don't feel, well, I haven't had that much, much experience with English, but I don't feel I have the right to, if the book's boring, well, it's boring, but no one has the right to criticize the assignment in this book. They—Harvard's been around a long time—must have a reason for this, this reading list. Although I would criticize the high school reading lists, which have been there since my father was in high school.

This student's open awareness of boredom and his use of venerableness as a basis for both veneration *and* criticism of Authority suggest more advanced development in which Opposition itself is possible (Position 2). However, these embellishments are founded in the prior distinction between knowledge and those who mediate it.

In this distinction, Authorities—as mediators—can even be indulged somewhat by being granted their peculiar interest in "theories" and "interpretations" but only so far as these do not seriously obscure the solid truths it is their duty to communicate. A freshman examines an item on the *Checklist:*

S.   (*Reads*) "If teachers would stick more to the facts and do less theorizing one could get more out of their classes."

I.   You agreed in the spring?

S.   (*Speaks in a flat tone, as if he were still reading or even lecturing*) A certain amount of theory is good but it should not be dominant in a course. (*Raises voice*) I mean theory might be convenient for them, but it's nonetheless—the facts are what's *there*. And I think that *should* be, that should be the main thing.

An instructor can be perceived as failing of adequate mediation on two grounds. The older and admittedly "experienced" instructors are usually perceived as "knowing their subject" but may be criticized for failing of that "teaching method" which outlines precise procedure:

S.   In high school they attempt to teach you, whereas here they let you patch yourself in as you want, or if you don't want to, they don't crowd you too much. In high school you'd learn, you'd have learned quite a bit more about calculus.

I.   But here they can't teach you, they just let you do it, sort of?

S.   Well, everybody else that I talked to, with very few exceptions, has about the same idea of the teacher of Math. He must have taught it for the past thirty years. He uses books, but they were, they were very bad. And the teacher himself didn't eluci-, didn't help us much at all. He came in and he would do problems on the board without thinking of whether the, it was ever getting through to the class. And it usually wasn't. And then we drew another one in the last term of Math which also should have been relegated to some other college, preferably the *West Coast*. (*Laughs*)

I.   In the water, about six feet?

S.   In the *water,* yes! He was all right, he's undoubtedly brilliant, but, ah, it's the way he teaches that doesn't get through to the class. Of course he would give problems, and then he would try to explain the problems, but he was thinking on a different level. He gave, he gave lectures that tended to be for the intellectuals, the people that were taking the course and, ah, really had an aptitude for mathematics and were interested in delving into it. He gave a lot of that, but the teaching method left a lot lacking. I never liked him. It wasn't that he was personally bad, he had a nice temperament and all, and he was very nice to talk to. But he couldn't teach math for beans.

The young teaching assistant, however, is liable to perception as an outright fraud, a kind of older-brother pretender who arrogates the perquisites of Authority without its justification in knowledge:

S.   I don't know how many guys feel that way, but I, I (*laughs*) feel, I think a lot of the students do. Just-ah, well, they don't have much respect for these section men. No kidding, they just don't. They really, they really think, they think sometimes that they just are, the worst things in the world. They ah, and, and I think some of them are not as, half as smart as some of the students there. The students can talk circles around these guys. And it doesn't really do your, do them any good. For one thing, Professor Black who taught us Christmas, you couldn't lose him on one point. Man, he wouldn't, you couldn't, you couldn't *find* a question *he* couldn't answer. I doubt. And you respected him for it. Not that you're trying to trick the, the section man, but you, when you come up with any kind of a reasonable question, *he* can answer it for you, and he can answer it *well.* Whereas the section men dwiddle around and, and talk a lot of nonsense.

I.   Sometimes you feel like they just don't even *know* the answer?

S.   I don't think they do. I don't think they know the material.

The existence of knowledge in the Absolute as an entity separate from Authority has therefore made possible the distinction between Authorities who know and those who don't. This dualistic distinction might set the stage for the question as to whether *any* Authority knows, and this question could so loosen the bond between the Absolute and standards of conduct as to precipitate a pervasive crisis. According to our records, however, it is the impact of *pluralism* that will later drive home this opening wedge, weakening as it does so Authority's mediational role, and finally throwing in question the concept of the Absolute itself.

One might suppose that this distinction between good and bad Authority might make possible the direct perception of pluralism in Authority's ranks. In the records expressive of the early Positions in our scheme, however, the assumption that there is one right answer to all questions seems too firm to allow of this assimilation. A revered professor who actually teaches a pluralistic or relativistic address to his own subject is initially misunderstood; he is perceived as "teaching us to think independently," meaning "to find the right answer on our own" (see Positions 2 and 3).

In our records, the confrontation with pluralism occurs most powerfully in the dormitory. Here diversity emerges within the in-group with a starkness unassimilable to the assumptions of Position 1 by any rationalizations whatever. The accommodations of structure forced by this confrontation make possible a more rapid and clear perception of pluralism in the curriculum. The following two excerpts are from the very beginning and end of a freshman's report:

I. So what would you say stands out for you most about the year, as you look back?

S. Well the one thing, I would say, that strikes *me* most, ahh, of course just, just one point-ah, there are many other ones, but I would say that what strikes me mostly is the fact that many guys sort of, ahh, don't have belief in a God. You know, that's the thing, don't believe in God. I-ah, before I came here, I met quite a few guys who seemed to-ah, most of them seemed to have some belief in, in a God-ah, even though it would be sort of a normative approach, in a passive, in a passive way. When you come, when I came here, I find that-ah I would say the majority of guys don't, don't seem to have a belief in God. . . . And then, of course, maybe not tying in with that but somewhat . . . relative to the moral, moral beliefs and that sort of problem. And I mean it interests me. That's you know, one of the main things, I think-ah more than anything else, are the types of fellow that you meet, their beliefs and-ah how-ah, I didn't realize that there was such a different approach. I more or less had sort of a *common* belief that there was a God, that had certain moral standards, but up here you find they're different.

———

I.   (*Reads item from CLEV*): "One thing is certain: even if there is an absolute truth, man will never know about it and therefore must learn to choose and venture in uncertainty." [Student had checked "Strongly Disagree" and "Easy to Decide" in the fall, "Agree more than Disagree" and "Hard to Decide" in the spring.]

S.   Yeah. Well, I can see, I can see a certain, a certain change of view here, I mean, here I was more, yeah, I can see sort of a change, there [in the fall] I was strong. Right here, "strong disagreement," it's easy. I would say that *before* I would have said that you *can* find it, yeah there, and here "even if there is an absolute truth. . . ." Yeah, I can see my philosophy course right there, see my philosophy right there. I'd say it's right there.

I.   Somehow this is connected with-ah your experience of the year, in terms of the new points of view you have seen . . . ?

S.   I dunno, it's sort of, sort of connected, different points of view. Then, of course, I, well, I hadn't read James yet. . . .

In an intervening passage of this interview the freshman provides a description of his experience which will serve as a summary of this description of Position 1 and set the stage for the developments to be traced in the remainder of the scheme:

S.   Well I come, I came here from a small town. Midwest, where, well, ah, everyone believed the same things. Everyone's Methodist and everyone's Republican. So, ah, there just wasn't any . . . well that's not quite true . . . there are some Catholics, two families, and I guess they, I heard they were Democrats, but they weren't really, didn't seem to be in town really, I guess. They live over the railroad there and they go to church in the next town. . . .

So in my dorm I, we've been-ah a number of discussions, where, there'll be, well, there's quite a variety in our dorm, Catholic, Protestant, and the rest of them, and a Chinese boy whose parents-ah follow the teachings of Confucianism. He isn't, but his folks are. . . . And a couple of guys are complete-ah agnostics, agnostics. Of course, some people are quite disturbing, they say they're atheists. But they don't go very far, they say they're atheists, but they're not. And then there are, one fellow who is a deist. And by discussing it-ah, it's the, the sort of thing that, that really-ah awakens you to the fact that-ah . . . (*words lost*)

I.   So that-ah really the discussions in the dorm were in many ways, ahh . . . instances and moments when this kind of thing came to your attention?

S.   Yeah, well, I mean, you—*that* way you meet it more personally. And of course then you can see it in the sort of attitudes of professors, I mean, but this is more personal.

I.   So really, where the contact with it is most immediate, but somehow you *can*-ah see it in the academic situation too. /Oh, yeah/ Is there any course in which that comes at you particularly?

S.   Well, I take philosophy, took Philosophy 1a and I'm taking Philosophy 1b this semester and of course-ah Philosophy 1b takes up, we've been-ah discussing the modern philosophies, introduction to modern philosophy, it includes-ah the reading of Descartes, Spinoza—Descartes, Spinoza, Hume, Kant and James, and so there, you see it right there, it's the same, same thing, it's, it's a very *wide range*. (*Pause*)

In short it appears that it is the extension of potential legitimacy to "otherness" that brings the implicit background of Position 1 into foreground where transformations in its structure may occur. Otherness in the implicit, unquestioned structure had been consigned to an unconsidered limbo—on the other side of the tracks. Pluralism forcefully demands legitimacy in the peer group or is more gradually accorded its legitimacy in the curriculum offered by Authority itself. Its assimilation requires accommodations in the most fundamental assumptions of outlook. These changes can be rapid or extended through time, but our records suggest that there are a limited number of paths through which these changes can lead coherently from Position 1 to a relativistic view of man's predicament. The linkages among the variant structures within Positions 2, 3, and 4 reveal these sequences. The progression is from thinking to meta-thinking, from man as knower to man as critic of his own thought.

—᷈— Position 2:
Multiplicity Pre-legitimate

The structure of Position 2 delineates in closer detail the first steps in that journey from innocence forecast in broad terms in the latter part of the descriptions of Position 1. This detail reveals a point of paradoxical incongruity between a process in personal development and the nature of modern liberal education.

In the past, a young person freed himself from his embeddedness in the homogeneity of family and community through "adolescent revolt." In this traditional revolt a person laid hold of the diversity of opinion in the larger world and used it as a weapon against the orthodoxy from which he struggled to emerge. The individuation which he achieved in this revolt then faced him with the complexities and responsibilities of his freedom. Well into the present century, this often productive revolt could be carried on through the college years, since each professor claimed to be teaching *the* truth, *the* facts of his subject.

The decline of orthodoxies and the intrusion of a loose pluralism into community and home has caused at least one writer to regret with well-founded nostalgia the loss of this strengthening experience of revolt (Friedenberg, *The Vanishing Adolescent,* 1959). In a modern liberal arts college, however, the change has involved more than a mere decline of orthodoxies. The majority of the faculty has gone beyond differences of absolutistic opinion into teachings which are deliberately founded in a relativistic epistemology (see discussion of examination questions in Chapter 1).

In this current situation, if a student revolts against "the Establishment" before he has familiarized himself with the analytical and integrative skills of relativistic thinking, the only place he can take his stand is in a simplistic absolutism. He revolts, then, not against a homogeneous lower-level orthodoxy but against heterogeneity. In doing so, he not only narrows the range of his materials, he rejects the second-

level tools of critical analysis, reflection and comparative thinking—
the tools through which the successful rebel of a previous generation
moved forward to productive dissent.

The irony is clear in our records. The student who, at these early
levels of development, takes his stand in Opposition to what he perceives globally as the "hemming and hawing" and "vague theorizing"
of academic Authorities takes a bold forward step in personal individuation, but then quickly finds that he has painted himself into a
corner. In contrast, the student who more blandly presumes that Authority knows its business and is presenting all these complexities as
mere exercises for the students' own good—this student takes a far
less radical step in personal development but finds himself later in a
much more flexible position for further growth. As a final twist, in
perceiving all of Authority's "on-the-one-hands" and "on-the-other-
hands" as a mere obstacle course set out to help students learn how to
reach *the* Truth on their own, this trusting soul is misperceiving the
issue just as thoroughly as the most stubborn rebel.

The structures of Position 2 illustrate the origins of this paradox
in the two minimal adaptations through which those of our students
who were moving forward from Position 1 first accorded meaning to
diversity. In the first of these, diversity and complexity are still perceived as *alien* but as elements introduced *within* the community by
willful Authorities who are failing of their mediational role. Where no
contrasting "good" Authorities can be found, and where the student
is either isolated among his peers or finds support only in a like-
minded minority, he perceives diversity and complexity not so much
as alien to the community but alien to *him*. It is this perception that
seems to lead most forcibly to the student's relocating his own stance
within the structure by taking a stand in Opposition.

The initial reaction may be simply uncomprehending complaint:

S.   I don't know . . . in high school, public school, I used to really
like history a lot. I used to be *very* interested in it, it really was one
of the courses I liked *best*. Ahh . . . I . . . I . . . got here and I don't
know what, I guess I must have changed a lot or else the *course* was
very changed, or different, but I . . . it's one of the subjects I *don't*
like. . . . I don't know, it's bringing in philosophy which I don't . . .
a lot of these guys what they think about and-ahh . . . what they . . .
I really don't think . . . I just don't find any use for . . . I mean they're
fine to find out but, their ideas . . . but I'm just not interested

in it. I'm interested in more about what-ahh . . . what the *real* things in history are . . . what the *real* causes are. And well, I mean they're, they're real interesting, but they get you all confused. They seem to be always in threads coming in and always. . . . Ideas of a hundred guys that you've never heard of before. They seem to just ah, confuse you more than help you, I mean . . . I think they're trying to get too complicated. They put a thousand little, they try to think of maybe a thousand little ideas that forced this and that. And I always tend to try and simplify. . . . It's, I don't think that there *are* that many reasons for history . . . or a certain event happening as they make it out to be. . . .

Greater strength and acumen, however, lead toward Opposition:

S.   I'd like to teach an English course sometime, just for people who would like to read some good books and not know anything about Melville's complexes. Actually it wouldn't have to be such an aimless thing as just for enjoyment, but . . . they seem—in this English course particularly—they seem to like to be clever at the expense of what they're studying at the time. They like to find a paradox, whether one really exists or not, and they'll twist the material so they can say something ironic. . . . He's a good lecturer, even though he doesn't say anything. He's just a load of bull, but it's beautiful bull.

And Opposition can find strength in scorn:

S.   One comes to Harvard expecting all sorts of great things, and then one hits these, these Gen. Ed. courses which are extremely, ah, I don't know, they're just *stupid,* most of them. I've taken two, I'm taking Nat. Sci. and Hum., both of which I found, well, it's an extremely confused sort of affair, nobody seems to know anything. . . . [about Nat. Sci.] It's supposed to teach you to-ah, reason better. That seems to be the, the excuse that natural science people give for these courses, they're supposed to teach you to arrive at more logical conclusions and look at things in a more scientific manner. Actually what you get out of that course is you, you get an idea that science is a terrifically confused thing in which nobody knows what's coming off anyway.

The same can be said, of course, of peers, but it would seem to require an unusual tenacity to be able to say so as late as junior year, as does this student:

> S. I have a friend who majors in history and literature, and he spends a lot of his time thinking about abstract concepts from poems and books, trying to drag the author's thoughts out of a book and understand them, but it seems to me his line of reasoning tends to be abstract and not, not always. . . . He is undoubtedly a thinker, but what he thinks about doesn't seem to be of any major importance.

The full revolt may flower in an outright stubbornness which calls also for the courage of individuality. A sophomore has been expressing resentment of the "liberalizing" pretensions of required courses in General Education:

> S. . . . for instance nobody in the world is less interested in natural sciences than I am. I don't want to know a *thing* about it.
>
> I. I take it that you feel that the distribution requirement is just an arbitrary set of things and it doesn't make any sense to the individual.
>
> S. Well, for *some* people I suppose it does, somebody who has a sort of better-rounded mind than I do, and less centered. They can't make *me* learn it. *It's going to do me no good!*

As a developmental step from Position 1, this is a bold lonely renunciation of Eden in loyalty to self. Like the two-year-old's "I *won't*" it may require for its maintenance all the felt strength of anger and of closing-up of boundaries. The combativeness may originate, however, in defense of growth rather than in defense against it.

The problem for such a student arises with the next step. If, at this early level, a student has taken his stand in Opposition against what he perceives as the vague chaos of Multiplicity gratuitously thrown at him by his teachers, he cannot use his education to work through the initial impression of needless confusion to the discovery of contextual Relativism. Where then can he go? In the years since this study it would seem that such students may have turned either toward the dogmatic activism of indiscriminate protest or toward the dogmatic inactivism of global "love" or psychedelics. In our own records, while some few students seem to have entrenched themselves in the absolutisms of reaction or of indiscriminate radicalism (see Retreat), most found some way to free themselves to move on to the challenges of more responsible dissent.

The road does not seem to have been easy. Where sheer fight was not sustaining, several seem to have experienced a depressing sense of being "out of it all"—an awareness of being frozen, somehow, relative to the movement of peers and the demands of the curriculum:

A freshman:

S.   I've noticed ah, dissimilarities between people I might not have noticed before I came here. Lot more variety in point of view which I, I find I'm much more insensitive to, I think, I just can't understand them. I can tolerate them fine, but perhaps that's only because I don't quite understand what people think sometimes.

A sophomore:

S.   And, actually, as I look at it, I'm on the wrong side of the fence here because it seems to me that, to its great distinction, I don't know, from Harvard or from other schools, is that Harvard gets away from straight facts and puts an emphasis on reading between the lines and interpretation. And I can't do that. That's the, that, that bothered me all the time too that, it seems to me around here that's what they want mostly, and I can't do it. Now I don't know, it must be me because everybody else seems to be able to do it. But, just grin and bear it, that's all.

Most poignant seems to be a haunting sense of "immaturity." A freshman:

S.   Well, in high school we took a course like that, a history course. In that course the teacher would be telling you exact facts and here it's altogether different. I don't know. I like the work better when they . . . I suppose it's more immature, but I like it better when they give you something concrete, exactly what happened—not go off on a tangent on some phase that appears on the surface not to have anything to do with the subject. I don't particularly care for that. So that's the way with almost all the courses that I've come in contact with. That's the way they give them; so they must be right and I'm wrong. So I won't argue with them. They know more than me; so who am I to argue?

And another:

S.   It just seems to me as if it's a waste of time, although in the back of my mind I really think it's good. I really think that I wouldn't want to go to a trade school or anything like that. I really think it's good, in the back of my mind, but I can't accept it.

In these last instances, the students' continued perception of complexity, diversity, and "interpretation" as alien seems to have been more the result of some delay in "catching on," and less the consequence of entrenched combat. Most of the students quoted did "catch on" in a year or two without a crisis of selfhood. Where a student has made a heavy investment in battle, however, the way out seems to lie only through radical conversion. A freshman describes his way into the entrenchment and the crisis of his deliverance:

S.   You start thinking, well, hell, if they—I came here and I don't know anything about this thing anyway, and if *they* don't know— my God! They've been at it long enough. Well, heck, bah!

I.   How come you didn't keep saying "bah"?

S.   Well, because . . . I mean you start thinking well, good heavens, what am I doing here anyway? Should I just sit here and waste it? I mean no matter what I think of the people in the courses there's still the libraries and, ah, here I am with some liberty to learn something so why not take it? And also the very fact that this stuff is handed to you in such a pathetic sort of way, you get mad eventually, I mean you get mad and do something. . . . You *can* turn people out on an educational assembly line, but I think it's much better if this person, something—suddenly something happens to him and he decides that what the hell, ah, his education is going to be his own, his own concern or it's not going to be at all. . . . You feel that you're going to have to fight if you're going to survive but you don't feel that you have to be so, ah, I don't know, spiteful and completely zany. That's good, that's very good, because if you spend all your energy being completely different and completely just the opposite from what they're telling you that they're doing, I mean you, you get into trouble. . . . I mean you're just being that way for the sake of being it. . . .

When you look into yourself as a freshman you see the terrific, terrific confusion that surrounds you, confusion that's within *yourself.* You realize that if you stay that way you're not going to get anything done at all. . . .

You realize that the stuff you were disapproving in [the instructor] when he was up on the podium just comes as a result of, ah, the *type* of thing he's doing. It's not *him,* I mean he's not the one that's that way, which is of course the whole problem, because he represents what you're going to be, or more or less what you want to be, in some way or another. And as, as soon as you realize that, that he's not the way the course is, you feel much better about it.

In contrast to this poignant struggle into which some students plunged by boldly rejecting Authority's palaver, others found a smoother path by perceiving their instructors' actions in a relatively bland and ingenuous way. These students supposed that Authorities were presenting complexities, diverse views and alternate possibilities as "something they want us to work on so we can learn to think 'independently'"—meaning "to learn to find the answer for ourselves."

A sophomore reports this discovery:

S.   I found that you've got to find out for yourself. You get to a point where you, ah, see this guy go through this rigamarole and everything and you've got to find out for yourself what he's talking about and think it out for yourself. Then try to get to think on your own. And that's something I never had to do, think things out by myself, I mean. In high school two and two was four; there's nothing to think out there. In here they try to make your mind work, and I didn't realize that last year until the end of the year.

I.   You kept looking for the answer and they wouldn't give it to you . . . ?

S.   Yeah, it wasn't in the *book.* And that's what confused me a lot. *Now* I know it isn't in the book for a purpose. We're supposed to think about it and come *up* with the answer!

Here, then, the student assimilates Multiplicity to the assumptions of Position 1 with a minimal accommodation requiring no change in his own stand as loyal Adherent to Authority. He accords pluralism of thought and judgment the status of a mere procedural impediment intervening between the taking up of a problem and finding *the* answer. In any epistemological sense, therefore, Multiplicity remains a mere appearance; difference of opinion is allowed into the family, but only because it is quite temporary, good for the mind, resolvable, and therefore ultimately *unreal.*

This perception remains tenable only within limits, of course. If wrestling with uncertainties is only a means toward the attainment of a certainty which Authority already has in its possession, too much can be too much:

S.   I mean, they wouldn't in other words, the problems wouldn't be *given* unless they were of some value, something you could get out of it, I mean. I mean, you can't, ah, you can't ask for peaches and cream *all* the time, you gotta take the bad with the good. I mean they [the students] may review the problem and feel that they came out with, say, the wrong answer, and say, "Well, it doesn't look logical." It could be that, or maybe they got it right, but say, "Gee, all that work for that! Just for *that* problem!" you know, "Why did they give it to us?" In other words, if there was another way of . . .

Indeed, if Management is suspect of presenting complexity simply as a covert way of eliciting more work, even these students might incline toward Opposition:

S.   (*Reads No.* 20 *from CLEV*): "It's a waste of time to work on problems which have no possibility of coming out with a clear-cut and unambiguous answer." It isn't a waste of time, I think eventually there's a time when you have to stop, but-ah I suppose it won't hurt for a while. I mean it's a little more of a challenge to see how much work . . . I don't think you should go on it forever, I think there's a time when you finally will have to give up on it but, I won't say it's a com-, it's a complete waste of time, but that's really hard, some, really is a hard question to answer. Some reason or other. Let's see, 21.

I.   (*Disregarding change of subject*) You, you feel that working on a question that might not have a clear-cut and unambiguous answer is really a way of-ah, eliciting more work . . . ?

S.   Yeah. It's also, also maybe may make you think more. And I, so it wouldn't be a waste of time, I think eventually, I mean you, you shouldn't intentionally just give problems like that, I mean if one crops up, certainly, work on it. I don't say you should make a habit of giving them though. I mean that's, that's just gonna discourage people eventually, and sort of give them a sense of frustration.

For several students the limit of uncertainty which they could tolerate seemed to lie between the precision of the sciences and the vagueness of the humanities, and therefore to influence strongly their choice of field:

A freshman:

S.   I'll tell you the best thing about science courses: their lectures are all right. They're sort of, they say facts. But when you get to a humanities course, especially—oh, they're awful!—those lectures. Oh, I can't see any relation. You're reading a book, and, ah, to my way of thinking, anyway, the lecturer is just reading things into it that were never meant to be there. They say that, ah, I can't see how they can draw a conclusion that an author living sometimes B.C. had any certain thoughts—predestination, whatever they read into it now, just made popular now—they seem to think for every word written down in the book there the author had a definite meaning, double meaning, ambiguous meaning. I don't know, I couldn't see that.

I.   And this has sort of grown more and more as you see these guys that are reading an awful lot of stuff between the lines?

S.   Without sticking to the actual, what's written down in black and white. . . . For what I want to major in, my field, I have to take certain courses, no matter how they give them. I just need them for concentration so I'll just take them, regardless. Well, when it comes to taking outside courses, I certainly won't take anything that I think will be just raving, in other words a lecture that won't have anything to do with what's supposed to be going on in the course. (*Pause*)

I.   You're beginning, I gather, to pick up some opinions about the way the place runs and what you're going to do about it, sort of, and—

S.   Well, I'm not going to do anything to change it. Far be it from me to change an established institution which is certainly—well, it's more than I could do to change it. Some things maybe I don't think are right, but I guess the consensus must agree on what's going on here, otherwise they would have changed it. It must be pretty good.

And the same student as a sophomore:

S.   Things like philosophy courses, I just couldn't go into those, I mean I'd do lousy, I, I'd do very badly in them because—like a Hum. course I had last year, they'd see things that I couldn't see in them and, and it's just that they're not for me. And I don't think I've changed that much; it isn't bothering me now because I don't have much of it.

I.   You just don't run into that so much?

S.   Some, I guess some of it, but not quite as much as I did in an English course. It's a, it's about recent modern American literature, and they, the professor explained that a novel or something, well, he'll put things in there that I actually didn't know were meant to be there. But if they're there, if he says so, that's all. But I mean that's where I've always had trouble here, writing essays. I can never write a good essay, I never could get any original ideas until—ah, in most essays around here they'll tell you to well, explain or give your opinion of this or take a book and say well, what did the author mean, and, I don't know, I can never see what they really meant. I can tell them what it says in black and white, the actual writing, but when they looked between the lines for interpretation I was very bad. That's why I could never write a good essay.

The word "interpretation" in this context always seems to refer, in a very particular way, to a vague undifferentiated activity that is sensed in the environment but not comprehended. It would be easy to suppose that the student quoted above simply lacked the imaginative and intellectual potential to be successful at it. Later performance of students who have spoken in this way, however, demonstrates that this supposition would be erroneous in a large majority of instances.

The irony is, of course, that the students, even as they talk to the interviewer, are *interpreting* their own experience. They have an opinion, they marshal evidence of a sort, and they are aware that other people come to different conclusions. However, the overriding expectation of dualism in which one answer must be right (in the sense of being "given," and all others wrong) leaves no *meaning* for interpretation of evidence in the ordinary sense of the phrase.[4] When, therefore, Authorities "interpret," it is "a huge amorphous mass they throw at you" that "doesn't have anything to do with the course." Also when "They ask you to interpret," it is "something I just can't do; it's not there in black and white." That *some*thing must be there and *some*one must be wrong is all too evident; other people seem to be able to "see what They want."

Science and Mathematics still seem to offer hope because they can still be perceived, at their elementary levels, as procedural rather than interpretive. Yet the very distinction between Science and other subjects involves a concession. Wide areas are relinquished to a Multiplicity regarded, however grudgingly, as potentially legitimate. A freshman has been complaining that different section men in the same course often cover very different material:

S.   Maybe my ideas will change after four years, though.

I.   But this year, this really seemed to you, ah, pretty doggoned unfair.

S.   Yeah, I don't like that idea, I don't know why they go ahead with it here, there must be a reason for it. I know my cousin was a graduate student in Anthropology here, gonna get his Ph.D. in a year or so. And he was, I guess, he was a section man in this Soc. Sci. course a few years ago. And he sort of liked this system because

---

[4]This ordinary sense of "interpretation," central to what we refer to as Relativism, is, of course, a method of assessment or adjudication among alternatives in a plurality of possibilities, all of which are made potentially legitimate by the context of uncertainty. At the level we are considering here, uncertainty is not yet perceived as epistemologically legitimate, hence the nature and function of interpretation cannot be perceived either.

... I don't, I can't remember just what he said, he thought it better for the teacher, teachers like it better and they could do a better job, be better for them, but ah . . .

I.   Yeah, to let them run their own course, a little. /Yeah/ But you feel that the injustice at the student's end is ah, sometimes considerable.

S.   In some cases, yeah, especially in a course like Math where it's, it's ah, just, well, not good. It's less subjective so I would think, I don't know, I would think in a course here like in the Humanities or Social Sciences, it might be more important for the teacher to make up his own program than it would be in Math where you just cover certain things. Or people. Everybody does them the same way.

I.   Uhuh. And there you don't see why things can't be laid out a little more rigorously?

S.   Yeah, I don't see why they can't give them a, a way they do in high school, where each teacher does the same thing the other one does.

I.   And you say in the Humanities that ah, somehow . . . are more subjective?

S.   Yeah, I think it's more important for them to have a chance to choose their own subject. Even there I, I would think that, I don't know enough about what these different section men are doing, things I've heard from other people. Even now I mean it's not too good if they can drift it around too far. Of course, they're all reading the same thing so it's not too bad.

Our records suggest that this trust placed in elementary Science can be sustained in advanced courses in a university setting only when supported by great computational talent. Even so, the discovery of theoretical relativism in advanced courses will be likely to re-create the crisis unless recourse can be found in more "applied" aspects of the field. The defeat of a student of less ability by the very Authoritative Science that had in high school offered him hope (and an initial sense of competence) can be heartrending, especially if it occurs while the student is in a defensive stance in the assumptions of these early Positions; he can see no other place to go.[5] He can, of course, search for a field he hopes will still be exact while somehow less exacting, like engineering, physiological psychology, or economics, but if the defensive necessities remain relatively high compared to compensating academic talent, the outcomes may not be very satisfying to either the student or his teachers. A senior discusses why he changed his major from physics to economics:

> S.   (*Discussing economics*) Well, it was, it was tangible, and also I thought it was—from that hand it had *value* to it. It, Ec. in my opinion describes the world around us very well. I mean I may be able to look around and then just—in my studies I can look around at the business around me and at the labor groups around me and everything, and now especially with the depression, or recession, or unpopular economic policies, it looked like it would be valuable to me. And it, it had a lot of tangible val-, tangible things. . . . Well, you can't say *around* me, it was just something off in a distance from you. Well, in that way the field itself is specific, but it's also vague. I mean it's not, not as specific as math or anything like that, but it has its other points that aren't clear.

If, however, a student is unfettered by defensive necessities, the discovery of legitimacy in even a temporary uncertainty can be liberating. Of those students in our samples who appeared to have entered college with the assumptions of Positions 1 or 2, most found it so:

> S.   After the first term in Hum. [the new] professor . . . and it's just a total reversal in the second term . . . would, would start talking on something. He'd say—we were reading Plato—and . . . he wouldn't say that, that Plato was wrong or Plato was right; he'd just sort of raise some problems and talk about them. And maybe he would say, "You know, yesterday, what I was saying, I don't think that's right. Today, *there's* the way I think, you know." And, (*laughs*) and you know, you just didn't know *what* to believe, and so you had to think it out for yourself. And decide what, what *you* thought.

---

[5]The same defeat can be experienced also in foreign languages, where a similar right-or-wrong clarity of procedure and a similar relation between work and reward can be found at the elementary levels, only to be lost when relativism emerges at advanced levels in literary criticism.

And maybe it didn't come out to be what he thought. That's all right. Ahh, doesn't mean that you're an idiot. . . . Maybe your section man agreed with you. And this is often the case. And so-ah . . . ahh . . . it, it might be annoying. I know it *was* annoying, a little bit, at the beginning 'cause it was new. I just-ah—but what'd I say? (*on CLEV*) "perhaps educational." Well, education means *self*-education. If you, you have to do some, some individual work, and not, not rely on the lecturer to interpret the book for you and tell you what to write on the hour exam, and just parrot back what he said.

And socially:

S.   It's a new experience to date eastern girls, in my book, I think it's entirely different. A mid-west girl, well, you can talk with them about the, you know, the discussion doesn't open up with about what you're taking in school, it—sometimes it opens up with "How ya doin', cat-nap?" (*Laughs*) That kind of stuff, see, 'course girls are the same no matter where you go, but generally here there's more emphasis on getting to know you as a person better. Ah, that's what one girl told me, anyway. She said that, ah, before couples get serious they have to discuss things, you know, and I think in a way it's a more mature attitude.

This sense of joy in the world's opening up and of discovering diversity appears in many forms, all of them charming. The experience of growth, of becoming more "mature," runs through them all and is associated not only with increasing breadth but particularly with the freedom for self-regulation. A freshman:

S.   I just realized that it's a more mature way of teaching. It puts responsibility right on your own shoulders. I mean-ah, if you're going to go in a lecture hall and sit down and sleep there, you're not going to get anything out of it. So, I realized I'd better keep awake and listen.

I.   And, you said, in a way, that you sort of feel you like this, or you don't. I mean?

S.   No. I *do* like it, now that I'm getting used to it this year. At first it scared me, and . . . it seemed like you were in a shooting gallery. And they were shooting at you. As I say, it's more of a mature way of teaching, and-ah . . . I think it teaches a person to become dependent upon himself, more than it would in high school, where somebody's holding a whip over your head, and sending you down to the office if you don't do anything right.

I.   Yeah. And this—and this seems to be OK now. You don't miss it?

S.   No, I like it now. I like this system now.

I.   Yeah. You wouldn't want—more help, as it were, in the way you go about it.

S.   No. Well, I wouldn't exactly say *that,* but—ah (*pause*). Well-ah, it just teaches you to become confident in yourself and doing it yourself.

Even the student in extreme Opposition to Authority's dictates finds a new freedom from enslavement to his own combativeness:

S.   I mean, if there'd been more restrictions here, like required attendance at classes, gee, I'd have been done for!

These are, of course, only first tentative steps into individual responsibility, and they are forced by Authority itself. Thus the experience is deeply ambivalent, and not always successful:

S.   The lack of-ah coercion and-ah compelling forces making you do things, it was more or less you were left on your own, your own initiative and what you wanted or else you could do the minimum work and, and . . . you were left free to make your own decisions as far as how you live and, and at times I wish I had taken more initiative and gone to see my adviser and talked to him a little more, you know, gotten really well-acquainted. Plus some of my teachers too, but sometimes the time just didn't work in so consequently I let it slip, and . . . I figure next year it, it'll, it'll be a lot different for me, I'll, I'll have my foundations, so to speak, here and then I c-, I can start exploring possibilities that definitely are offered here, which I wasn't able to do this year as I was building my foundations, so to speak.

Authority is still there to help and to tell you what to do, but one must now go to Them; They won't come to you. Again:

S.   I mean, you, you, you accept things as they are. You, I mean everything here, everything you do, you do on your own. I mean, if you, if you feel that you're in trouble in a course, or anything, it's up to you to see the professor and see the section man, the grader, and find out if he can help you out, make you understand what you're *not* understanding.

I.   Then it's kind of ah, up to you to . . .

S.   Yeah. All the work that has to be done. Nobody's going to tell you, nobody's going to tell you it has to be done. You *know* it has to be done. If you don't *do* it, it's your own fault, that if there's further—that the consequences are disastrous.

Even where it is assimilated to the basic structures of Positions 1 and 2, this new freedom to "think" in specified ways, to find "the answer," and to manage one's work "on one's own" represents change. Often the change is enough to reveal to the students themselves the nature of their previous assumptions. The dictum drawn from LeChatelier holds: "If you want to learn about a system, try to change it." It is therefore here, in Position 2, that the clearest picture of the nature of Basic Duality is given. The change reveals the previously undifferentiated fusion of knowledge, values, and conduct. Authority has been the source of all, as if they were one; there was no difference in being told what is, what is good, and what to do. The introduction of the new value, to "work on one's own," brings these assumptions into sharp relief—nowhere more poignantly than when one senses that one's allegiance to the old assumptions is somehow preventing the attainment of the new value.

A Radcliffe freshman discusses the CLEV item, "The worst thing about a vague assignment is that you can't tell how much the professor wants done":

S.   I mean, there I would have said the worst thing about a vague assignment is that, and I still believe it, you're unclear about what books to read, or something like that. But I realize now that my idea is probably pretty much based on marks, although I do do more than the assignment usually. . . . But I mean I think I realized what my motivations towards classes are. Don't much like them. Well, I really need direction more than that, because I'm not quite capable of doing things for myself. I think I just get confused, and if there's anything I dislike it's confusion in myself. (*Laughs*) . . .

(I. then refers to her earlier statement that positive opinions are more important to her than "this wild liberal tear." . . .)

S.   Yeah, they definitely are because I just can't run my life when I don't know what I'm doing. I think this is one of the doubts I feel about majoring in history because I know that isn't where I'm going, and I think I'd feel rather undirected and I *have* to be directed, damn it. (*Laughs*) Which is too bad, too. Well, I think so. I mean I should be able to order my life myself and I shouldn't need the external . . . symptoms, (*laughs*) of order but I do. I just can't live like that. . . . I'm independent, but I just do need something around which to center my life. But it almost doesn't matter what. And in an assignment, I like to have a direct assignment so that I know what I'm doing, and know when I've got it done. I just hate vagueness and it's all wrong, damn it. (*Laughs*) And I just shouldn't feel that way about it but I do. . . . It's just wrong in that it makes me not a leader, it makes me kind of a vegetable (*laughs*), and there again, that's the way I feel. . . . I have no objection to being a leader, it's just that I'm incapable of it. . . . I think basically this year shows me that I have potential that is unused. Very. (*Laughs*)

In this structure, then, Authority and Absolutes are still assumed to be readily available, and the new value of "independence" is felt to mean simply that one should not lean on them too much. A freshman:

S.   I don't "live in," I'm a commuter, and commuters, you know. . . . Over there [at the commuters' center] it's great, because you get to meet all the fellows. In fact I think there's one advantage in that, I meet upperclassmen, whereas a freshman living in the dorms doesn't get much chance to meet upperclassmen. Over the year I get to know the ropes a little bit. You know, they tell me what's going on. Maybe it's not good to know. Maybe it is, but ah, I know a couple of seniors, sophomores, juniors, they tell me what's going on. Sometimes I ask them for help, maybe I shouldn't.

Likewise, uncertainty and groping are legitimate and respectable only within strict limits. One should, after all, know the answer or be able to find it quickly:

S.   Ah, let's see, I, I think that there's been a tendency this year, because of all I've learned, etc., to keep my mouth shut more-ah . . . I'm not sure why, I'm not sure whether that's a good trend, but-ah, it seems to be there. I seem to be taking everything in and weighing it and there . . . seem to be so many conflicting doctrines and opinions that I guess that the tendency is just to keep quiet until you really know just what the answer is.

Indeed, one could better tolerate fooling around with the gratuitous frills of Multiplicity if only They would first lay out the real answers clearly as a foundation:

S.   This term the Hum. course, let's see, what's his name, L—he of course is another man who's very brilliant and very good at what he's doing, but now he brings so much in that nothing happens, I mean he takes all sorts of stuff that, that isn't directly connected with what he's talking about anyway, so he says—it's all very nice if you can appreciate it, but that still doesn't do it—so you get just a sort of a huge amorphous mass of junk thrown at you which doesn't really mean much until you actually have some sort of foundation in what the man is talking about.

But despite all bewilderment and protest, a major concession has been made: *some* complexity, *some* groping in uncertainty has been given a place. Multiplicity of opinion, experienced as an annoying impediment or as an intriguing area of interest, has been allowed into the family's address to the Truth. As long as it is still conceived as a temporary exercise or a narrow area of freedom for exploration, Multiplicity has of course not yet attained the status of epistemological legitimacy; the Absolute remains secure and close at hand. The concession, however, has opened a path toward doubt.

Along this path new perceptions will be readily assimilable in a sequence of steps that gather momentum: (1) that in finding the answer to some problems, groping in uncertainty may be quite prolonged; (2) that uncertainty may therefore be a human problem proper even to Authorities, who themselves may not have arrived at some of the answers *yet;* (3) that in the meantime . . . etc.

Each of these extensions will require elaborations, accommodations, complications of those fundamental assumptions about man's relation to the universe with which the person began. These cumbersome elaborations of a dualistic structure will result in a system of increasing complication and incongruity. There will then come a point (Position 5) when even the intricacy of a tentative contextual Relativism will provide a simpler fit with experience.

Our records suggest that this development becomes a positive experience only where two processes run in parallel: (1) The confrontation with diversity occurs in ways which allow a person to moderate its impact by steplike assimilations and accommodations (Positions 2–4); and (2) the analytical and synthetic skills of contextual thought are developed (Positions 4–5) to provide an alternative to helpless despair in a world devoid of certainty.

—◦◦◦— Position 3:
Multiplicity Subordinate

A sophomore-to-be is speaking of his preference for physics:

> S.   I'd feel (*laughs*) rather insecure thinking about these philo-
> sophical things all the time and not coming up with any definite
> answers. And definite answers are, well, they, they're sort of my
> foundation point. In physics you get definite answers to a point.
> Beyond that point you know there *are* definite answers, but you
> can't reach them.

In the concession "but you can't reach them," this student makes
room in his epistemology for a legitimate human uncertainty. It is a
grudging concession and does not affect the nature of truth itself (only
man's relation to it!), but the accommodation has loosened the tie between Authority and the Absolute. Uncertainty is now unavoidable,
even in physics. As a consequence, a severe procedural problem becomes unavoidable too. How, in an educational institution where the
student's every answer is evaluated, are answers judged? Where even
Authority doesn't know the answer yet, is not any answer as good as
another?

This is the problem which preoccupies students looking at the
world from the structure of Position 3, a structure in which uncertainty and complexity are no longer considered mere exercises or im-
pediments devised by Authority but seen as realities in their own right,
plumb in the middle of Authority's world. The new perception seems
in some cases to derive from direct observation of instructors involved
in that very act of puzzling previously thought fit only for students—
"Here was this great professor, and he was groping *too!*" Often it is me-
diated by such vehicles as the history of science or current discoveries
which imply (so obviously in retrospect) that many "answers" are yet

to be revealed. In any case, it is understandable that the first issue raised should be of evaluation. It affects the student right in the midst of the guidelines of his daily work.

The blow is considerable. So far Authority has been perceived as grading on amount of rightness, achieved by honest hard work, and as adding an occasional bonus for neatness and "good expression." But in the uncertainty of authorized Multiplicity, coupled with a freedom that leaves "amount" of work "up to you" and Authority ignorant of how much you do, rightness and hard work vanish as standards. Nothing seems to be left but "good expression":

> S.   If I present it in the right manner it is well received. Or it is received . . . I don't know, I still haven't exactly caught onto what, what they want.

And:

> S.   I've been handing in papers that if I were grading I would have given an extremely low mark. Some of them perhaps I wouldn't even have passed. But they've been coming back in many cases with extremely good marks. So since I can't explain that, I certainly can't explain how any marks, ah, would be worked out.

Authority's maintenance of the old morality of reward for hard work is called into serious question:

> S.   A lot of people noticed this throughout the year, that the mark isn't proportional to the work. 'Cause on a previous paper I'd done a lot of work and gotten the same mark, and on this one I wasn't expecting it. . . . I just know that you can't, ah, expect your mark in proportion to the amount of work you put in. I, I've seen that occur with my friends—some people can sit down and study for, go to the library and spend eight hours a day studying for an exam and get the same mark that somebody else would that spent maybe, ah, three hours studying. In prep school it was more of a, more, the relationship was more personal and the teacher could tell whether you were working hard, and he would give you breaks if he knew you were working. It wasn't grading a student on his aptitude, it was grading somewhat on the amount of work he put in.

This amount of uncertainty can again raise Opposition:

S.   This place is all full of bull. They don't want anything really honest from you. If you turn in something, a speech that's well written, whether it's got one single fact in it or not is beside the point. That's sort of annoying at times, too. You can put things over on people around here: you're almost given to try somehow to sit down and write a paper in an hour, just because you know that whatever it is isn't going to make any difference to anybody. If you make one good point in a paper, one ten-word sentence, somebody will think it's very nice, and that's so silly, really, because it's completely meaningless.

And temptation is set in the way:

S.   You also get the feeling, I mean on an exam they'll give you points for writing your name down, practically. Of course I don't object to this because I don't know anything when I go to these exams anyway, and if it weren't for that I wouldn't get through, but still, looking at it from a purely objective standpoint it looks to me like it's (*laughs*) kind of not very good, you know? I mean you can't help but take advantage of these things.

Part of the difficulty seems to derive from the fact that the initial impact of complexity and diversity is experienced in terms of sheer quantity. Just as the salient aspect of assigned papers is their "length" and of assigned readings their "amount," so it is also for the intellectual virtuosity of instructors:

S.   I found that my section man, out of two lines, could talk a whole *hour*. And at first I didn't see where he got it all. I said, where did *that* come from? Two lines just, and where did *that* come from?

Perhaps it is because this sense of quantity is so pervasive, or even overwhelming, that little room seems to be left for perception of the instructor's fine discriminations. In any case, complexity and diversity are first experienced as raw and unstructured, an aggregate in which each item such as a point of view is *sui generis* and irreducible. This is the pluralism we have chosen to call Multiplicity and which confronts the student at this stage of development with the necessity to discover the grounds on which his own opinions are being graded.

The solution to this problem is technical, and the student will discover in his next steps the technique which "They want." Only later will the student come to perceive in this technique, which he first learned as a mere procedure, an expression of the nature of human truth itself.

In the meantime, until the procedural problem is solved, the student must somehow bear the stress. He still sees the world of truth and value as the domain of Authority; in a subordinate but real part of this world he perceives the fact of uncertainty, compelling for Authority itself. Now epistemologically relevant, uncertainty implies the legitimacy of a multiplicity of answers. And yet Authority continues to grade one student's answer against another's, even in respect to problems to which the Right Answer is unknown. The incongruity provides a power *vis à tergo* to the student's search for a more satisfactory ordering of his experience. His search will focus on an effort to reappraise what it is that "They want," and he will now listen with more open ears to what his instructors say they are up to.

Note: I pause here to remark briefly on the use of the terms "perceive" and "conceive" in this report. In the past 30 years the traditional distinction between perception and cognition has become increasingly problematical. What a person perceives, even in viewing a physical object or event, is known to be influenced by the generalizations he has developed from experience, that is, by his concepts. Two persons with different notions of the solar system may be presumed to see different events in perceiving the same sunrise (Kuhn, 1962). And yet, as constructs, "concept" and "percept" remain useful referents to the poles of a process.

In this report the ordinary difficulties are compounded. The development of a person's theories of knowledge and value occurs at a level of abstraction that should place it firmly in the arena of cognitive psychology, but, strikingly, this fact does not free our analysis from the problems arising from the interpenetrating functions of cognition and perception. On the contrary, this interpenetration continues to be the very object of study itself.

First of all, all the ordinary first-level difficulties of inference obtain. The assumption is made that, for example, what a student thinks knowledge to be like strongly influences, limits, or even dictates his perception of what his instructor is up to. Perception being always meaningful, a student who conceives of knowledge as a collection of right answers (that is, responses which directly correspond to the absolute reality known to his instructors) has available a limited number of ways in which he can "perceive" an instructor who is presenting several valid alternative views of his subject. In general, then, the data of this study are not restricted to the students' abstract conceptual statements; the students' reports of their social perceptions are considered relevant first-level data from which to infer their conceptual systems.

The difficulty, however, is not confined to first-level interaction of concepts and percepts. Already in the early Positions of the development, and increasingly as the students move on to the capacity for perspective over their own thinking, we shall be focusing on meta-thought—at a second, third, or even fourth level. Here it should be easy to say that we were beyond the perceptual, receptor modalities and dealing therefore only with concepts about concepts. It turns out, however, that an analogue of the concept-percept relation functions at these levels as well, and that the term "perceive" must be used even in this abstract cognitive realm.

For example, I may *conceive* of knowledge as relative; I can also *perceive* knowledge *as* relative. The mere fact that both these activities occur at highly abstract levels does not vitiate the distinction between them. Phenomenologically, they are very different. As I "conceive of" I am more aware of my activity and of alternatives. In my "perception as" I experience relativism more as an attribute of knowledge "out there," I am less aware of my activity of attribution, I feel more subject to the "fact" and less conscious of alternatives. Our records suggest that, in this phenomenological sense, our students conceptualize more frequently in periods of transition or confrontation with incongruity, and that when a new high-order concept has proved itself generally viable, it tends to embed itself into the new *perception* of "how things are" until dislodged by some fresh incongruity. (See the experience of a student considered at length in the section on Position 5.)

A brief example of this evolutionary process:

S.   Well, I read Freud and I went whole hog. I mean this was it and I looked around and saw everything differently, kind of a revelation . . . everything looked different. And it was only this year I discovered . . . one day I just saw the contradiction in Freud's thinking, in my own thinking, between the theory of personality and the theory of therapy. And I said, "Gee I've got to stand back and have a look." And I've been looking and I've been thinking, and I can see now what Hartmann and Erikson and everybody have been struggling with.

Here, the relation between a cognitive frame and the cognitive analogue of perception is stated in "everything looked different." But when a contradiction is discovered (perceived?) in the cognitive frame, and the decision made to "stand back" so as "to have a look" and "to think," it is as if the cognitive-perceptual continuum has been *moved up* or back a step. What was previously a considered concept becomes itself the object of *perception*. Then, in turn, a new high-order concept makes possible new perceptions of what is "out there."

Precision not being possible at this level, I shall use the terms loosely in this report with primary reference to this phenomenological distinction between them:

To perceive (and such correlates as "see," "see as," "realize," etc.): an interpretive act in which the interpretation is experienced as an attribute of the "object" perceived, rather than as something one has attributed to the object. The "object" can be concrete in the external environment or an abstract concept in the internal environment, but is experienced as existing in its own right, its attributes part of its "so-ness" or own nature. Most perceptions are relatively compelling; one is usually unaware of one's act of interpretation and senses little freedom of choice in the matter. When a perception changes, it seems to do so spontaneously (as does a reversing figure) even when the change is the result of a deliberate and conscious shift of one's own internal frame of interpretation (Rubin, 1958; Wittgenstein, 1953). As long as one "sees what one sees" (e.g., an act as immoral), one cannot see it as something else without risking a separation from truth (Polanyi, 1958).

To conceive (to conceptualize, to think, to consider, etc.): an act of interpretation in which various possibilities, combinations, and orderings are tried out with a relatively active sense of alternatives. When the reordering involved lays the ground for new perceptions, the latter will appear as "realizations about" objects. That is, the new perceptual interpretation will appear not as one's creation but as something that was in the object all along. A creation of thought, therefore, no matter how original, may, when completed and itself objectified, be perceived as supra-personal, and an object or a truth in its own right (Polanyi, 1958).

This form of the distinction will be relevant, however, only in the phenomenological sense evidenced in the way a student is speaking. In the analytical sense, the analogue of the conventional concept-percept relation will also be considered valid in the sense that a student's conceptual assumptions remain inferable from his "perceptions" of other concepts even when he is not aware of his assumptions or voicing them explicitly.

⚯ Position 4:
Multiplicity Correlate or
Relativism Subordinate

In endeavoring to account for man's relation to knowledge and value through the structure of Position 3, the students left major issues unresolved. In daily experience these issues were represented to them most pressingly by Authority's insistence on continuing to pass judgment on their opinions even on matters about which Authority itself acknowledged ignorance of the Right Answer.

In developing some rationale which would account for this anomaly, our students split into two groups, each developing a distinct restructuring of the world. We considered these alternative views as developmentally equivalent in that each represented an ultimate extension or accommodation of the old fundamentally dualistic structure before its capitulation to the vision of a generalized contextual Relativism—the revolutionary restructuring in which the students reunite in Position 5.

As in the bifurcation which occurred at Position 2, the choice between these alternative structurings in Position 4 seemed to be dictated by the balance between a student's tendency toward Opposition on the one hand and Adherence on the other. Once again, too, the developmental advance in individuation and independence implied in the more Oppositional alternative is paradoxically balanced, or even overbalanced in the long run, by the greater openness of the Adherent structure to the acquisition of the *skills* of independent thought taught by Authority.

As I remarked in the discussion of Position 2, we suppose this paradox to occur in the setting of modern liberal education wherever it is institutionalized. In these settings, Authority, no matter how ambivalent it may be, is committed to the development of the students' intellectual independence based upon the skills of comparative, and hence relativistic, contextual thought. Ironically, then, it is the students who conform, at least to some extent, who can derive most readily from the best of their instruction the tools of intellectual independence. In contrast, the students who fight for their independence "from" Authority at this stage of their development must pit themselves against the enemy within the very dualistic structure which they perceive Authority (all palaver aside) to be imposing upon them.

At this point of development, then, the less combative student, perceiving Authority as "wanting" him to think relativistically, will cooperate in his instruction with anything from compliance to eagerness and more readily "catch on" to the skills of critical thought. This achievement hardly makes him independent in any spiritual sense. A certain creative judgment and a willingness to risk are of course required by any critical comparison of competing interpretations of data, even where the critique is narrowly analytical. However, when such thinking is performed purely *in the context* of "what They want," it remains an act of conformity, with final responsibility lying outside the thinker. What such a student will do with the tools of independent thought once he has acquired them will remain for him to determine. He may use them in establishing responsible independence and in working out thoughtful Commitments including those of productive revolt. He may, however, use them in opportunistic avoidance of any commitments at all (see discussion of Escape, p. 211). As the successful arts of examsmanship reveal (Perry, 1963), the forms of independent thought are readily imitable by any bright student. In Authority's turn, even the most shrewd and experienced instructor, when faced with an agile and scholarly manipulation of the forms, is in a poor position to ascertain the spirit in which it has been presented. Even if he knew, he would be helpless.

The students' souls, as I remarked before, are safe even against being saved. The educational community may do much to nourish the probability of a favorable outcome by acquitting its own responsibilities to the student in addition to that of training him in intellectual expertise. These responsibilities would seem to involve more than the provision of models for emulation; we infer from our students' reports that the most urgent requirement may be that of providing the student with recognition and confirmation of his community with these models, a community earned not only through his expertise but through his courage in the face of doubt (see Chapter 6). Even with these provisions, however, the choice, as an ultimate spiritual choice, remains irrevocably with the students. The second half of our scheme of development will trace the forms through which our students worked out their resolutions of this challenge.

Here, in considering Position 4, we take up the outlook characteristic of the modal developmental position of the students in our study at the time when they first talked with us at the end of the freshman year. The mean point of development of freshmen of the Class of '58 (computed from the judged interviews) fell between Positions 3 and 4; for the Classes of '62 and '63, it fell between Positions 4 and 5. Position 4 represents therefore the modal "starting point" in our students' accounts, the view of the world from which they most typically reported in the spring of their freshman year. Of the two structures of this Position, I shall consider the more Oppositional alternative first.

Multiplicity Correlate

In Position 3, the student perceived Multiplicity as a temporary fuzziness in Authority's domain—a limited area of ambiguity in which They will someday soon uncover the underlying Laplacean order. However, a student with a bit of Oppositional gumption in him will recognize a playground when he sees one. As long as the area of ambiguity remains, he will have a right to his own opinion in it, and They will have *no right* to call him wrong. Moreover, as he finds the area to be ever larger than he expected, and the day of revelation of The Truth ever more remote, he may claim for Multiplicity a domain of its own, over against Authority's domain, and of equal epistemological legitimacy. Then, in Authority's domain, where Absolute answers are known, epistemological and moral law may still read, absolutely, "You're either right or you're wrong"; but in the domain of Multiplicity, where answers are (as yet) unknown, the epistemological and moral law will read, with equal absolutism, "Everyone has a right to his own opinion."

This restructuring provides for a recapitulation and broadening, at an abstract philosophical level, of an earlier adolescent revolt which had been limited to a reactive espousal of the *opposite* to whatever Authority said. The raising of Multiplicity from a subordinate status to that of a legitimate domain of its own seems to promise freedom from the bondage of simple reaction, and the energy of revolt can now be invested in an imperialistic extension of the domain of total freedom at the expense of Authority's claims.

The prerequisite for this structuring, in contrast to the alternative to be considered later, is some realization of the extent of Authority's ignorance. A freshman reports on the experience:

S.   (*Quoting from CLEV*) "Educators should know by now which is the best method, lecture or small discussion groups." Guess they don't.

I.   You agreed in the fall, and you disagree in the spring. . . .

S.   Maybe because I, well I guess as you, you look at that-ah . . . no one does know really, although it would be *nice* if they *did* know. I agree that they should know but I, I could see, I can see now realistically it's hard to know, some ways.

I.   What do you mean?

S.   Well, in-ah, small groups are more the individual attention, but you also are limited in what you can cover. A, a lecture you might give what's general, and in the sections, it's more particular or more explanation. But it's really hard to say which is the best 'cause, b-both have their place.

I.   And so it depends on what you're trying to do, is that . . . ?

S.   Yeah. Probably it'd depend on the course and it'd depend on the individual and it's really a hard, hard question to answer. But I, I was surprised, (*chuckles*) that's just, I guess I, I think they *should!* It would be nice if they knew by now what was the method, but I guess you can't.

From here it is but a short step to freedom. A sophomore:

S.   I mean if you read them [critics], that's the great thing about a book like *Moby Dick*. (*Laughs*) *Nobody* understands it!

The context in which the student made this remark suggests that he meant it without the qualification that some understandings of *Moby Dick* might be preferable to others. Had he been pressed on the matter, he might have acknowledged the possibility of "better" and "worse" in this domain (perhaps on such grounds as "expression," or even something approaching plausibility vs. sheer irrelevance), but the inference to be drawn from his own report is that he was operating on all-or-none assumptions. He was saying, in effect, that if authoritative opinions differed at all, no one "knew."

In short, this new structure, consisting of two domains, represents an accommodation of earlier structures which preserves their fundamental dualistic nature. Instead of the simple dualism of the right-wrong world of Authority, we now have the complex, or dual, dualism of a world in which the Authority's dual right-wrong world is one element and Multiplicity is the other. The categorization of all epistemological and moral propositions in accordance with this structure remains atomistic and all-or-none.

The student has thus succeeded in preserving a categorical dualism in his world and at the same time has carved out for himself a domain promising absolute freedom. What, however, has he done with the problem with which he began, namely what meaning will he ascribe to Authority's evaluating his opinions in areas in which They acknowledge ignorance of The Answer? The meaning provided by this structure abandons the search for Authority's *grounds* by substituting the proposition that "They're unjustly doing what They have no *right* to do."

Some students, only mildly oppositional, seem to view Authorities with generous complaisance, even from this structure. They seem to say, "Oh give them what you figure they want. They're good guys doing the best they can." The more reactive students see Authorities as imperialistically extending their biases and prejudices over the underdog's rightful freedom. In the intellectual realm the fight is against the constraint of the threatened (unjust) low grade; in the moral realm it is against the constraint of (unwarranted) guilt.[6]

---

[6]Consider here the conventional misuse of the discovery of comparative cultures: "Since it's all right for the Trobriand Islanders to do thus and so, you've no right to make me feel guilty about what I do sexually. It's *purely* a matter of individual decision." Far from being immoral or amoral, such pronouncements are made in a tone of moralistic absolutism (Inhelder & Piaget, 1958) which reveals the continuity of the emotional aspects of the structure. Such propositions "make sense" only in the context of Multiplicity as distinct from the context of Relativism.

Here again, then, it is difficult to see how the Oppositional student can assimilate from this structure a perception of contextual relativistic thought. The data in our records are diffuse, but they suggest centrally that the student becomes entrapped by his own argumentativeness. Unable to leave well enough alone, he demands that Authority justify itself by *reasons,* and, most fatally, by *evidence.* Unwittingly he may then be caught in the necessity to do the same.[7]

In addition, the student's perception of all Authority as bigoted and dogmatic cannot readily assimilate the impact of a careful teacher who refuses to be baited into behavior that can be read as arbitrary. In relation to his peers, also, his assumption that in uncertainty "any opinion goes" cannot give meaning to his daily encounter with students who have "caught on" to "interpretation" and who are considering the relation of opinions and data in terms of varying degrees of "fit."

However, the structure does derive strength from the daring behind its creation, and it is a strength that can serve the student well in the future. The establishment of a domain separate yet equal to that of Authority, in which the self takes a stand in chaos, will provide (once contextual thought is discovered to provide some order) a platform from which certain Authorities may be viewed with entirely new eyes.

By whatever means it is discovered, the bridge to the new world of comparative thought lies in the distinction between *an* opinion (however well "expressed") and a *supported* opinion. One item on CLEV read, "Where authorities differ, a student's opinion should be graded only on how well it is expressed." A freshman who had agreed in the fall and disagreed in the spring remarks:

---

[7]Recently some students of the extreme radical left have avoided this trap by shouting down or forcibly preventing the expression of any "reasons" but their own, justifying the tactic on the premise that the Establishment uses reasoning purely as a weapon of entrenchment. Whether or not this particular premise may be frequently valid is not relevant to this report. What is relevant is the absolutism of the *form* of the premise and the consequences of its universal application. The foreclosure of all debate with Authority on any subject makes it impossible to consider the degree to which the premise may be valid in a given situation. As a closed system, indistinguishable from that imputed to the enemy, it would appear to derive its prototype from the structures of Positions 1 and 2 as described in this scheme.

S.   Well—it's an opinion, but it's got to be an educated opinion. Have something behind it, not just a hearsay opinion. I mean, you can't form an opinion unless you have some knowledge behind it, I suppose.

In this transitional statement it is not yet clear that a better opinion would not still be one which simply has "more" knowledge behind it in the purely quantitative sense; and yet an "educated" opinion is surely something else than a right answer or a wrong answer or *any* opinion. The step to truly qualitative comparison is now a short one.

Relativism Subordinate

There is, however, another pathway from Position 3 to the vision of Relativism. This path, which the majority of our students followed, does not involve setting Multiplicity, as a world of its own, over against the world of Authority. Rather, it allows the discovery of Relativism in Multiplicity to occur in the context of Authority's world where Multiplicity is still something "They want us to work on":

S.   Another thing I've noticed about this more concrete and complex approach—you can get away without . . . trying to think about what they want—ah, think about things the *way* they want you to think about them. But if you try to use the approach the course outlines, then you find yourself thinking in *complex terms:* weighing more than one factor in trying to develop your own opinion. Somehow, for me, just doing that has become extended beyond the courses. . . . Somehow what I think about things now seems to be more—ah, it's hard to say right or wrong—but it seems (*pause*) more *sensible.*

Here the correction from "what They want" to "the *way* They want you to think" signals the discovery of the articulation of the "concrete" with the "complex" in "weighing" in Multiplicity—a mode of thought which is the structural foundation of Relativism. The weighing of "more than one factor," or, as this student later explained, "more than one approach to a problem," forces a comparison of patterns of thought, that is, a thinking about thinking. For most students, as for this student, the event seems to be conscious and explicit; that is, the initial discovery of meta-thought occurs vividly in the foreground, as figure, against the background of previous ways of thinking,[8] and usually as an item in the context of "what They want."

Now the capacity to compare different approaches to a problem in "developing one's own opinion" is presumably the ordinary meaning of "independent thought." The paradox for liberal education lies in the fact that so many of our students learned to think this way because it was "the way They want you to think," that is, out of a desire to conform. Can one learn to think independently out of obedience to Authority's demand? This particular student does say that this way of thinking "has become extended beyond the courses," but his primary experience is within the context of Authority's "wants," as is suggested by what he says next:

S.   I guess I'm thinking specifically of one course I took this year, this required humanities course. It's a literature course, and tries to outline an approach that can be used on almost any kind of literature. I started off a little bit less well than mediocre, because I couldn't see what they were trying to do. In the papers we wrote you were supposed to use this particular approach to reading material that they were trying to outline for you. And as the course went along, my grades got consistently *higher* as I understood their approach. Finally I came to realize about the middle of the second term that they were trying to get you to look at something in a complex *way* and to try to weigh more factors than one, and talk about things in a concrete manner. That is, with words that have some meaning and some relevance to the material you were studying. And all of a sudden my grade just *shot right up* and stayed right up.

I.   This was a lift.

S.   It was. It really was . . . (*voice rises*) . . . for *that* to happen. To understand all of a sudden. I mean, to realize . . . the *realization* of the understanding was what was quick . . . just what the club was driving at and then to use that in the course and suddenly see the

---

[8]Its later tendency to recede into the background will be remarked upon in connection with Position 5, together with further excerpts illustrative of this transitional phase in which Relativism is explicit as foreground.

grade go right up. That was really a great *lift,* a matter of extreme personal satisfaction!

In short, independent-*like* thought gets good grades. Genuine independence of thought, with all its implications, is an issue to be met later. It is enough for the moment to assimilate, under Authority's guidance, the discovery of coherence and congruence in reasoning in the indeterminate.

For it is "reasoning" that provides the lever that will move knowledge from the dualistic realm to the qualitative. Until now a question has either *one* right answer or *any number* of answers with equally legitimate claims to rightness. The requirement that an answer or opinion be reasonable raises the possibility that some questions may have *some* legitimate answers. The difficulty of making a dualistic determination as to whether a given opinion is reasonable *or not* will then lead inevitably to the discovery of degrees of reasonableness visible only in the light of relationships among assumptions, contexts, purposes, and observations (Relativism, Position 5).

But at first the complexity of "reasons" is experienced as quantitative. A sophomore:

S.   And now I realize it . . . as I say, there's a lot of answers for a certain question, and ah, by reasoning things out you can come to a variation of the answers /uhuh/ and-ah, it depends upon which way you're looking at it. That's right. I mean there's no . . . you can't come right out and point to one thing and say this caused the Industrial Revolution. And that's what I was looking for last year— one sentence that would tell me what caused the Revolution.

I.   One cause.

S.   But there is no such thing. It's a combination of factors and-ah, people vary on their ah, on looking at it, and ah, that's what I couldn't realize last year, and I can this year.

Many students first experienced the demand to articulate their opinions with reason in their negotiations with their peers. A freshman:

S.   Before, I used to think that Christianity was the only religion in the world—*the* religion—but when you talk things over you find out the Catholic view, the Unitarian view, different views on religion;

why they believe there is a God or why they don't; why they don't accept Jesus Christ, and why some do as well as some don't; why some don't even believe in religion period. I never had been exposed to this kind of thing before.

I.   What did it make you feel like when you ran up against some beliefs like these?

S.   Well, in a way it requires a lot of thought in what they say or what you say. But, ah, since I'd never really discussed these things—in public schools, the majority of them, those discussions aren't held on that kind of plane—it's something really new and you sort of tried to draw the other fellow out to present his views. You tried to present yours and you tried to find out just what he was thinking, and at the same time try and not make yourself look as if you were ignorant of it all, you know.

A junior looks back:

S.   I was very idealistic in the freshman year, and with very little substance to it: just the ideals. Just things that I wanted to be right. And I wanted to be very liberal and very open-minded, and thought that there would be absolutely no harm in being completely open-minded. Well, if you have more troubles you get more cautious in thinking (*laughs*).

A junior sees but still resists, preferring the immunities of Multiplicity:

S.   I'm beginning to discover that I can't follow a reasoned argument at all. I've never had to. I can't read philosophy. It's a sad state of affairs, but . . . I tell myself that this is no way to, ah, really prove anything, anyway—logic is really meaningless. I'm a great believer in intuition rather than science or logic.

Another junior, originally in science, has found a competence in the ambiguities of economics, but sees the humanities in the old way:

S.   I think everyone [in economics] that writes or everyone that speaks has their opinion and they, they see one meaning to it, but that's why they assign different writers with different opinions. And the lecturers even, as I say, they, they have their opinions but they, uh, because I mean they're big enough to be able to let you know there are other opinions. And, ah, it doesn't, in these English courses, in an exam, you read a novel for example and they assign all sorts of significance, and insight and foresight and all sorts of things between the lines. Well I—the way I think, either it's there and I don't see it and everybody else does, or it isn't there. It's one or the other. That's the way I—I think it isn't there. It could be that I'm dumb and it is there for everybody else and not for me, or I can't make up my mind about it and they can, but I don't know which is right.

Yet for most, the experience is liberating, and in a way that seems more meaningful and solid than the false promise offered by chaotic Multiplicity. This senior had said flatly in his freshman year, "I don't like ambiguity":

S. When you get in a narrow shell or something you sort of just can't break out, you're just, just looking around. It's like being in a room with all the windows down and all of a sudden you're let out. You, you open the windows around you and you can see things around you, and it impresses upon you the fact that the things you held for just normal, everyday things have become so much more important to you. . . . Ah, I think college has opened the shell for me, let me out. I can see things that I've never seen before and think about things I never really thought about or thought were important. It's just opened up so many, so many different roads for me. It's not only the learning itself, it's the paths that it opens up for you.

The distinction between an unconsidered belief and a considered judgment now becomes explicit. A freshman is discussing one of the items of CLEV:

S. When they say "personal beliefs" here, do they mean just beliefs that they believe because they want to believe them, or beliefs which are based on, on good rational solid reasons? It, it depends on what you mean by the word beliefs. If you just mean beliefs which you, which you had because you've been told to believe that, that's a different matter. . . .

And so responsibility also becomes explicit. It is still a limited responsibility, practiced within Authority's care, but it is practice for the more strenuous issues to be faced later. At this point responsibility is experienced primarily in matters of petty conduct, and always with reference to Authority, which "lets you" be responsible:

> S.   I mean there's nobody pushing you to study for a certain course, not like in high school. Over here it's different. You're on your own and that's what I like. You get all the, all the responsibility is on you. If, if you want to pass the course, if you want to get a good mark, you're going to have to really study; you can't go out gallivanting around, you know, I mean, ah, there's no, when you, when your section man doesn't come up to you and say "Look you're falling behind." I mean, it's not up to them, it's up to you. There is a lot of freedom and everything, you know; and-ah, you go to class, and there's responsibility . . . well, I have work to do and I have to do it, you know? And some guys are going out to the show, and you say, ah, "Sorry, I can't go out tonight, I got, I've got a paper to write or I got ah, something to study for tomorrow." I get, I got a lot behind in my work, I needed to sit down. /And make these decisions/ Yeah. And ah, ah, and then it's, it's that idea of responsibility, that idea, that aspect of freedom you get, with nobody pushing you.

Or if Authority did not appear to stand back, the same condition was won through Opposition of the traditional form. A sophomore:

> S.   Last year this friend of mine and me were having a race to see which of us could go to the least classes a week and things like that, but that's not going on this year. Last year I might go to one class a week, or sometimes get up at one o'clock in the afternoon and go to lunch, go to the ball game in the afternoon, come back and go to a bar. Go to bed and get up the next day at one o'clock. Just not too good. This was, ah, sort of getting out of prep school, where you have to be in at eight o'clock at night. It was sort of going hog-wild, I suppose, showing that you were free now, big man, grown up. I'm more used to being free now, more used to being allowed out after eight o'clock. But I think last year was sort of necessary, blowing everything out of your system.

Sometimes Authority's standing back and one's own revolt can be experienced together:

S.   I certainly appreciate the freedom aspect of this. I don't think I could last a week in a school that didn't have this kind of freedom.

And:

S.   I think, ah, that I might have dropped out if Harvard had had some strong pressures like, ah, insistence on going to class.

And finally, a sophomore:

S.   I think at this point that my mother has given up the case, so to speak (*laughs*) and I actually did try to provoke this a long time ago. I just wanted people to say, "Well, that's the end of that. Let him do what he wants, and let him work it out. We won't be responsible any more."

Responsibility for conduct merges, however, with the expanding responsibility of studies:

S.   Last year there weren't any directions, I mean everything was sort of muddled around and you ah . . . had to try and make a direction, but this year every-, everything's set up. In the house. And it's not run by anybody, it's there for you to run, and if it flops, it flops 'cause of your interests. And that's, I think it's a good idea. Also I think it's been easier this year, the academics, have. . . . My courses have been harder, but ah . . . oh, I don't know, I . . . think I've got to, I've gotten sort of the knack of . . . how to take a test and . . . which I didn't have last year. And sort of what each type professor wants. And a paper. Ah, oh I haven't got them figured out or anything like that, but it's a, there's a marked change in my marks, they've gone up and ah . . . I'm much, of course I'm much happier with my courses. That's one of the best reasons.

Diligence alone, however, will no longer produce security; the risk must be faced:

S.   In that course I was given more than I could think about in a lifetime, I guess. A very fine reading list. I might say, because it forced me to take and look at ideas that have been expressed by people since the beginning of recorded history, about the nature of people and their place in what we call the world, and I have had to think about them for themselves without any interpretation. As I say, I've had to make my own interpretations. I don't know how good I am at it, whether I should have been let loose on those things, but I think in the long run it's, it's high time I did begin to think for myself and, ah, I really think it would be better than getting a recipe for the course. I resented it—it's frustrating because, well, shucks, you do like to pass exams and know what to say on papers, but that isn't the real thing, that's not what it is. I mean I have visions sometimes of perhaps not being able to come back here because I didn't, wasn't able to think clearly enough. But I will know then that if I won't be able to come back it will be because it isn't in me to do the kind of work that's to be done, and not just because I didn't happen to remember the formula.

I think it's just perhaps becoming a little bit more aware of what's inside. If I find that I haven't measured up to the standards expected it won't be because I haven't tried. It will be because, because my proficiencies are oriented in another direction. Perhaps I'd make a better garbage man or truck driver than student; this, this may be. I won't know, but I'll have a better idea than if I'd just sat down and written out the formula. I think it's a gain almost in that feeling of "Shucks, if this happens I'll, ah, have a better idea of why than, than before."

If courage was previously thought of as physical courage, or the guts to stick with a job, it now derives a new moral quality from the intimations of choice. The experience can be conscious:

S.   Well, the problem I was talking about last year was "What am I going to do, what shall I think about this?" So now I say that, well, I'm going to just have to choose. I'll read the topic for a paper and then I'll choose a side, or choose a point—and another thing, I'm not as scared to, to differ with them and say "Well I don't think so." Ah, I think the courage came with sections; I think it's easier to disagree in sections than it is when a lecturer is saying such and such from his podium. In sections we have differences of opinion, and there are arguments on one side and the other, and you see the section man himself sometimes changing his opinion, and this is encouraging.

Sometimes courage fails, or seems as if it might easily fail:

S. Every now and again you do, do . . . do meet pe-people who just give up and try and find "answers" . . . I mean . . . it's hopeless.

So far, in describing our scheme, I have indicated no direction for a student to move except forward. In later sections on Retreat and Escape, I shall describe in detail other directions in which some students moved, so it seemed to us, in the experience of despair, or anger, or alienation. However, since the forward motion in the main development can best be understood through an awareness of its alternatives, a brief note about these alternatives may be useful here.

In Positions 1–3 the available structures have offered no way "out." Resistance could express itself only by a stubborn entrenchment within the dualistic world itself in alignment with, or in opposition to, Authority. Any such stand, in the face of powerful environmental pressure to move forward, would call for an emotional fortification of near-violent energy, a mustering of a sense of inner strength and categorical righteousness best experienced in resentment, hate, and moral rage against otherness. Here, then, would be found the all-or-nothing worlds of the dogmatic reactionary and the equally dogmatic rebel. Detachment, in contrast, would be impossible, for there is no place in which to stand back. Even passivity, if it is not to consist of mere obedience within the system, would have to take the extreme form of a numb, catatonic non-being, and no student who had chosen it would have survived in the environment.

Position 4, however, opens up a new possibility—escape through detachment. Multiplicity, as a quasi-legitimate world of its own, offers the haven of a bland personalism where "anything goes." Here one is not responsible even for thinking. "Intuition" will do; "it's all up to the individual anyway." Relativism also, if left at the level of conformity to Authority's demands, can be exploited in gamesmanship: "I guessed it would be good to seem in favor of the book, but I didn't forget to be balanced." Here, then, the capacity to think about thought offers a position of detachment which can be exploited, as the sophists learned to exploit it, to evade responsibility.

It is interesting therefore to search the records for what the students find that makes the risk of going on worthwhile. It seems to be some loyalty to truth, a feeling that if the truth is really dubious, it is better to have a dubious truth than a false certainty. A freshman:

> S.   (*Discussing changes in his answers to CLEV*) "If professors would stick more to the facts and do less theorizing, one could get more out of college." Well, it's [student's disagreement] based on the idea that if you present more theories you can, ah, more or less, sometimes you can arrive at a *better* answer. And if you just present one side of the question then you're just left up in the air with one side.

In this new world of "thinking," there can develop, also, a new sense of community among peers. This community is based in a real sharing of ideas, rather than in the banding together of "we" against "They." Indeed, the ground is laid for a community in which "we and They" can merge. A sophomore reports:

> S.   I think the House has done a great deal, ah, being with upper-classmen of senior and junior level, also being in a field [with] people ah, that are . . . all have the, you know, same interests in, academic-wise so to speak. And you sort of get the feeling of a, not a clique but a, a very important group feeling that you didn't have last year. Ahh, you have a tutor, he has about 30 tutees say, in the sophomore class and you all know each other and talk over these papers and, and then with the upperclassmen. You get to know very quickly those that are in your field, they're going through the things that you will be going through, like general exams, theses, and so forth. And you get to know them, their problems on graduating, where they're going.

A sense that everyone is in the same boat will be of comfort as the student allows himself to see the full implications of his recent learning.

—⁓— Position 5:
Relativism Correlate,
Competing, or Diffuse

Our scheme must now account for a drastic revolution. Up to this point the students have been able to assimilate the new, in one way or another, to the fundamental dualistic structure with which they began. The new, to the extent that it has been anomalous or contradictory, has naturally forced them to make certain accommodations in the structure, but these have been achieved either by the elaboration of dualism into a dual dualism or by the addition of a new subcategory of "critical thinking" to the general category of "what Authority wants."

These developments, however, have been enough to make the system unwieldy. Like the Ptolemaic cosmology, it has become overelaborate, and it has taken into itself incongruities which are the seeds of its own destruction. The time is ripe for a more economical address. The students will find this address in the radical reperception of all knowledge as contextual and relativistic.

The students appear to achieve this revolution in their view of the world by making a transposition in the hierarchy or forms of Position 4. They promote Relativism from its status as a special case (or subordinate part within a broad dualistic context) to the status of context, and within this new context they consign dualism to the subordinate status of a special case.

This form of revolutionary restructuring has been revealed as a characteristic of the evolution of scientific theory (Kuhn, 1962).[9]

---

[9]Example: Properties obtaining to certain anomalies of measurement within the old context of Newtonian mechanics are reperceived as expressive of universals within which Newtonian mechanics are a coherent special case.

Strangely enough, we have found no explicit description of this kind of transformation as a phenomenon in human personal development.[10] As a strategy of growth it would seem to deserve a prominent place, not only in theory of cognitive development but also in consideration of emotional maturation and the formation of identity.

In our scheme of development this striking event takes place between Position 4 and Position 6. In Position 4, the student had assimilated Multiplicity and Relativism into the framework of a world he still assumed to be dualistic. In Position 6 he will apprehend the implications of personal choice in a world he assumes to be relativistic. This revolution is precipitated by the failure of a dualistic framework to assimilate the expanding generalization of Relativism.

What is the experiential course of this revolution? In their reports, some students are not enlightening of detail, for they appear to have realized the personal implications of the new structuring contemporaneously with the revolution itself. In one year they were judged to speak from Position 4; in the next, from Position 6. In Position 6, unfortunately for us, they were far more concerned with the personal challenge of their new vision than with explaining how they developed the vision in the first place.

Many students, however, were more informative, precisely because they had moved into the new relativistic framework without having noticed its demand for personal choice. The world as they saw it was broadly relativistic, and they spoke implicitly and explicitly from that assumption. This structuring of the world, however, was devoid of that focusing element of individual relevance that characterizes later developments. Loose and vulnerable as it is, this generalized relativism appeared in the reports as a sufficiently stable structure to form a position of its own, Position 5. The reports of students in this Position provide our best evidence for a description of the revolution, even though there are special reasons why this description must remain to a large degree inferential.

A student who saw Relativism as "subordinate" in Position 4 saw it as a special way of thinking about certain special problems. He had discovered that a comparison among several interpretations of data (e.g., the wording and metrics of a poem, the offices and powers of a

---

[10]A possible exception may be found in a sensitive portrayal of stages in psychotherapy by Franz Alexander (1941).

governmental system, the complexities within an economic or historical event) is "the *way* They want you to think about such things." He had discovered not only a Multiplicity of points of view *about* such matters as literature, history of politics, but a patterning *within* each point of view, an interdependency of parts within the whole, which gave each "point of view" its special character, its coherence, its integrity.

The discovery brought him a new sense of power. Not only had he "caught on" in his studies, he could now think about thought: he could spot a false dichotomy, talk about assumptions and frames of reference, and argue about the degree of coherence of interpretations or their congruence with data.

But in making this new discovery, the student had, by necessity, to assimilate it in some way to the extant major structure of his previous world view. To perceive it at all, he had to construe it from where he stood, in short, to see it as a particular, a figure seen against the old background.

He saw Relativism, therefore, as a special case: a way of thinking about a certain class of problems, a way of "making sense" in otherwise chaotic Multiplicity, and most of all, a special procedure (among other procedures) that "They want here."

The old dualism was still intact. It was of course a complex, or dual, dualism. On the one hand there were still those things that are either right or wrong, and to which "They know the answers"; on the other hand were those indeterminate matters about which "They want you to think" in the new relativistic ways. The latter "ways" had not yet challenged the former. Authority still reigned, asking for performance in both.

In sum, the student perceived Relativism as an item *in the old dualistically structured context.*

In the next step, Relativism is perceived as the common characteristic of *all* thought, *all* knowing, all of man's relation to his world. Against this ground, dualistic right-or-wrong thinking, and even "ideas of absolutes," become special cases *in the new relativistically structured context.*

This event presented us with a paradox: the revolution is both the most violent accommodation of structure in the entire development, and at the same time the most quiet. It involves a complete transposition between part and whole, figure and ground, and yet almost no student in our sample referred to it as a conscious event, a discrete experience, a "realization."

The inferences suggested by the reports of students in Position 5, however, gain in credibility by offering as their corollary an explanation of the paradox itself. What seems to happen is this. Relativistic thinking, self-conscious in its newness in Position 4, gradually becomes habitual. This seems to occur first in those specific courses or situations in which the student has perceived such thinking as appropriate. At the same time, however, the student discovers new areas in which it is appropriate, perhaps in bull sessions in his dormitory on subjects like religion, politics, or morals. As the sophomore quoted in Position 4 remarked, "And I find this way of thinking to have become extended beyond the courses."

In Position 4, indeed, the generalization of relativistic thought does seem to receive this kind of conscious notice:

S.   Besides your meeting people, it's, it's the way of thinking. I mean just by the process of going through the school, the courses are lined up so they make you think, especially when you come to, say, hour exams and you have to take them. This rubs off not only in taking an exam, but when you, when you meet people and have to talk to them the process is in your mind and then you can think about things and be able to come up on your feet.

And:

S.   It's a method that you're dealing with, not, not a substance. It's a method, a purpose-ah, "procedure" would be the best word I should imagine, that you're, that you're looking for. And once you've developed this procedure in one field, I think the important part is to be able to transfer it to another field, and the example that I brought up about working with this, this crew of men. It's probably-ah, the most outstanding, at least one of the achievements that I feel that I've been able to make as far as transferring my academic experience to the field of everyday life.

This expansion, at first conscious, deepens the tendency of the activity to become habitual. When it becomes a habit, then, like any other procedural skill that has become automatic, it ceases to demand self-conscious attention. Attention is freed from "method" to "the matter at hand."

This state then furthers in turn the process of generalization. For example, a student may enter a course on the history of science and automatically respond with his new tools, not noticing that he is assuming relativistic structures in an area he had previously considered the domain of right-or-wrong. Through this sort of expansion he would quite coherently emerge with the assumption that all human knowledge is relative without ever having noticed the route by which he had started out with a special case and ended with a premise.

The records suggest that, as a generalized abstraction, this is a fair description of the normative course of the revolution. To illustrate in a particular student, we can take up the thread in the report of the sophomore quoted at some length in Position 4 (pp. 111–113). In that Position he reported his discovery of Relativistic thinking and its initial generalization (requote):

> S.   Another thing I've noticed about this more concrete and complex approach—you can get away without . . . trying to think about what they want—ah, think about things the *way* they want you to think about them. But if you try to use the approach the course outlines, then you find yourself thinking in *complex terms:* weighing more than one factor in trying to develop your own opinion. Somehow, for me, just doing that has become extended beyond the courses. . . . Somehow what I think about things now seems to be more—ah, it's hard to say right or wrong—but it seems (*pause*) more *sensible.*

This discovery, which the student reported, in retrospect, as having occurred in the middle of the year, was made in the context of Authority's "wants" in a particular course. That is, he at that time perceived Relativism as a subordinate particular, in the manner characterizing Position 4.

Later in the same interview the student speaks again of the matter, this time not in retrospect but in his present way of thinking (early June). He is considering how generally applicable his new complex thinking is—that is, what its proper limits may be:

> S.   I don't know if complexity itself is always necessary. I'm not sure. But if complexity is *not* necessary, at least you have to find that

it *is* not necessary before you can decide, "Well, this particular problem needs only the simple approach."

Here then it is the "simple" right-or-wrong that has become a special case. He now finds it safer to assume complexity as a general state and then to discover simplicity if it happens to be there. This is as explicit a statement of the transition to Position 5 as appears in our records.[11] The last statement would indeed represent the fully developed structure of Position 5, except for the fact that the "simple," when it occurs, is still assumed to *be* simple and not itself a derivative of complexity (e.g., 2 + 2 *does* equal 4; the simplicity of the proposition is not perceived as a derivative within a relativistic theory of sets).

Yet even for this student much of the revolution seems to have come on unnoticed. He happened to be one of a few with whom we reviewed, just following the interview in senior year, selections from recordings of previous years. One of the particular passages we selected for his comment was the first one quoted above. We looked on it as a significant passage, expressed with freshness and charm. His interviewer was dismayed, therefore, to find him react with surprise and intense scorn. The interviewer protested, and the student explained his reaction as follows:

S.   Well, we're talking about . . . if we're talking about the value of a liberal education, maybe one of the things is that you kind of take complexity for granted, or it teaches you to do this. And therefore you kind of dismiss . . . You, you can't even *talk* about taking a simple approach to something, you just kind of, I mean it's just a way of looking at things which *is* complex and therefore you can't talk about being complex as, as a *conscious policy.* I mean it's *not* a conscious policy, it's, it's just something that's been absorbed into you.

---

[11]Other students who remark on the status of either-or, all-or-none binary functions in a relative world do so in the context of decision-making in action. That is, such functions appear as a special case forced by the exigencies of action in a relative world: "You can't analyze, consider and balance things forever; sooner or later you've gotta decide and *act.*" This is not, however, a transitional statement; the establishment of a relativistic world-context is already complete.

And this, and that's why this seemed kind of superficial conversation, or seemed just to lack intelligence, because I don't think you can say, well, I'm going to take a simple approach to *this* problem and a complex approach to *that* one, I mean, looking at things, if it's just the way you *do* something.

So ingrained had his "way of looking at things" become that he had come to take it "for granted." He had forgotten his discovery.[12] More than this, the way of looking seems almost to be at one with the way *things are*. The ambiguity of reference of the pronoun "which" in mid-paragraph ("way . . . which *is* complex?"; "things which *are* complex?") seems in the spoken record to emphasize this congruence. In this sense, he has not only forgotten his discovery, he cannot imagine how anyone as old as a sophomore could be involved in making it.

The confrontation of the student with his sophomore self in this interview was fruitful in suggesting to us the way in which such a revolution could take place without a student's notice, but it taught us to be very careful in inviting students to hear their records. The restructuring of the world revealed here entails a revolution in identity as well. In the new perspective, developed unawares, the old self may have become unrecognizable, alien, and "not what should have been."

We can see no reason why this revolution should not occur explicitly in consciousness—we feel sure from our work as counselors that it often does. For example, students whose need for certainty has caused them to focus narrowly on science can experience severe shock in advanced theoretical courses; and the conscious question "Is *every*thing relative?" can lead to the question "Even me? My own values? My own certainties?" Some courses in psychology or cultural anthropology are known to precipitate explicit crises of identity. Our particular set of records in this study, however, although they document the problems of identity in a relativistic world (Positions 6 and following), would suggest that students commonly find themselves in a relativistic world without an explicit memory of how they arrived.

---

[12]That is, his experience of discovering. He is no longer aware of conceptualizing *about* the complexity of things; he simply perceives things *as* complex (see pp. 102 ff.).

Within the general description of the transition given above, we thought we detected two structurally different paths. The first path leads logically from Relativism Subordinate in Position 4. The discovery may be of the form "Not only do 'They want' us to think this way, They have to think this way too. We're all in the same boat."

The second is a development from Multiplicity Correlate in Position 4. Relativism is discovered in this Multiplicity (which was set over against Authority's world), and becomes Relativism Correlate. Then Authority is discovered to be engaged in the same kind of thinking, and the revolution is complete.

In either case the revolution may be initially unstable. Our judges found interviews in which a student spoke at times as if he construed the world dualistically, at other times as if he construed it relativistically. The contrast could be striking, yet the student would appear not to notice the incongruence and would make no effort to reconcile his statements. It was almost as if two different people were speaking. This suggested a transitional state in which the two systems existed independently in the student, each with its own integrity, in competition.

Our heading for Position 5 reads: Relativism Correlate, Competing, or Diffuse. Both Relativism Correlate and Relativism Competing should properly be thought of as containing unresolved elements of transition. The completed revolution is designated by our title Relativism Diffuse. In this more generalized structure, all knowledge is perceived or "accepted" as relative; Relativism has become context, a permeating property of man's seeing, thinking, knowing and valuing. We chose the word "Diffuse" for its connotation of vagueness or lack of focus, for it is just this quality that distinguishes this structure from the developments which are to follow. The student has not yet faced, or come to grips with, the personal and social implications of his discovery. He may, of course, feel lost and confused in his new world, but he is still without a clue as to what he might do about it. Most commonly in our records, he appears simply too busy with the development of his new competence and too intrigued with his immediate interests to notice the implications.

The excerpts that follow illustrate salient qualities in students' reports of their experience in this Position: (*a*) breakdown of the old structure and identity, balanced by a realization of growth and competence in a relativistic world; (*b*) changed relation to authorities; (*c*) new capacity for detachment; (*d*) unawareness of a path toward a new identity through personal commitment.

Breakdown of Previous Guidelines and Identity; Compensations in a Relativistic World

A freshman reviews his year:

S.   It has involved the tearing away of a lot of beliefs in what has been imposed by convention and I think that it does come down to you tearing away your faith in the fact that-ah . . . [seeing that] conforming to any standard, that other people have decided, is selfish. I'm (*laughs*) not trying to drum it up into an emotional issue, but it's that on the important questions of what you're going to do, well, then I think you do see that ideals that have been set up elsewhere aren't necessarily the right thing. And you're exposed to more-ah, perfect ways of life that contradict each other. And you sort of wonder how could *all* the things be perfect?

You know, in the past months, it's been a matter of having really . . . having reduced to the level where I really wasn't sure there was anything in particular to follow. I, you do begin to wonder on what basis you'd judge *any* decision at all, 'cause there really isn't-ah . . . too much of an absolute you can rely on as to . . . and even as to whether . . . there are a lot of levels that you can tear it apart, or you can base an ethical system that's a, presupposes that there are men who . . . or you can get one that doesn't presuppose that anything exists . . . and try and figure out of what principles you're going to decide any issue. Well, it's just that right now I'm not sure that . . . of what the-ah, what those de-, how to make any decision at all.

You can completely forget them [decisions] and go ahead and live a good, quiet life, but that doesn't seem that you can completely ignore . . . especially when you're here and are having the issues sort of thrust in your face at times. As to, and probably the thing that's-ah most impressed [*sic*] is . . . that is, just seeing the thinking of these men who have pushed their thought to the absolute limit to try and find out what was their personal salvation, and just seeing how that fell short of an all-encompassing answer to, for everyone. That those ideas really are individualized. And you begin to have respect for how great their thought could be, without its being absolute.

A sophomore:

S.   I think the main thing that was interesting this year was questioning basic assumptions. . . . It was interesting in anthropology, particularly, which I didn't go into very deeply, but what I saw is the very basic differences, things that never occurred to me to question before. I don't know whether I'm questioning them now, but at least I know that it's possible to question.

That is a frightening thought to say it didn't occur to me to question. Sounds like 1984 or something. Well, it didn't feel *out,* or anything, before. So I'm sure there are things that I'm not questioning now that I should be. Whatever "should be" is. . . .

A junior:

S.   I mean I've just merely settled down to work, and since as I say . . . at home had too many darn things *done,* in my case, I suppose I have to think about it that much more.

But, sure your way of thinking pretty definitely changes. You work and I think out of your courses, as applied to life in general . . . you may apply them, maybe not specific points, but I suppose your way of thinking does change in a way that can't really be visualized . . . no pattern or anything. If you try and see too many things in a . . . set pattern, it isn't good. If you, you, you lose your perspective . . . (*clears throat*). That's what, 'cause I used to like, still do in a sense, but not as much as before, like to . . . fall into a set pattern or a nice ordered system in particular ways, what everyone likes to do, 'cause this is more comfortable or convenient that way. But in, in fact they don't.

You have to have *some* degree of order to things, as you look at them, but I think it's more accepting, it's a little more accepting things as they come. . . . Be o-open to a little, say, more tolerant viewpoint . . . Not this narrow one.

The sense of expansion contrasts not only with the felt narrowness of the past but with any anticipated narrowness into which one might "settle" in the future. The fear of losing the new breadth by becoming too specialized or set-in-one's-ways may itself contribute to the stability of this otherwise unstable and diffuse structure.

A sophomore:

S.   And I believe, for myself—as again I've got to repeat—I've got
to say that it's just a value judgment, because I see, I come in contact with so many people who-ah think that *their* idea of the public interest or *their* idea of a certain action is the *only* idea. But I
believe that as long as I'm thinking about problems which involve
my life, and which will involve the rest of my life, then to a certain
extent I'm alive, and to a certain extent I'm whole. You see. And this
is probably where this fear of, ah, specialization comes to me, from
this realization. And whether this is not practical, whether this is
ridiculous at this point, does bother me to a certain extent, because
I'm afraid that when I go on into these, into these specialized fields
and choose one-ah . . . that-ah . . . I will be shown *in black and
white,* that it, it isn't practical to think that way. And this could be a
hurt; this would be a, a emotionally upsetting, or whatever the devil
it could be. But at least now I, I believe that, when someone says
something, or when I read something, if I'm thinking about it, and
it piques me, this is good.

Another sophomore:

S.   This year I think I've been crawling around the university and
investigating all the libraries and crawling on rooftops and seeing—
I mean, there are great big areas that I haven't seen, but maybe these
are areas that could never become a part of me. I would like the
freedom to explore and then not to be held back.

The sense of expansion, and of being at least in touch with the
problematic quality of life, a quality experienced as "things as they
are," appears to compensate at a deep level for the confusion and even
for loss of control.
A sophomore speaks very softly:

S.   I know that, ah, there is more to me, and more to the things
about me, than I knew before. I won't say I understand them; I just
know they're there and that I may never fully understand or appreciate them. Before, I had ideas about where I was going and
what I was going to do. I had a plan. I had a certain program I was
going to fulfill. I was going to go through four years of college and
get a degree in this, and then I would know this thing and this thing

and this thing. And I would be well adjusted, a real honest-to-goodness all-around human being. Ah, and I would come out with a complete set of the things that I had come here to get.

Well, what I've appreciated is this: that I may get something I wasn't planning on, and that some of the things I'm planning on I may never get, because it isn't in me to do it, and I may not even particularly want to, deep down. I won't say that I've become, ah, what you might call a fatalist. I'm not saying that whatever I do, something is bound to happen. What I'm saying is that I don't think I'm in perfect control of myself and the world anymore. And I think I'm probably the better off for it, because if something should come up, if the bottom should be pulled out, I wouldn't have been aware of the fact that this could happen.

Ah, I was beginning to feel this last year, but I hadn't thought it out. I still have a lot of thinking to do about it; I'll probably spend the rest of my life thinking about it. But at least I've started to think now.

A junior reports the lasting quality of the experience:

S.   Well I think-ah . . . probably the way I'm thinking now-ah, *when* I'm thinking-ah . . . at all, probably pretty close was last year at this time, which was sort of a radical change from the year before-ah. I still, well, you look at something not quite so simply as you did . . . first of all—as you did probably freshman year, and I think I am still thinking about . . . well, it's somewhat more chaotic . . . (*laughs*) in that—I mean I, I, in the-ah present day-ah I'm not sure I wanted to be a writer, although I don't think I knew too much about writing. And about-ah, well, philosophy was another thing that I didn't know too much about at all. . . . Gov. 1b was a beginning there, and then I think the material that we were introduced to . . . and were encouraged to read in Soc. Science 8 was for me new and-ah . . . interesting, and also-ah, a little bit of tearing down of some of the old patterns of things and recognizing patterns as such. . . . (*Laughs*)

Commonly, the first compensation for the insecurities of relativism is that of immediate competence in the management of studies. In our counseling work we had observed a curious irony: students often first discovered an effective relativistic address to their courses through having neglected them. Without time for redress of their sins through the old obedient ritual of reading every assignment word by word, they were forced to "cram for the exam," and in the process to select what they guessed would be on the examination—in short, to consider the thinking and the problems of knowledge addressed in the course. For our counselees, the success that followed upon this scandalous activity was clouded with guilt and a sense of fraudulence. They would often resolve to do their work regularly and honestly in the future, not noticing that they were throwing out with the bath water of their negligence the infant discovery of thought. In the following excerpt, a junior confesses the guilty circumstances of his discovery—his disobedience in Eden. However, his commission of Original Sin does not prevent his claiming his new exercise of judgment. He has been clarifying for the interviewer the difference between his old and new experience of study:

S.   Then, it was just the weight of the thing. *Now* it's, it's not so much how many pages there are on the reading list, it's more what the books are worth. What sort of ideas do they have. I mean, I can read a book now, without regard for the pages. And read it pretty rapidly and get the ideas. That is, I'm looking for the ideas rather than plodding over the words and . . . /How come?/ And, well, the ideas are what count, and unless it's a particularly well-written book, you're not going to get that much pleasure out of how the words are put together. And after all, I've finally decided that you don't read a book just to say you've read it, just to say that you've gone through it. But you read the book for what it's worth, for what it has in it. And this, this doesn't count on any, for exam purposes, that is, it's a broad outlook really. I mean, before maybe I was reading, whereas *now* I've, tend to generalize the thing and get the main ideas and concepts, and then pick up a few illustrations here and there, and amplifications when it seems worthwhile. But it's the broader picture. /Uhuh/ It's just not reading to have read, but reading to learn something. Perhaps.

I.   And if this is sort of a dichotomist's picture of "the before and the after," as it were, any ideas about where you reached these conclusions?

S.   Well, (*laughs*) it may have been a pure accident in that ah, well, last year see, let's say I got a little bit behind when we were going into the reading period! And I had to move pretty fast, to finish. I still had the idea of finishing the reading list, but then, again, when I had to read it fast, then you get the other business about getting a general picture, and there maybe the two come together. This fall, I began to realize that in so many of my exams, as I reflected back, the facts were really *part* of the *issue*. And so, then, although I had the time to plow through it all, and to read it very slowly, I began to read for the over-all picture. This led to another thing where you tend to try to put the courses together, and the thoughts. And since I was taking three fairly related courses, this helped a lot, and there were a couple left over from the spring which pretty well tie up, and you can draw on them for your thinking in the others. And perhaps this was fortunate that it came at this particular time, but I began to get the, or at least to try to get the general picture, and the overlying tie-ups, general education.

Expansion and competence, however, are hardly enough in themselves to balance the loss of all fixed landmarks and guidelines.
A freshman:

S.   [If a teacher] is teaching third graders about communism and democracy, I think he would have to make some sort of a value judgment, just for giving the children some security, something to base their lives on, and he'll just have to grab ahold of the one that's nearest to him. It goes back to the doctrine of the mean—the one that's closest to you, the one that you don't have to reach for. If it's arbitrary, you might as well take the one that's closest.

And the same student as a sophomore:

S.   I could take one side of an argument one day and then three days later I might take the other sides with as much conviction or lack of conviction.

I.   Uhuh. But that doesn't give you any concern; you, you sort of feel that you're an open system yet—?

S.   Yeah, well . . . yeah, it could be also an open sore in a way. (*Both laugh*)

Lostness and loneliness threaten, and only community can provide the required strength:

S.   Being willing to accept tentative answers depends so much on your own personal situation. The way I feel about my family, my friends, the whole set of ideas; my willingness to accept them or not depends on my personal situation. As soon as I become integrated into a new community and learn my way around and become able to control it, then I'm more willing to accept tentative answers, the double answers. And, well, I'm less willing to accept them when I'm completely unintegrated, when I'm in a completely new atmosphere and have no connections. After a while, when I've really become worried about this, then I'll want the sure answer and try to grasp for it.

And:

S.   The college here is a place where your ideas are questioned, where you're put under quite a bit of pressure to do well and it's hard to really excel. I think this is an experience which, which does tense you, makes you question these old values. It's hard here, but here you have other advantages too which partly make up for it. You have other people going through somewhat the same experience, really, intelligent people who have similar interests. In other words you're in a kind of community of people somewhat like yourself, and that makes it easier in a way.

Fortunately, the possibility of a new sense of community is provided by the new structure itself, a community shared not only with peers but with authorities.

Changed Relation to Authorities

The unexpected rewards of disobedience, and the tolerance of authorities, confirm the implication of the new relativistic epistemology: namely that authorities must themselves be groping in a relativistic world. The hierarchical relation to authorities is now balanced by a horizontal relation in a shared context.

The result is a changed structure of community. If authority no longer rests on "knowing" fixed truths but rather on an experience and expertise in groping which are only more advanced than the students' own, authorities have lost their cosmic aura. In our coding, Authority becomes *a*uthority, a social function.

The first step may be experienced as forced by Authority itself. A freshman:

S.   I think what it is, an awful lot is the shattering experience at the very beginning. You know, of where just everything—suddenly you're away from home, suddenly you're faced with, with this dire choice of, of what you're going to take, you know, I had a great problem when I came, I, I didn't know wh-which way I was going at all. I just didn't, didn't, I was completely lost, and I went to my freshman adviser, whom we'll be anonymous about, and ah, he said, "Well . . . " and I said, "Look, I, I've, I, I don't know what I'm going to. What should I do?" And he looked, and he looked at me, and said, "Ah, well, I can tell you about the courses," he said, and I said, "Well I, yeah, but, but what should I do?" You know. He said, "Well you've got to decide that for yourself," and-ah, I just couldn't understand it. Then, you know, that, that here I was completely lost and he wouldn't help me.

I.   You were saying, help me.

S.   Yeah, yeah and, and he just wouldn't and, and he was, well now as I look back on it, this was the first time that anyone had ever done this, you know. You say "help me," and they'll, they'll sort of pat you on the head, coddle you right along, you know, help you with something that's wrong probably, but, but help you anyhow. So, at any rate looking back on this, he, he was of course right and the whole University's right, cause I think this is an awful lot the spirit of the University, this, this sort of, oh, which I thought was neglect at first, no one cared, 'cause it's so big. [But it's] something that grows out a great deal of care; they, they care about you as an individual, think because you're an individual you have a right to, to make . . . decisions for yourself to, to live your own life, and decide this. And, and I think, I think that this, this, this realization and th-that it was me, it was I, that has to make these decisions for myself. And, and the ability to do this, because I had to.

Sometimes the student is ahead in acknowledgment. A freshman had in school days perceived authorities as what they are in a relative world, but had found, or stirred up, such resistance in them that he had settled for artful dissimulation. In college, to his delight, his pretense was rejected:

S. The first time I liked it was when I . . . I wrote a paper for Nat. Sci. on, on philosophy of science, and I maintained that there . . . there weren't any absolutes in science, which, of course, was something that my chemistry teacher in high school would deny. He would maintain that there were all sorts of absolutes, I guess, and ah . . .

I. That's one of the reasons they would have called you radical if you had written that there, huh?

S. That's right, though I wouldn't have had much chance to write; there was never any reason for it, but I handed this paper in to him [instructor in Nat. Sci.] and one place in the paper I said, well, he's a science teacher, I'd better make him happy. So I stick in the word "absolute" once, just to make him happy. So I got back the paper with a B+ on it, and the only mark on the paper, a big question mark over that one "absolute" I put in. And from then on, I said, well *that's wonderful!*

The release, however, makes evident the need for new controls for behavior. A junior is talking about his instructor in tutorial:

S. His tendency toward, toward leniency with, with not . . . you know forcing me to do my assignments and not really being very strict about it. And, and my inability to, to quite, you know I, I wanted to so much because he was a friend, but at the same time I, I, you know, I just somehow couldn't help myself taking advantage of it, because it wasn't a stringent requirement, you know. I just knew he'd understand if I couldn't, so, so I, I, you know, so I *couldn't* usually, or I didn't.

The new controls, as they come into function, carry a different meaning:

S. I still study a lot. I think I study more now because I want to study, because I want to learn particular things instead of just studying because it's assigned to me, I think. But this year for the first time I've left some of my work undone. At the end of the year I was behind and I said, well, I'd do a certain thing. Before, I would have said, "It's assigned: I gotta do it."

The new structure of community results in a new dignity. It dissipates old humiliations, especially that involved in asking for help. A sophomore:

S.   I don't have, ah, so much false pride anymore, I guess you might say. I'm not—or at least I like to think I'm not—afraid to go and say to someone, "Now look here, I have something that bothers me. There's a question in my mind. I don't understand what you mean by this, or what so-and-so meant when he said this. Could you point me in some direction, or could you clear this point up?" Of course maybe I'm a dummy, but I'd like to be shown at least in what respect. And if something within myself, if I should think I was becoming neurotic or psychotic or something I'd go down to the hygiene department and have someone ask me, "Do you like girls?" I have a little more confidence in those outside me and I don't feel bad about going for help when I have a problem. This I think is just taking, making allowances for myself.

And a junior:

S.   I think when I was younger, when people in general are young, there's so many problems that they feel they don't have to face, and that's why they're indifferent about them. Either it's something that somebody else—the hierarchy, like the family—worries about, or it's something in the future that isn't any problem yet. And then you, when you mature you begin facing these problems for yourself, and looking at them, and then the family just becomes a help to people . . . with more, with a lot of experience. To help you, and not to take the brunt of the problem or something that's *your* worry.

For the student who has found himself entrenched in Opposition, the new relation is a release from the tyranny of reactive combat. A freshman (previously quoted):

S.   You feel that you're going to have to fight if you're going to survive, but you don't feel that you have to be so, ah, I don't know, *spiteful* and completely zany. That's good, that's very good, because if you spend all your energy being completely different and completely just the *opposite* from what they're telling you that they're doing, I mean you, you get into trouble . . . I mean you're just being that way for the sake of being it.

Another freshman:

S.   The most important of the . . . things, well, first of all the fact that there wasn't a system to fight. I got along fine with the teachers, with, with all the faculty. And even when they disagreed with me it wasn't a matter of ah, "I disagree with you, therefore you are stupid," it's "I disagree with you, but you might be right." [In high school] it was very personalistic. I could never get in a philosophical argument without it ending up in a debate over whether I was a bum or not (*laughs*).

The structure of the new community, based in a relativistic epistemology, provided a new meaning for individuality. If authorities must address the student in these terms, so must the student address those for whom he is an authority:

S.   My brother, my brother has always sort of looked at me askance. (*Laughs*) He's younger than I am-ah . . . I'll tell you something interesting about my brother that I realized up here too. Ah, *before* I always had so much that I wanted to teach him, had to tell him this, had to tell him that. I don't have to do that, really, I don't think, anymore. I mean he's living. He'll find out. And he probably won't believe me if I tell him anyway. He'll find out himself. I really don't think I ought to rob him of that experience. I got that here too, I think.

Of course, authorities still exist, with their functions, and must be addressed—realistically. Being human, they will have their own preferences, bias of thought, or even prejudice. Some may still consider themselves Authority. One can be aware of this, however, and still develop effective mutuality:

S.   You get involved with, with section men, people, yeah. (*Laughs*) In English C, certainly, you have to develop in relation to your section man, have to write for your section man, and get to know what your section man thinks is, is good, and what you think is good, and what you can hand to him that's good, that you'll *both agree* is good. Certainly you have to get to know your section man there. I suppose it's that way in any course. Particularly with writing papers.

I still enjoy papers above all, because it's something beyond the book . . . that I think is valuable. /Something for you to do./ Yeah. It's also something that distinguishes the . . . the men from the boys, the slackers from the, from the, from the, you know . . . people who are willing to work. It takes a certain amount of creativity to get out a paper, and imagination, no matter what the subject. . . .

Capacity for Detachment

In the structure of the earliest Positions, detachment was impossible. The structure provided no place to stand back in. One could, of course, make certain judgments, even of oneself (for example, diligent, lazy), but the standard of the judgment and the assumptions underlying it, being "behind the eye," were invisible. As the students put it in retrospect, "it was a kind of oneness."

To observe both an act and its context, one requires an alternate context in which to stand. In offering a plurality of contexts, Relativism provides the ground for detachment and for objectivity. Although the objectivity obtainable is always qualified by the nature of the contexts in which one stands back to observe, it is nonetheless a radical and powerful departure. It may well rank with language as the distinctive triumph of the human mind.

Students in this Position remark on this achievement, often with mixed feeling. For some it promises a rationality to balance the stress of emotions:

> S.   When everybody goes through college I guess sometimes they try to formulate some type of idea of why, for what reasons. To me, it seems to me that the more I-ah . . . go through this place, the more I work here, the more I feel that what I'm trying to do is-ah become what you might call a detached observer of various situations, of any type of situation that you go into. And by that I mean-ah, one who can, to the utmost of his ability, detach himself-ah emotionally from the problems and look at the various sides of the problem, in an objective, empirical type of way—look at the pros and cons of a situation and then try to . . . analyze and formulate

a, a judgment—a value judgment it could be on your part . . . bringing into consideration in this judgment-ah, well, what the other person would feel and why he would feel so. I think it all boils down to trying to remove emotionalism from your decisions and from your life as much as possible. . . .

It's just a matter of whether such a method of learning can go on working anyway . . . can be transferred from the college atmosphere to . . . to . . . everyday work situations. I should hope that some of this would, would stick with me, even if I don't stay in research work or something of the sort.

Others sense the loss of immediacy that is the cost of detachment:

S.   I think that I'm a little more objective in formal thinking now, than in the past, and I'm more aware of what I'm doing perhaps, but I'm doing it for what I think is good in some ways and bad in others. . . . Objectivity makes a lot of things clearer I think . . . like where I'm heading. I think it's one of the main references of clarity, and (*pause*). For instance in the Government course I think that-ah . . . working in a very broad, general look at everything from the outside, it gives you almost a sense of purpose, if there is such a thing. . . . Then I, I think that subjectivity, that comes in on the other side, in the writing. It's much better there . . . well, not being completely subjective, but I mean you have to be objective, to step out and look at it, but I don't know, I think that there's a spirit, a subjectivity, which . . . well it certainly holds you . . . but not more to enslave you. I think for instance, last year, I know in my Gov. 1b, I was . . . well, I don't know, whether you call completely, but I did the assignment every week, I mean just like it was supposed to be done, and I got *caught up* in it, and I think that's good. I liked it very much, but perhaps I didn't *judge*-ah as much as I'm planning to do this year.

I.   Is this-ah lessening of . . . subjectivity perhaps the . . . the drawback with what you felt was in some ways bad?

S.   Yeah, that, that would be the . . . partial drawback I think. I don't know, maybe I'm just being soft, on myself, but I think it's more fun to, I don't know, just, just get caught up in something . . . and just . . . flow with it. . . .

The same student goes on to search for some balance, or some way of accepting the stress:

> S.   In the past what I used to do is, well I'd read something and then I would get lost completely within whatever it was, I mean I would accept it completely without asking any question, and . . . I still have that tendency, and I think it's good, because it makes you look for what's good in something, and I think that's something that's sometimes-ah neglected. But . . . the objective viewpoint, let's say in literature or something, too . . . gives you the chance to get outside the world and then look at it . . . get outside the poem or whatever it would be and look at it and see what it . . . how it's handled. . . . It's well, for anyone interested in the arts you have to have both . . . and then tension comes, I think. Perhaps if you like something . . . (*laughs*) and then you look at it, and see a mistake.

If detachment has its costs in immediacy and in the pleasure of "getting caught up in things and just floating," it can also offer its own temptations for irresponsibility. A freshman:

> S.   Sometimes you get in some discussions and you're sort of forced by the nature of the task to take a decisive stand. When you're not forced to take a stand, you don't, and you don't feel compelled to argue for one side or another. The discussions become freer. More ah, more relaxed, I suppose.
>
> My roommate has a, has a rule. I, you, if you qualify yourself enough, you're sure to win an argument. (*Laughs*) And it's, it's true to a degree. I mean, if you keep hedging, and hedging, and hedging, you can get the guy to agree with you, eventually. All you have to do is to put in enough qualifications. (*Laughs*) He'll come halfway along.

One can, of course, apply the same rule in an argument with oneself. The consequences of such manipulation will be illustrated in the section on Escape. At Position 5, however, a certain looseness in the exploration of Relativism is not a sign of negativism or deliberate irresponsibility. The question of developing a "stand" is simply not yet a real issue.

Unawareness of a Path Toward New Identity Through Commitment

For some students the first exploration of Relativism, the initial practice with the new tools, is still too engrossing to allow of worry about where it is all heading. They may feel a little at sea, but not lost enough to wonder what compass will serve them. A sophomore:

S.   Actually come to think of it, it's probably a little childish for me to expect to be able to peg myself along a broad spectrum. Not desirable.

I.   You mean as, as a general position as opposed to specific issues?

S.   Yeah, maybe the trouble is if I had a, you know, axiomatic ideology which I used to, used to determine what position I took on any, on any specific subject, I'm afraid it would probably become dogmatic. Maybe I should just decide on the merits of each individual case.

And another:

S.   Well, I, I'd say that I've stopped trying to figure the angles, and I've sort of woken up to the fact that there's always something unaccountable. Not always, but there may be. You can't count on the unaccountable happening, happening either, it's just—you have to wait till it happens and plan as best you can. And you can always be ready to ditch it.

But the stirrings of some unnamed malaise can be conscious:

S.   I think it's very difficult for a person to examine his own beliefs. It's been very difficult for me to say that I have a certain belief, or to recall the changes in my belief. It's hard to examine yourself in that way, ah, it's quite unnerving, I think, to put yourself under a microscope, because every time you think you've accepted this, or done that, an experience you went through or something, then you begin to question the truth of it. How much did you really go through this experience? And you question these answers you've come to. It's quite a difficult thing to examine your belief, or your outlook.

And a Radcliffe sophomore:

S.   I never, I haven't yet felt that I'm ready to put things into a system, yet, I don't even know if it's possible. Sometimes I feel about ready to put it into questions! (*Laughs*) I can't even put it into questions. I've been trying, but it's so confused and unclear and so self-contradictory. And yet there *is* something, there is really something bothering me. I, (*laughing*) I don't know if I've gotten it across, but (*almost unable to talk from laughter*) there is.

Often it feels as if the disorder might vanish if one knew "what one wanted to be" after college:

S.   You see I'm very undecided as to the future after college, well, what I would like to be and it hasn't, couldn't point to anything particular and say, "I really liked this, I want . . . I want to be a doctor, I want to be a lawyer, I want to be this." I, I can't decide, so I can't say what I like, but I can just say what I don't like. So I keep away from what I don't like and hope that something else will appeal to me. . . . I don't know if at my stage in the game more people are decided about what they want to be, but I don't know at all what's over what. I don't know if I could be a doctor, if I could be a lawyer, or anything under the sun. I have, I make no future plans yet, and that's not, that isn't too good I don't think.

Or the sense of drifting can be more general. A sophomore:

S.   You see I've got myself into the position that any relativist gets into, that is he's, he's bound to be set up in a position finding whatever he says, "Well, look at this, and look at this," and it all balances, and you've got a, you've got yourself thinking this on one hand, but then again you might be thinking this on the other—it's ah, it's just the old idea that if, if you don't have an absolute truth, what is truth, and I don't know. (*Laughs*) And if you don't know-ah, if you don't have some sort of-ah-ah, a standard outside of yourself, what is going to be your standard? And so I don't really have one, and admittedly I'm in a lot of difficult problems, and (*laughs*) I can't-ah—as I sit and talk to you now . . . because what can I say that can give you my emotional responses? And it's the only thing that I can-ah-ah-ah, the only thing that I can even argue on is the value of emotional responses. This is where my, my relativism has taken me. . . .

And a junior:

S.   And . . . fallacies and things. . . . You know, sometimes, the other side is right, you know, and . . . this thing is not all one side or the other. So this was a progressive thing. I think that's . . . for me, it has, I guess it will always, and always and always become more and more complicated as it goes on. But . . . I think one thing I've . . . not really done yet is become committed to, you know-ah . . . I'm registered as a Democrat in Philadelphia, but that doesn't mean anything. I could vote any way . . . ah . . . and I guess you don't have to become committed to a party, but I'm not sure I'm committed to an ideology yet, either. I guess you don't have to do that either. I don't know. Maybe that's the meaning of much more-ah . . . freedom . . . that sort of thing.

Although some of these statements do carry intimations of a need for Commitment, they carry no intimation of how it may develop. As an act, Commitment is not really "foreseen." Only the stage is set. The backdrop for the rest of the drama has taken its final, and usually irreversible, form. In our records no student who had once accepted a relativistic epistemology as context showed evidence of a generalized "regression" to absolutism.[13]

I have put the word "regression" in quotation marks above to indicate its use specifically within the terms and developmental values of our scheme. A question might be raised as to whether one might not go beyond Relativism, or transcend it, by using the old dualistic frame on a higher level. For instance, one might commit oneself in new ways to a religious absolute, consigning Relativism to a subordinate position limited to secular affairs.

---

[13]For a discussion of regression to a loose Multiplicity, see the sections on Retreat and Escape. Regression to dualistic absolutism does occur in life, of course, but it would seem to be specific to situations, especially those in which intense moral investments meet with frustration or threat.

I should therefore pause here to mention the problem of religion. For a student in Position 5, what answer can there be for the problem of a religious Absolute? None. The relativistic structure in this diffuse form offers no assimilation for an absolute in the old sense. As an alternative to the usual loss of belief, the only possibility lies in the unstable dissociated condition of Relativism Competing, and any attempt at integration of the competing systems would be fatal to one or the other.

The role of religious Absolutes in the subsequent Positions of Commitment is a special subject. There are data in our records illustrating several dispositions (e.g., "leap of faith," "liberal religion," etc.). In this report, however, it is enough to make two observations:

1. Theologically speaking, Position 5 represents the point of critical division between "belief" and the possibility of "faith." Belief requires no investment by the person. To become faith it must first be doubted. Only in the face of doubt is the person called upon for that act of Commitment that is his contribution, his faith. In Position 5 one can no longer "believe" in the simple unquestioned sense.

2. If one later commits oneself to a faith in an Absolute, *there is a criterion which reveals that this Commitment has been made in the context of a relativistic world.* This criterion is one's attitude toward other people with a belief or a faith in a different Absolute. They cannot appear as alien, as other than human; one must, however paradoxically, respect them. In one sense they "must" be wrong, but in another sense, no more so than oneself. The moral obligation to convert them or to annihilate them has vanished.

This phenomenon points up once again the power of the revolution in which the "special case" of Relativism became the broader context subsuming the previous Absolute world as itself a "special case." The capacity to make this kind of reversal may well be man's most potent tool for transcendence.

The attitudinal consequences as they appear in our records can be impressive:

S.   I had, you know, well, you know, political views that, I had religious views, and . . . moral views I think, all these sort of things that, you know . . . you have when you're younger . . . you have . . . you accept it as a oneness . . . so to speak.

I.   Yes, it's all—

S.   And it . . . I don't know, it's just sort of a separating, breaking up, and you know. . . .

I.   I see.

S.   A hashing out before you make your own rehashing, and I guess I haven't done that yet, but . . . at least I've had the opportunity to see . . . different sides.

I don't know whether it, it was reading material I went over, seeing so many different people defining good and evil in different ways, and the realization that they, they couldn't put their fingers on it, on a universal, or, or *what* exactly. I don't know what it was. But I know that it happened to me while I was here, while I was here. . . . And I consider that a basic part of my education too. I know people . . . that spend an awful lot of time reading and discussing and so forth, trying to get someone to tell the . . . what it is, what a universal truth is. (*Long pause*) And I'm glad that I don't have to do that. . . .

I seem to respect everything more, I think, that's the key note. (*Pause*) I had an awful lot of trouble with respecting things before because I would always try to punch holes in it, and I always could. I don't think there's anything that somebody can't punch a hole in, and I don't look for those holes much anymore.

I.   Could you give me an example of, of the kind of . . .

S.   Well, sure, I've already talked about this, the guy that lived downstairs. This, as I said, was a fellow that had . . . a number of-ah rather odious characteristics. He, oh, he wouldn't bathe sometimes, and he tried not to cooperate with the group, and that sort of thing-ah. And seizing on these, I could really develop a very unnatural hate for him . . . ah . . . (*pause*). Well, after a while, as I said, I realized what I was doing, and it left me in pretty much of a quandary about Peter. I didn't know exactly how I felt about him, and then again with, with this realization and understanding, I find a lot in him to respect. He has made the *Crimson,* he is on the Dean's List; understanding that he was being attacked he went to the library and took out a book by Dale Carnegie, called *How to Win Friends and Influence People.* He realized that he had a problem. There is a lot in this person to respect. I don't haze him any more.

And the same thing, then, can be said of oneself:

S.   [In the beginning] just the fact that, that, whatever you pride yourself on being, there's someone who in that particular thing is probably much better, you know, and is much more established in it. So you begin to, well you see these epitomes of something or other, you know, and you compare yourself to it, and you think, well, I guess I'm not quite that good there, you know. And then turn someplace else, and well, I guess, I'm not quite that good there either, you know. But I, well I think, yes, I think that first of all, it is this sort of destructive comparison. I think you feel really lost at the very beginning, you know. You feel, you feel-ah, oh I don't know, and you want to go back home, at least I did. People would sort of just look at you and smile, you didn't have to do anything you know.

   But then, but then after a while you begin to, you begin to sort of build up faith in yourself again, and it's a new sort of faith, it's a much nicer faith, 'cause it doesn't come out of, out of so much what people have been telling you, but out of something that you truly believe yourself.

The challenge of finding what "you truly believe yourself" forms the theme of the subsequent drama.

—ᨳ— Position 6:
Commitment Foreseen

A sense of identity seems to require some feeling of continuity in what "I" know and what "I" value (Erikson, 1959). If one comes to look upon all knowing and all valuing as contingent on context, and if one is then confronted with an infinite universe of potential contexts for truth and care, one is threatened with loss of identity. From one context to another what one will see as true and what one will care about will be discontinuous; one will not know who "I" am. Reciprocally, for lack of a stable locus, or "point of view" for the observer, whatever is seen "out there" will swim also.

If one construes knowledge and values as relativistic, one is therefore threatened with the possibility of humanly unbearable disorientation. Other than denying relativism itself, the ways of preventing this disaster would seem limited to three. Two of these are defensive, involving denials of responsibility. As forms of alienation, they will be considered in detail in the section on Escape. Briefly they are: (1) To "go limp," denying any need for meaning beyond one's immediate, passive responses; to leave responsibility for context, and thus meaning, to the vagaries of environment; to drift from context to context without acknowledging one's wish to reconcile incongruities. In this mode, orientation can be adequate within each moment; the cost is to know one's self as a self through time. Furthermore, this cost must carry with it a cost to knowing, in any deeper sense, other people's selves. (2) To exploit the situation deliberately by becoming an active, self-avowed opportunist. Here a limited selfhood is achieved ("I am an opportunist"); the loss is to depth of feeling and to the social responsibility that springs from compassion.

The third solution is transcendent, taking the form of Commitments. In this study the term "Commitment" refers to an act, or ongoing activity relating a person as agent and chooser to aspects of his life in which he invests his energies, his care, and his identity. In common usage the word often refers more narrowly to the object of Commitment alone rather than to the whole act or relation. Thus, "a man's commitments" may suggest his wife, children, job, and whatever obligations or causes or expectancies he has undertaken. If, however, one includes not only these external objects but also a man's acts of choice, and the personal investment he makes in them, the word refers to an affirmatory experience through which the man continuously defines his identity and his involvements in the world (cf. Polanyi, 1958).[14]

The word "Commitments," then, refers to affirmations: in all the plurality of the relativistic world—truths, relationships, purposes, activities, and cares, in all their contexts—one affirms what is one's own. As ongoing creative activities, Commitments require the courage of responsibility, and presuppose an acceptance of human limits, including the limits of reason.

Commitments are creative in that through choice and affirmation the individual generates meanings and relationships neither presupposed nor entailed by the structure of the relativistic world itself. The structures of Relativism (as distinct from the chaos of Multiplicity) do provide, by definition, wide opportunity for the exercise of reason. Reason reveals relations within any given context; it can also compare one context with another on the basis of meta-contexts established for the purpose. But there is a limit. In the end, reason itself remains reflexively relativistic, a property that turns reason back upon reason's own findings.[15] In even its farthest reaches, then, reason alone will leave the thinker with several legitimate contexts and no way of choosing

---

[14]There are, of course, aspects of identity that appear to be passively acquired and none of one's doing, such as one's height, one's limp, or the fact that as a child one was never schooled in the arts. The question is, however, one's address to these facts: One can refuse to "accept" them, investing one's honor in stubborn battle against the irremediable; one can "resign" oneself, denying any responsibility; or one can affirm, "I *am* one who is so high, limps, and wishes he had been schooled in the arts as a child. This is part of who I am."

[15]The predicament to which our students address themselves in the remaining excerpts in this report is considered in that current of western thought running from Kant (*Critique of Pure Reason*) to Camus (*Myth of Sisyphus*); see Polanyi (1958).

among them—no way, at least, that he can justify through reason alone. If he then throws away reason entirely, he retreats to the irresponsible in Multiplicity ("Anyone has a right to his opinion"). If he is still to honor reason he must now also transcend it; he must affirm his own position from within himself in full awareness that reason can never completely justify him or assure him. In affirming his values, reason may help, but it will not in itself convince him that these values are better than any others; he must commit himself through his own faith. In choosing his career, he must risk his life to his own best guess; reason can never tell him fully about the roads not taken. Yet in the nature of the world as he has come to see it, he must commit himself or abrogate responsibility.

Position 6 in our scheme describes the moment of this realization. In Position 5, Relativism had become the diffuse property permeating man's ways of knowing and caring in his universe. Against this background now appears, as figure, the responsibility of the individual in relating himself to such a world. The word "Commitment" as we use it refers to the structural properties of this figure-ground relation.

It may be well here to summarize very briefly the anatomy of Commitment as described in the passage from the *Judge's Manual* in Chapter 3.

1. Commitment (as distinct from a more generic commitment)[16] refers to an affirmation made in a world perceived as relativistic, that is, *after* detachment, doubt, and awareness of alternatives have made the experience of personal choice a possibility. It is an act in an examined, not in an unexamined, life.

2. Commitment requires a coming-to-terms with one's past in two ways: (*a*) it requires a decision as to the degree to which one will continue with the values of one's past and the degree to which one will break with them; (*b*) it requires a decision as to how much freedom of choice one can or will exercise in (*a*).

3. Commitments are commonly thought of in terms of their content, that is, the area of the environment in which they are expressed: career, marriage, religion, politics, friendships, social

---

[16]I will use the upper-case "C" hereafter wherever the context does not in itself suggest this distinction.

endeavors, and general values. (This usage is included in the larger definition given here.)

4. As acts, however, Commitments also manifest stylistic attributes in address to tensions both external and subjective. A Commitment involves a choice of balance in these tensions as well as a choice of content of object:

   a) External balances:

   narrowness vs. breadth

   number vs. intensity

   self-centered vs. other-centered

   etc.

   b) Subjective balances:

   action vs. contemplation

   immediacy vs. detachment

   stability vs. flexibility

   continuity vs. diversity

   control vs. openness

   maintenance vs. growth

   etc.

5. Identity derives from both the content and the forms, or stylistic aspects, of Commitments, for example, "I am a politician" and "I find I really prefer a wide range of acquaintances to narrowing down to one or two close friends." The stylistic, however, often feels to the person more proximal to the self, being experienced as the origin of choices in content, for example, "I'm just the kind of person who ought never to get married." Being proximal, stylistic affirmations usually feel less open to alternatives than the area in which they find expression: "It doesn't matter what I'm doing so long as I feel I'm building something."[17]

---

[17]The relation is often most evident in disjuncture, e.g., "I'm not going to take on that many things at once, not *me*," or . . . spoken by an experienced typist in elevator on way to work, wearily, "I should never have been a working girl. I should be some man's er, er . . . *something or other.*"

In Position 6, Commitment is foreseen as the resolution of the problems of relativism, but it has not yet been experienced. "Finding out what I want to do" may be yearned for as a settlement of present confusion; however, "having to choose" may be apprehended as a narrowing, a loss of freedom defined as the freedom *to* choose. The following excerpts illustrate the experience of this position under (1) Discovery; (2) Areas: studies, vocation, moral values, and religion; (3) Stylistic balances; and (4) The phenomenon of Commitment to Commitment.

Discovery

The realization of the individual's contribution to meaning in his life is often quite explicit in our records:

> S.   There was one other thing I expected—I expected that when I got to Harvard—I was-ah slightly ahead of my time in that I was an atheist before I got here—I came up here expecting that Harvard would teach me one universal truth . . . (*pause*). Took me quite a while to figure out . . . that if I was going for a universal truth or something to believe in, it had to come within me, and I don't know whether Harvard taught me that or not.

A new and different sense of responsibility for one's own life and for others can lend urgency:

> S.   I would venture a guess that this problem bothers everybody except for-ah, very, very small few, this, this constant worry about whether you can face up to it, and, and I think the earlier you find out that you can . . . I think the more important it is /uhuh/ ah, life is not, life is getting longer of course, all the time, but . . . life is much too short, oh, to, to waste ten or fifteen years of your life wandering around in a, in a, in a partial vacuum, not knowing-ah . . . whether when you do get out of your little vacuum that you can, you can face up to your responsibility to yourself and your family and the world around you, and I know some people are, are put on their own, very early in life through a variety of circumstances and forced out to make their own living-ah . . . fight their own battles without their, without the help of their parents-ah, or without the help of somebody very close to them, and, and they

make it, therefore, and I think it's, well it's not always desirable for this to happen, but I think it's a very good thing, ah, a sense of responsibility is something which, I don't think . . . you're, necessarily are born with, it's-ah . . . something that you're aware of . . . but . . . it's never very pronounced until you're on your own and until you're making your own decisions, more or less, and then you realize how very important it really is.

As a generalized realization, lacking as yet a focus in some specific content, the vision seems to derive from the felt exigency of "action":

S.   Once you get to be past twenty-one or twenty-two if you haven't begun to get control of yourself, you can't, if you haven't begun to get a certain amount of direction, you can't expect these internal evolutions to just develop and then suddenly bloom, you've got to work at it, I think, and he hasn't, and that's kind of bad.

You've got to do something, you've got to act. You've got to act these things, it's just like, I don't know, James, or who's a pragmatist? Moore said that if you don't translate these beliefs into action, you don't . . . if you have these thoughts, and you don't act on them . . . nothing happens.

But how to begin? The same student goes on to imagine that the first steps may require an almost arbitrary faith, or even a willing suspension of disbelief:

S.   You just have to jump into it, that's all, before, before it can have any effect on you. And the farther in you force yourself to get in the first place, the more possibilities there are, the more ideas and concepts there are that can impinge on you and so the more likely you are to get involved in it. Actually you have to make some kind of an assumption in the first place that it's worthwhile to get into it, but . . . and that you're capable of doing something once you get into it.

And yet the structure is compelling:

S.   It's hard to imagine what an absolutely standardless college would be like, any more than it's possible to imagine what a standardless society would be like. It's, it's the same problem in miniature, and it seems that-ah, it, it would be impractical. I was discussing Nietzsche with my roommate the other day, who's a firm believer in Nietzsche and I pointed out that if, if supermen were allowed in the world, were not persecuted, as Nietzsche seems to think they are, and would be, then everyone would take it into his head to be a superman, and while to condemn such a policy seems to be priggish in the extreme, yet if everyone takes it into his head to be a superman, the resulting anarchy will make it impossible for anyone to be superman, so the best intentions defeat themselves sometimes. And the absolute relaxation of standards would defeat themselves in the end. There are some things that are important.

But what "things"?

Areas of Content

Compared to these abstractions, the vision of some concrete investment offers a more immediate and less problematic transition.

STUDIES. Most immediate can be a vision of Commitment to the job at hand. Here the distinction between the old obedience (or disobedience) and the new investment can be vivid:

S. The sophomore year I was doing nothing, but in a different way. This year I'm beginning to see that you don't ever get anywhere unless you do work. You, you just can't sort of lie back and expect everything to come to you. That's the way I was trying to let it work, but that doesn't work.

The vision awakens yearning:

S. I went into a Chinese art gallery, and I enjoyed very much just walking around for the afternoon trying to make some sense out of the things I saw. I wouldn't give up what I've learned, the truths I've learned, I'm just sorry that I haven't been able to do anything with it. I have a feeling that I may be able to do something with math.

The new yearning, however, does not always find clear sailing. It must come to terms with time and competing demands:

S.   You've got to make a choice, let's put it that way, between getting good grades, I mean really good grades, or doing pretty much
with your life, and even though, if you try to see a perspective, and
say, "Well, I'll get good grades now, and I'll have the rest of my life
to do what I like and I'll have that *cum laude* diploma under my
belt," all right, but these four years are—if you have any sort of intellectual interests—this is the best place in the world to be with it,
and the idea that it has to go to waste, that time, time can't be spent
in, indulging more in them is unfortunate. But I don't know as
there's really any solution to that. I guess you, you've just got to
make your choice.

At this point the college can feel to some as if it were even holding
one back in too diffuse a relativism. A senior:

S.   Well, let's ah, let's talk about something that's concrete, something that I've thought recently. I wrote my last paper about two
weeks ago, and it was for an English course. And in this particular
English course it seems that ah, they want each sentence or the, the
party line in the course, seems to want each sentence just loaded
with the ambiguities of the particular novel. In other words, your
sentences have to be as complex as the novel was, and have the same,
same double meaning, and the same ambiguity, and it seems to me
unless you carry this through you're likely to get the word "over-
simplified" written at the end. They, they don't seem to like you to
take a position, and try to defend it. They want—admittedly there
is a position, there is a position implied in taking both sides, or trying to see both sides—but I, I sometimes tend to feel that novelists
stress one side or the other, just as political theorists stress one side
or the other—Hobbes stresses the sovereign over the individual,
although the individual is there, things like that. It seems to me that
writing this sort of work, isn't quite as valuable as, as being able to
take a position and defend it in a particular case . . . for instance
if I were running for political office tomorrow, I couldn't take the
other fellow's position—I might see it, but I couldn't take it. It
seems to me that a great deal of success or a great deal that, that
will determine success, any factor that determines success must be
the ability to take a position, to articulate one side of one issue, because you can't—because it's foolish to, to take both sides. It would
destroy *your* position, no matter how much you sympathize or see.

It seems to me that much that I've been forced to do here, this taking of two sides at once, just suspends my judgment. There is a value in it; of course there's a value in, in seeing any perspective, or any one particular facet of, of a problem. But there's also a value in, in being able to articulate one side more than another.

VOCATION.   The sense of impending choice of vocation most commonly offers the central hope of order. A junior:

S.   This year I began to channel my thoughts more in line. I want to take, ah, some courses in general culture and a few courses in art next year, and finish my history major. And I guess nearer graduation I'm more interested in what I'll do afterwards. I've done some thinking about what kind of law I'm going into, and where I'm going to practice, and where I want to go to law school. I'm not absolutely certain about that, but I'm fairly certain I'm going into law and I'm very certain I'm going to practice at home. But I'm not certain what kind of law I'm going into.

However, extracurricular activities can precipitate the experience:

S.   I'd be lost without the newspaper work, frankly, or without something like it. Without something of this type I would *really* be lost. My feeling is that if you're going to be in something like this you might as well really tie into it, be a part of it. I mean I really can't see the people that just sort of hang around and do a little work, say once a month write a couple of stories or something, because if you're not really going to be a part of it, then don't be a part of it at all.

S.   Just about the most important thing about this whole sophomore year for me, was, when I came into it I had no idea where . . . ah, why I was studying or where it was leading me. I was enjoying it. I wasn't particularly anxious over the fact that I didn't have a goal, but . . . I still had the feeling that I wasn't particularly perfecting myself in any, any way I was going to fulfill later. I always had the idea that ah, that if you were ever going to realize your potentialities to the extent that you could really feel satisfied with it, you'd have to start pretty young, and yet here I was banging around, in one thing and another, and I didn't know exactly where I was going, or why I was studying this or why I was studying that, aside from the fact that it was interesting. And then ah . . . um, it's a funny thing, my Dad always wanted me to . . . always thought that, ah, I'd probably get oriented if I wrote more, but he would never tell me this (*laughs*). He didn't want to give me the feeling he was pressing on me, but . . . I told him I was going out for the *Crimson* for two years, was his observation, and then as it turned out that it did give me a whole new orientation at this, because every time I sit down and I work-ah, I work with my typewriter and I look at a new way of, of approaching the problem, or a new way of smoothing out my language or, or of improving my expression, it makes me feel as if I'm actually doing something now, whereas before, when I was studying the Monroe Doctrine I wasn't sure exactly why I was doing it, except that it was interesting, I didn't, didn't know what relevance it had to me, ten or fifteen years from now, aside from the general abstract relevance of improving your knowledge and things like that.

MORAL VALUES AND RELIGION.   The breakdown of the old familial background and its replacement by a diffuse relativism can bring into sharp relief cares which one recognizes, after all, as one's own:

S.   I'm going to become independent as soon as I can. It's not that I don't want to feel obligated; that's something else again. I mean I don't mind feeling obligated, but I do want to give my parents the, the chance to enjoy themselves with their own money, you might say. But I don't mind making a debt to somebody, my parents or anybody else.

Another:

S.   It depends on the type of situations you come upon. Ah, I think it's just a matter of taking a calm look at what my father and mother have told me and what you learn all your whole life—the atmosphere—you sort of transfer it to spheres of college living, and throw out or disregard what you think is right—or what you *don't* think is right—and the things you think are right and correspond to your college a little bit more, you figure that they're the best things to follow through life.

At the same time the change makes possible the emulation and espousal of new values:

S.   [Also] I think I've become a little more aware of and contemptuous of intellectual sham. Reading the school paper sometimes is nauseous for this reason. Every once in a while I'll read something that just turns my stomach, and a lot of it resembles very closely a lot of the things that I used to do myself. The pure use of words for the sound, just for the sound they make. If it's pretty, fine, but if it's trying to get somewhere and impress people it's pretty nauseating. I don't know whether it's sour grapes because I can't get away with it or whether it's a frank and honest evaluation of the thing—I really don't know.

I think what I've become most aware of is the matter of— well, refinement. What's traditionally described as gentility, I guess, the quality of being a gentleman. Knowing something, and yet not knowing it ostentatiously. I admire that. I know a great number of people around here who have it to a great degree, and I'd like to cultivate it myself. I have difficulty doing this.

Nobody here is afraid of being an intellect. I won't say an intellectual, but an intellect—no one is afraid of thinking for himself, even though he doesn't go around telling everybody about it. I think it's a help here, where everybody is seriously trying to do that sort of thing. It sneaks up on you, as so many things do, and that's why I'm glad this place is the way it is. It's more or less taken for granted, I think, that people here do think for themselves, and whether they think the way they're supposed to or the way the rest of the people do is of little consequence.

In this Position many students report a confidence in the eventual return of lost religious cares. The prospect includes the feeling that they will return in a more meaningful form:

S.   I . . . ahh . . . I believe in taking a stand now. I've modified this from where, where you jump from no stand at all to taking a radical stand. I mean this year it's been, it's melted in somewhat . . . sometimes I take too strong a stand, but if it's too strong it's something that I feel I know a good deal about and that somebody's just talking out of his hat. My courses—that's something that's come in this year is . . . causal, and relative thinking—that this has got to tie up with something to be important. It's come into my thinking. This history tutorial has given me . . . it's put into me almost unconsciously a . . . sort of system of thought . . . system of . . . looking at something and, of course it's much easier to do in a history course but I still can do it in my natural science. . . .

I think this year I've looked a great deal at religion . . . have tried to reason it out, and I had . . . it hasn't been disturbing me at all, it's just been something that I've tried to do. . . .

Religion has fallen with me as a necessary force in my life right now. I don't feel that this is a definite necessary force. I'm not, I don't feel I'm really rationalizing when I say that I think that religion has . . . is just sort of faded out for these years and that I will take it up again, and when I take it up again, I feel that . . . I will get much more out of it, that I, I will meet it, I will not just accept it, I will meet it and develop it and really bring it into my life. Where it's never been brought into my life before. . . . It's the one place where I've really been unsuccessful . . . but I think that, that's going to come out after I get out of college. I'm not worried about it. But . . . in my courses I think that I'm in a . . . just a process now that I'm caught up in. A way of thinking, that is going to keep developing.

A Radcliffe student who had always taken it for granted that she would join the ministry describes the transition from the old unexamined commitment to the prospect of a new:

S.   The thing is, when you have a bunch of beliefs sort of handed to you, you don't really do that much thinking. I mean I was never even concerned with philosophy, I never read a single thing, I didn't have to. I mean, I accepted the Christian faith because my parents were Christians and I believed that, well, you know I never even thought, well, maybe there isn't any God. I mean it doesn't enter your mind. You just think, well, there's a God, you know, and he has a purpose for everybody's life and Jesus is his son. Then, oh, everybody's basically sinful, this is another thing that bothers me now, you know, people are horrible, (*laughs*) but anyway, you'll go to heaven you know if you're, if you follow, if you believe in Jesus. But the thing is, I didn't know what I was really gonna do with my life. My life just sort of seemed, well, the main purpose was just telling everybody else that they had to believe in Jesus or they weren't going to go to heaven. This was, this is the main, what they say you should do all your life, and this was really the only thing that I thought. They make you feel like you have to do this or you're being sinful or something. It's just that I was always going to be . . . working with the church, you know, but, I, I never really thought about what is my, you know, place in the universe, or anything. And, but the thing is, it really hasn't been unsettling, because . . . I mean starting to think about all these things, because . . . ahh . . . well, I don't know, now I'm more . . . somehow now I feel . . . I don't know, just more *honest* about, about my beliefs, now that I'm sort of getting them on my own. So I'm very happy. I'm with this . . . best parts of the year.

Stylistic Balances

Inasmuch as Commitment has not yet been experienced, only foreseen, its implications can only be imagined. The consideration of Positions 7, 8, and 9 will provide the sensible place to illustrate the stylistic properties of the experience itself. Students do, however, apprehend some of these qualitative issues in advance—often in a different balance than in the later experience, and their imaginings illuminate the challenge they are about to meet.

As we observed the way the students spoke, they seemed to express the qualitative experience of Commitment in polarities: narrowness vs. breadth, certainty vs. tentativeness, and so on. They were, of course, describing an equilibrium in a complex matrix of many vectors—as some students made explicit—but in speaking they had to describe one tension at a time, as it occurred to them. In our own thinking, we followed suit, and I shall illustrate here separate aspects of the matrix in terms of the polar stresses in which the students seemed to search for an optimal equilibrium.[18] Terminology for these polarities, however, may tend to overlap or interlock, as indeed the stresses themselves must do within the whole.

NARROWNESS VS. BREADTH. The prospect of "giving up" an infinite range of potentials for some specific actuality often raises the specter of narrow constriction. It is as if one were entering a funnel. The sense of impending loss and regret cannot be balanced yet by the confidence,

drawn from experience, that "once you get in, things open out again."
Though an occasional student can foresee this phenomenon, the common apprehension runs as follows:

> S.   Just have to sort of make the most of it, as it comes, and I say
> that's one thing you learn out of college that life is, is not one set
> narrow little plain. You just have to sort of, it's a very big thing, you
> just sort of have to ma-make your way through it as best you can
> after you've, experience of course is always the best teacher. That's
> just a question of, well, say, broadening your outlook and learning
> to be yourself.
>
>   Everybody they say as they get older tends to get more set in
> their ways but we hope not. If, if we can stay flexible as much as
> you can, it's better. It's not good to get too narrow-minded or set
> in your ways . . . as a child. That of course comes if you're domi-
> nated too much by your parents or by older people.

In short, the focus provided by Commitment still cannot be conceived as distinct from that unconsidered "narrowness" from which
one feels one has so recently escaped.

STABILITY VS. FLEXIBILITY.   Parallel to the polarity of narrowness vs.
breadth, with the added dimension of time, runs the tension between
stability and flexibility, or capacity to maintain vs. capacity to adjust:

> S.   Of course you have to make some commitment somewhere. I
> mean a very interesting thing, that if you take any strong point and
> stand on it, someone will, sooner or later, probably knock it out
> from under you, or at least shake it a little bit. It's the idea of not be-
> ing flexible to the whole thing, but not ah, to the point of not
> standing on anything. Being able to, at least at this point, I don't
> know, maybe later on you may be, I'll probably perhaps will be-
> come more set.

If "flexibility" were thought of as more than a defense against the
collapse of too rigid a "stand," it could be seen as a positive provision

---

[18]This presentation appears also in Allport, G. W. (1965), in which he speaks
of such tensions as "whole-heartedness vs. tentativeness" in commitment.

for growth, set over against the need for continuity. In this Position, however, our students do not make such a vision explicit. Possibly their concern about narrowness or vulnerability is still too preoccupying.

SURENESS VS. TENTATIVENESS. Similarly, students perceive the need to choose some point or range in a scale of confidence between certainty and total doubt:

> S.   Well, you see that's the fun of the whole game. Whether you want to call it fun—but I guess it's the, what you'd call a fascinating aspect of the problem. Because you never, you never decide . . . on one . . . set answer. I guess it's like the old liberal philosophy of "the facts are not all in." And I, you add and you detract as you go along. You never really make a single decision as to what is best and what is worse. That to me would be, would be a, a, an *emotional* factor. And unnecessarily adding to the situation. Because of course . . . of course you can't—like asking the old skeptics, how do they live—I mean you can't hang in the air, leave your, your answers suspended all the time. You've got to make *some* sort of decision, but this decision isn't final.

ANALYSIS VS. SYNTHESIS.   If, then, the aspects and detail of any situation may be elaborated forever, decision requires a stop to analysis, somewhere, in favor of some coherent synthesis from which action is possible. Just where the optimal "somewhere" may lie is a delicate judgment in which, once again, the individual must commit himself in a style of his own.

> S.   Then you go beyond questioning the small things, accept the small things and well, as an example, in religion my freshman year I was questioning the whole concept of the Virgin Birth and all that stuff, which, you know, I think now is pretty inconsequential. It doesn't mean a darn thing. So I guess you just get to accept a few things and not to worry about them, and become more selective in your concerns. And this year again, the last year I've become much more active politically in my thought at least, and I'm going to be working this summer, campaigning.

The integrative force of Commitment can weld into a coherent whole what might once have been fragmentary or piecework.

S.   I think almost anyone has the basic talent to be a great artist, so I think it has to do with your whole psychology. It's sort of fitting your emotions with it, and the feelings you have, and the memories. . . . Of course there's a certain amount of discipline associated too, but you can put up with just about any amount of discipline in anything if you have all your emotions associated with the goal that's going to come out of all this discipline.

DETACHMENT VS. INVOLVEMENT.   Closely related to the stress between analysis and synthesis is the problem of maximizing the products of detachment and involvement. A freshman gropes for a way of expressing the structure of some resolution:

S.   It comes down to whether you believe that an individual can detach himself from the network of liberalism and conservatism, or any other two extremes in life, for that matter. But to assume that sort of detachment, well it's dangerous, I mean—what we've learned about psychology in this century—the idea of somebody standing back or up or out, it's not as convincing as it was in earlier times. In my particular case I wouldn't call it a third position exactly, I'd call it a pre-doomed attempt at detachment. Because in practice you've got to be one or the other. And it comes to me more naturally to, well, neither comes to me more naturally. It is closer to a third position. But a conservative liberalism, if you will, rather than a liberal conservative. It's a nuance, but it's there. It seems more . . . more probable.

CONTINUITY WITH ONE'S ORIGINS VS. BREAKING WITH ONE'S PAST.   In establishing a self through one's own choices and affirmations, how much will one espouse from the years in which one lived an unexamined life without the possibility of decision one now enjoys? Will one now attempt an identity in radical departure from familial definitions or one expressive of continuity in them?

S.   I listened to both sides of the question, I've sort of analyzed what my beliefs were and, ah, I mean not as much as some guys, but, ah, I think the over-all advantage has been toward a strengthening of my beliefs.

Or:

S.   Who would have thought I might end up a scientist?

Subjectively the experience can be one of considerable latitude, a freedom of choice about who one will be that is one's first experience of existential loneliness:

S.   I don't guess most everybody goes through this phase, but a lot of people must go through a phase of sort of finding themselves alone in the world, in a way. Sort of splitting away from their family to some extent, if it's only geographically. Sometimes not geographically; he could be at home and the same thing might happen, but geography emphasizes it. And, and then they must work out new relationships to the world, I think, but depending on their past life with their family, their life with their friends and their personality—how much of an extrovert they are and so on.

Objectively, in the light of modern personality theory, one might suppose the latitude to be less than the subjective experience envisions. Of course modern deterministic theory makes an emergent system out of genetic factors and environmental factors, and has a tough time with notions of the will and creativity. The question of how much freedom one is exercising is especially poignant for those who would choose to affirm their continuity with their past. They ask themselves whether they are really choosing at all, or whether their feeling of choice is just one more expression of their past conditioning. The student mentioned in the *Judge's Manual* (see p. 38) made the point. Once he had chosen to commit himself anew to his old "taken for granted" expectation of being a doctor, he had to commit himself also to his judgment of how much he would believe this to be an act of choice at all.

The Phenomenon of Commitment to Commitment

Early in the judges' work they uncovered a form of Commitment we had not anticipated. In one of their first protocols they found a student who, they felt, spoke of his experience with a sense of Commitment expressive of Position 7 (Initial Commitment). In discussion, they found that they had settled on the same passages in his report as evidence. Yet they were puzzled. The student mentioned no specific area or content for his Commitment. Indeed he seemed to speak of all such Commitments in the future tense, an outlook which would express Position 6. In the discussion the judges agreed that the paradox lay in the fact that, though he had not yet made specific external choices, he had nonetheless done more than "foresee" Commitment. He had somehow committed himself internally to living a life of Commitments: "I've decided that this is the way I will live." It was decided that for future protocols this kind of affirmation would be accepted as a form of Commitment itself, expressive of Position 7.

Problems remained. Is this form of Commitment also capable of being "foreseen" as from Position 6? Furthermore, the form involves a kind of confidence, a Commitment to one's self as a point of origin for other Commitments, and is therefore difficult to distinguish from a sheer trust in one's competence. Passages like the following were difficult to place:

S.   I think in part that . . . it's true . . . they were . . . probably . . . in my unquestioning acceptance of the scientific world, I dismissed anything else as a lot of bunk. . . . It's been part of my life, all along accepted without question.

I.   And, now, now you're questioning that assumption? Why do you suppose at this time, do you think you're beginning to examine these assumptions?

S.   Well, possibly one reason is that I feel more independent. Another reason is that I've begun covering work in the courses that . . . most definitely are preparation for medicine, and, I can examine it in terms of ah whether I want to go on with the preparation. . . . Well, perhaps it's the natural outgrowth of just growing up . . . maturity. . . .

I.   When we say "just the natural process of growing up," it's a rather complicated process, probably. . . .

S.   Well, perhaps let me phrase it again. . . . You get perspective on the world. . . . You have more facts at your command on which you can make decisions . . . hence you are no longer forced to rely on hearsay. . . . You can actually consider the questions yourself. . . .

I.   Uhuh. And that's another kind of independence, in a sense . . . where you're not so dependent on the facts as presented by other people. . . .

S.   Yes, you can exercise your own judgment.

Or:

S.   I know that, ah, if I really wanted to do something I could find a way of doing it, so I feel much more at peace with the world.

In the end, the judges concluded that such statements were coherent variants of Position 6—"Commitment Foreseen."

This consideration of Commitment has of course not been exhaustive. Any one student, also, in foreseeing Commitment, may apprehend several of its facets and polarities. In the following passage, many of the elements mentioned above interweave in the portrayal of a delicately poised moment in a student's life.

S.   A commitment, well the reason I changed the word so from commitment is because I believe commitment, I like to think of commitment as something much larger, a term that you would apply to something that involves your life, or your life's philosophy, or your idea of what life is, and means, and . . .

I.   Yeah, exactly, what I wondered was about the process that goes into making such a commitment, if you get . . .

S.   At the moment I think a commitment that would involve anything that involved your . . . your life or your, your idea of what life means . . . involves a sympathy and that sympathy not only in intellectual understanding, but a realization that past and present and your ties and so forth and so on, all lead to this, making this conclusion or coming to this commitment. And that, that's why I think a commitment's so important and it's a big word in my vocabulary. It means something is there, something else that we can say about—that—you would like to have time for, and would like to find, would like to lead toward. . . . People are-ah trying to . . . giving things much more thought, having to come to new commitments and it's awfully hard on them, and I sympathize with them completely. I understand that they're having a hard time because I have too, and I haven't come to any conclusions yet as to positive . . . steps to take, I mean it's so hard to arrive at a—use the word some commitment—of what you think should exist, then think of a positive step to take because all of a sudden and actions seem to change moral situations or moral values. And they don't get, they're not nearly as high as you would think they were as you begin to act because, well, you have to deal with other people, and sometimes underhanded means are the only way to accomplish what you think is right, you know, in the means or . . .

Also in this term in a terrific fit of depression . . . (*laughs*) I was reading Max Weber who's so tortured by the idea of a value system you know-ah, where are my cigarettes? and-ah . . . He was so tortured by the idea of a value system in politics, and I was very interested in this thing because I wanted to, it, of course H. Stuart Hughes says there's an answer to all the lies and relativism, but you hate to-ah, think of that. Of course I'm sure, that is certainly to an extent, maybe there are some morals, some moral standard if you take, well a Christian society, a society that's supposed to be Christian anyway, orthodox Christian at least. Today there are some in the Ten Commandments, something like that . . . and if people professed to believe in these things, there you have your standard. Of course that's not considering other religions, Confucianism, and so forth; I mean that, that, that I think that you don't have to let relativism go . . . away that far. I mean you have to realize that if a whole society is professing one thing, then that should be the standard regardless of other parts of the world, and that aspect of relativism—but if that doesn't exist, it certainly shows a moral degeneracy in the society, or if not, in the degeneracy certainly a need for a new set of standards or a new commitment on standards.

That's the thing I'm in. You get in a position where you become completely passive, you're not able to act. And that's what I wonder: well am I able to go back South, can I act, you know, can I go back and face it all because—it really is, is—once I've gotten out of it, it's quite a problem for me to decide whether to go back into it because it's a hell of a mess. . . . (*laughs*) I don't know if I want to get into that again. Mercy! . . . it's like I . . . it reminds me of a Henry James character, all of these books have one of these characters, begins to, who's already discovered life for some . . . that . . . what's that fellow's name-ah, Ralph Touchett in-ah *Portrait of a Lady*? and he's rendered passive by this thing. He can't do anything, now that he knows that evil exists and so on. Well I don't think that's necessarily true—people can rise above the passivity of finding out about evil. . . . That's what the heroine of the book does, she goes back and faces it. But it's a terrific—Henry James realizes what a terrific sort of-ah moral change it was in her case. It, it demanded in her character to be able to face the reality of it all, and it is something that everyone has to come to.

Now I could very well . . . it would be the easiest thing in the world for me never to go back. Because if I stay in education, or if I begin to teach, it would be easy for me to get jobs out of the South. Or as a fact, it would be, would be more probable that I could get jobs out of the South. And not because they, they would pay more. And it would be an advantage to living in the North simply for the material standpoint, and it probably would be bet-just more enjoyable.

There's a lot to consider about going, acting, besides yourself. (*Pause*) If things get more and more relative when you would rather they not be relative . . . you know what I mean? (*Laughs*) Things get more and more relative in that you have to take into consideration other people's opinions, people that you care about and don't want to violate or injure. And you have to back down on some of moral standards. Things are not, and that's the reason I brought up the idea of-ah, ah, my thoughts of course were wandering because I don't have anything to go by—I brought up the idea of that I was authoritarian when I first came up here. I definitely was I'm sure. I answered that value sheet mostly on authoritarian terms. But I could, I wouldn't answer it that way at all now. . . . But then if I ever take a stand, you have to go somewhere—an authoritarian, just a liberal authoritarian—take a stand.

Positions 7, 8, and 9:
(7) Initial Commitment,
(8) Orientation in Implications of Commitment,
(9) Developing Commitment(s)

In the drama of maturation we have been observing, the setting has now become stabilized. From this point onwards, our records reveal no major restructuring of the background of life. The assumption is established that man's knowing and valuing are relative in time and circumstance, and that in such a world the individual is faced with the responsibility for choice and affirmation in his life.

The drama of development now centers on this theme of responsibility. The hero makes his first definition of himself by some engagement undertaken at his own risk. Next he realizes in actual experience the implications of his initial Commitments. Then, as he expands the arc of his engagements and pushes forward in the impingements and unfoldings of experience, he discovers that he has undertaken not a finite set of decisions but a way of life.

The development is therefore more qualitative than structural, and its steps are not readily demarked by major changes in forms. Accordingly, Positions 7, 8, and 9 express degrees of ripening in an art. They describe degrees of seasoning which we felt to be broadly distinguishable in our students' reports.

Position 7 describes that state in a student's life in which he has undertaken to decide on his own responsibility who he is, or who he will be, in some major area of his life (for example, "I have decided on medicine"). He is at the moment rather taken up with the impact of the content of the Commitment. Internally he typically experiences a relief in settled purpose, and at the same time he feels strongly *defined by* the external forms typifying the role he has chosen (for example, medical student, doctor).

Position 8 describes a level of experience in which the stylistic issues of Commitment have emerged in greater prominence over external forms (for example, "So I've decided to be a doctor but how many ways are there of doing *that?*—and the rest of life!"). Position 9 describes a maturity in which a person has developed an experience of "who he is" in his Commitments both in their content and in his style of living them. At the same time that this experience has "settled" him, it has left him aware that, to a degree that is partly his own to determine and partly in the hands of fate, he is to be forever on the move. His past decisions may have settled to some degree what he is doing, what he may do, and what he can never do; but how he does it emerges from himself in the particulars of each moment. He will be far too busy, of course, to contemplate each moment in these terms, but the fact that he takes many of his responsibilities for granted does not reduce them for him. Indeed the very degree to which he will balance his emersion in action with times of contemplation will express in itself one of his Commitments to "the kind of person I am."

We hardly felt that the circumstance of being a college student would provide a basis in experience for the seasoning described by Position 9. Rather, it seemed to round out the scheme by extrapolation, much as did Position 1 in the other direction, and its inclusion seemed also to enlighten the character of Position 8. As it turned out, the judges did use Position 9 on occasion—thirteen times out of a total of 120 ratings of the twenty senior interviews in the sample of four-year reports. In discussion, the judges revealed that they looked on such a rating as a kind of tribute—a statement that a given student expressed a degree of maturity beyond the judge's own: "I just wanted to say, 'You're a better man than I am'!" One senior received an average rating of 8.33.

In view of popular notions of this particular generation of students as "uncommitted," "alienated," or "silent," the finding shown in Table 1 of this study seems impressive: on the basis of their average rating by the judges, *75 percent of our sample were judged to have attained the degree of Commitment characterized by Positions 7 and 8.*

In junior year, nine men of the twenty received average ratings between 6.5 and 7.4.

	Position	N
Average rating	6.5–7.4	8 seniors
Average rating	7.5–8.4	7 seniors
TOTAL		15

Table 1.   Number of Seniors with Average Rating in Positions of
Commitment
(Total sample N = 20)

It is beyond the scope of this report to document the striking contrast between this finding and the popular portrait of college youth of the fifties and early sixties. Within the confines of the study itself, however, a sense of the meaningfulness with which the judges used the concept of Commitment to describe the maturation evident in the students' reports may be derived from a frequency table (see Table 2).

It should be remembered that the reliability of ratings was proved to be independent of the judge's knowledge of a student's year in college (see summary of findings, Chapter 1).

Short excerpts fail to illustrate the evidence on which the judges relied in discriminating among these three Positions as they were expressed in the records. Position 7 is of course identifiable in simple content. The student says, "I've settled on law," or "I've developed a set of values," or "I've decided to get married—next week yet!" But this provides only a base line. The breadth, depth, style, and maturity with which the student makes his affirmation can be assessed with confidence only in a context of some length. The excerpts illustrating Positions 8 and 9 must therefore be read as suggestive of the tonality of the broader context in which the judges made their decisions. The excerpts will serve also to augment the stylistic categories in the anatomy of Commitment begun in the section on Position 6.

Initial Commitment: Position 7

S.   This may sound sort of silly, but I've developed a sense of, ah, a set of morals. I never had to use them before I got here, but since I got here and, ah, have seen what goes on—they may be unusual, sort of, but I don't think so—I, ah, had to develop them because it's something I never ran into before. It's, well, I'm out of high school now, I'm out of that sort of thing, kid stuff I might call it now. I'm a freshman in college, I find that kid stuff kind of ridicu-

Position	Fresh.	Soph.	Junior	Senior
7 (Initial Commitment)	3	11	48	42
8 (Experience of Implications)	0	0	14	55
9 (Developing Commitment)	0	0	0	13
TOTALS	3	11	62	110

Table 2.   Instances of Individual Ratings in Positions of Commitment (Six judges, 20 students = 120 ratings per year)

lous. Ah, here I'm out in the big world, more or less. And I've come to things and decisions I've never had to make before, and I've made them. And afterwards, thinking it over, I've said I've done this because, well, it was right, and the alternative wouldn't have suited me and I wouldn't have felt good about it. Ah, maybe somebody else wouldn't have cared, maybe somebody else would have told me just the opposite.

A junior:

S.   There are so many values you can't possibly line up all of them. Maybe what you do is pick out one, or two, or three, after a while. It's not a fast thing. It's slow. But you pick out something that you kind of like after a while, rather than trying to do what you see is being liked. I mean, you come here, and you get a total view of everything, and you see a whole lot of values. I mean, you're confronted with them. Every one of them is a good thing in its own way and so you instinctively want to be at least a little bit aware and take part in all of them. But you can't. I mean, it's impossible just from a pure mechanical point of spending time. You kind of focus on the type of career you want and when you think about that, then if you're going to work toward it, it has its own imperatives. It means that you have to drop certain things and focus more on others. If you want to teach, that means you emphasize studies and drop clubs, and a certain amount of social life and some athletics. You just let these things become peripheral. (*Pause*) And you're sure about that.

Initial Commitments may emerge from one's past, or from recently discovered interests, or from identifications:

S.   I started dating a girl from Boston State Teacher's about three or four weeks ago, and we did a lot of talking, not along these lines exactly, but more or less basic philosophies. I'd never sat down with anybody and tried to figure out, you know, exactly how I felt in things, or told anybody what I felt about things and we sat down and I enjoyed very much talking with her, and very fond of her. And it was really quite enlightening to hear myself say things which I'd always thought, but you know, I'd never said out loud. And I was frankly amazed that I had such firm convictions on many things and was actually able to even back up a lot of them with, what I consider logical reasoning and sensibility. And . . . of course again I have to give credit to the, the college background that is here, the way that you have to prepare for courses and for . . . everything. It's just . . . just moves in completely with, with your life. . . .

I'm really glad to find that, you know, to see that these are things that are tied together, and that I'm not, this isn't just a separate four years of my life that I can say, "Well, here's where I am and here's where I came out, and this won't ever be important to me, I had four years here, and . . . didn't do much for me except I just learned a lot of facts," but *it really is working*. I mean it's just, just become a part of my life actually, which I didn't think this was going to be.

S.   I've always had a lot of doctors in my family, and my father meant to be a doctor and then, ah, quit during the depression. And he'd always wanted me to be a doctor, at which I had rebelled. And well, I had a board and room job this year, taking care of kids and, well, it just came slowly to me that this is really what I want, and for the first time I had a little direction. Right now I'd like to go into pediatrics; I'm really set on this deal.

S.   What do I think influenced me to decide this way? Well, one thing would be people I met, for instance, my sophomore tutor in government. He had been actually a section man of mine in government the second semester of freshman year. He was at Dudley House and I was in his tutorial. I got to respect him so greatly as a person that I tended to think that what he was doing was somehow very desirable.

I.   What things in the man appealed to you?

S.   Well, this is not going to sound rational in any way, but his manner for one thing. He seemed to talk so knowledgeably about things I was interested in, and he seemed to be saying things that I thought I would never be able to say. Probably I couldn't ever say them because he was a brilliant person, and he had a quality of perception and insight which somehow I don't think I'll develop. He had it naturally, so to speak. But this impressed me. I think that was very important. One of the first days I was here, I was sitting in Dudley House, alone. He came over and sat down, and we started to talk, and he just introduced himself, very nice about the whole thing.

There is also a growing sense of agency in respect to making meaning in one's life:

S.   Then by a few months or a few weeks ago, feeling new kinds of resolve, you know, just grabbing hold of myself and saying, "This I want, that I don't want, this I am, that I'm not, and I'll be solid about it. . . ."

I'd never believed I could do things, that I had any power, I mean power over myself, and over effecting any change that I thought was right. I'd artificially try to commit myself to something, or I would intellectually realize something about myself, intellectually understand that I was this way, and then a few months later, the realization would come that yes, I really *am* that way. They're two different things, one's intellectual and comes fairly easily; one is emotional and is a process of absorbing something, the things inside just sort of slowly shifting around and there's a lot of inertia there.

Stylistic Issues, Positions 8 and 9

Initial commitments do not settle as much as they seem to promise:

S.   I don't think it reduces the number of problems that I face or uncertainties, it just was something that troubled me that I thought was—I always thought it was an unnecessary problem and based on my limited experience with a broadened world. . . . [Now] I don't see it as something that is passed; it is something that I have to decide continually.

Identifications themselves turn out to be only a first step:

S.   That was just about what it was. Somehow I wanted to emulate [such people] because they seemed in some way noble people, and what they were doing seemed somehow noble and lofty—a very moral and superior type of thing. I think I fastened on this.

One thing I have found *since*, is that it's not really *right* to make decisions on this basis, because you may come out doing something you don't find yourself suited for. It's really strange. I'm committed for next year to go on in political science at Berkeley in California, I have found myself thinking, "Well, if the only reason I decided on government was because I like certain people and because what *they* were doing seemed good, then I think that I have neglected entirely my own abilities and capacities." Shouldn't I think about other things like business school and law school? And I've been doing this, but it's a whole new vista, so to speak, opened up.

Yet the specter of narrowness still haunts the corridors of choice, even geographically:

S.   I'll tell you one crisis of conscience that I had, that is I decided to come back to Harvard to graduate school, which is the thing that I thought two years ago I didn't want to do at all. But I didn't of course know about the traveling fellowship when I made the decision [not to come back], but I was doing it on the gamble that I would get it. Just the thought of coming right back to Cambridge next September is appalling beyond words. So I, I took that risk. I, I decided to do it. . . .

Simply the thought of another four years in Cambridge, four or five years in Cambridge! It's not that I don't—that I specifically don't like Cambridge, but I do have this feeling as I was saying before, knowing it backwards and forwards, and I suppose when I get back from my, from my year of traveling most of the people I know, who are even, most of them are either juniors or seniors, will be done and it will be different. But I wonder how much it really changes beneath the surface. You get the same kinds of people, I'm sure, year after year. I'm just a little bit frightened by that. I mean, if, if I feel now, that I've come to the . . . to the ridge of, come back and see everything, what's it going to be like looking over that ridge for another four years?

Well, of course the-ah . . . experience of being educated as a graduate student is something new and extremely challenging. But . . . that's only peripheral to being alive in a place and feeling with it. And that I'm not so sure about. . . .

One's worried about getting too comfortable. I mean I've got to the point now at Lowell House where I walk in every night and you know, I feel as if I'm not simply dwelling in E–42, the whole place is-ah, my paternal estate or something. I come in with a paternal smile on my face, which is an enormous, vast—I have to keep reminding myself that it's an enormous, vast, and impersonal place that it no longer seems at all. And this, this comfort is a mixed blessing at least. I expect to be discomforted a little in my year of travel.

If by comfort you just mean-ah-ah getting along easily, and the wheels are all running smoothly, then that's perhaps not so bad, but if you mean comfortable in the sense of a comfortable rut, I mean where you no longer have to take the trouble to, to . . . to think about living where you are, I mean just to, you know, you just go along existing. I don't think that's very good. I mean you do get the feeling that it's . . . kind of stagnation, isn't it?—to get settled?

Students frequently find a fruitful restatement of this dilemma in terms of "focus":
A senior:

S.   Well ah . . . I don't know exactly if there's any one thing that's central . . . this is the whole point that ah . . . there are factors in the whole . . . you group all these factors . . . I don't know that there's one thing about which everything revolves . . . but it's rather just a circle.

I.   It's the constellation that ah . . . you try to maintain?

S.   Yeah. Right. Yeah, you think of the old ah . . . the balance of powers you know . . . you know it's not . . . north and south or black and white . . . it's . . . it's not a simple thing. It comes in any given occasion . . . and . . . it's different. . . . This is what makes things exciting—it offers a challenge.

Another senior has been groping to describe the new sense of living with trust even in the midst of a heightened awareness of risk:

I.   And I take it, part of this mellowness that you speak of, is being able to live in peace with this complexity . . . if it isn't so simple. . . .

S.   It's not as frightening as it may have been. . . . If you feel that-ah, whatever you do there's going, there's going to be much more to do, more to understand, you're going to make mistakes . . . but you have a certain sense of being able to cope with a specific or rather a small fragment of the general picture and-ah, doing a job, getting the most out of it, but never, never giving up, always looking for something.

What is required is some balance between tentativeness and whole-heartedness:

S.   Well "tentative" implies . . . perhaps uncertainty and, and, I mean readiness to change to anything, and-ah, it's not that. It's openness to change but, but not looking for change, you know-ah. . . . At the same time-ah, believing pretty strongly in what you do believe, and so it's not, you know, it's not tentative. . . .

And again:

S.   So it's a commitment. It's a real, definite commitment, with a possibility of (*laughs*) of withdrawing from the commitment, which I think is the only realistic kind of commitment I can make, because there *is* a possibility of change here.

And between contemplative awareness and action:

S.   I don't . . . I don't brood. . . . I think that's a waste of time (*laughing*), I mean I'd rather do something than just sit around and . . . brood about it. Sometimes I . . . I'm just about . . . sometimes you do hasty things . . . it's a certain amount of relief to . . . just . . . just to do something. But . . . now the only . . . the only broodiness is sort of an inward broodiness . . . about whether . . . whether . . . whether I'm on the right tack . . . the right field. There are all kinds of pulls, pressures and so forth . . . parents . . . this thing and that thing . . . but there comes a time when you just have to say, "Well . . . I've got a life to live . . . I want to live it this way. I welcome suggestions. I'll listen to them. But when I make up my mind, it's going to be me. I'll take the consequences."

It is not always easy, however, to be debonair about the consequences. The new responsibility can challenge one's depths.

A junior:

S.   What you have to do is set up a set of rules for yourself that you're going to live by, and that you're going to, that you've got to, to-ah, you can't lose your self-respect! . . . You've got to be willing to use everything that your, every means that you command to achieve-ah, to survive, and to. . . . In essence survival includes a whole range of things, accomplishing goals that are important to you in a society and, yeah, survival, survival means that you don't lose your self-respect, because once you totally lose your self-respect, you're destroyed and you might as well be dead. And so you have to operate within a certain set of rules, a certain set of principles, or, or you're going to lose your self-respect. You still have to recognize that all these things that you learn, all these odd things about yourself and other people are potential tools for destruction or construction, and that you've got to be very careful in the way you utilize each one of them. They are things that you, that's one way of perceiving them, that you are, you are capable of using them. You don't go around turning on compassion and turning it off like a water faucet. You, you can use it. People . . . people just aren't conscious enough of their roles, that's all. They don't, don't try. There's such a thing as being too self-conscious, but, but you've got to be able to see the effects you're having on other people, and the effect other people have on you. And you've got to be careful about how you use all these things you've developed. And most people aren't. I'm certainly not careful about how I use things, but a recognition of your own qualities and what effect they can have on other people is very important. . . .

In the face of the crisis, however, the students seem to find themselves aware of a new inner strength:

S.   I wasn't *deploring* the fact that my interests were narrowing, I was just simply *observing* it. I don't see how I could get by without it. You know what Keats says in one of his letters, he says when he's sitting in a room and everybody is talking brilliantly and he's sitting in the corner and he's sulking and everybody is whispering to each other, "Oh that poet Keats is sitting over there like a wallflower," he says in moments like that, he doesn't care about that because he's aware of the, the resource in his breast. I think that's the expression that he uses. And what goes along with this narrowing of the purpose is the greater and greater sense of, that resource in my breast which is, I don't suppose that everybody needs it, but I need it. You know, it just, it just puts a center and a focus into your life, into what you're doing. And it hasn't really anything to do with where you are or what particular society you're living in, because you would like to think that it would go on, this "inner life" (which I think is really bad to call it) that will go on no matter what you're doing, whether you're traveling around the world or whether you're sitting in your stall in Widener. So I know that it must seem like a disparity, but I don't feel it that way.

The loneliness, again, is balanced by community:

S.   It seems to me much harder to think about something like that, unless you can look at what other people are doing and judge from the way they handle it, gives you so much more ability to accept the fact that you are gonna direct your efforts in such and such a way and if you know that other people hold some of the same things valuable, it makes it much less of a strain, you don't have to question it intensely, whether this is all something you dreamed up to meet a special situation, accept it as something you believe in, and other people believe in.

And yet the larger community also includes those who think differently, and one must both believe in one's own commitments and somehow acknowledge others' even when they contravene one's principles:

S.   Personally, I tend to think more or less in political terms, in terms of social good. I think a person who spends his time at cocktail parties, and spends four evenings on the telephone getting dates for the other three evenings is not accomplishing anything. He's not being at all constructive. I always tend to think that this person is not being the *citizen,* or the *man* he ought to be. And so I can reject this way of living because I think that you should really do more in the way of work. But on the other hand, I would have to say that there is no absolute moral right and wrong to this. I can't condemn such a person on any *final* grounds.

And:

S. I'm really just one of the mob, and I don't know whether it makes me feel more self-assured or not, but I feel happier knowing that, well, we're all really not too sure, and those that are are either pretty remarkable or kidding themselves, one or the other. I like to think—perhaps this again is erroneous thinking—I like to think I've become more tolerant, I don't know. Last year I had written out in my mind what I must have called a set of standards, a code, and, ah, I'm afraid I looked down on anything that didn't conform. I'm aware now that that isn't the best attitude. You can't let go of your own standards, but you can't really afford to look down on anyone who has a different—I won't say lower anymore—a *different* set of standards. Perhaps it isn't tolerance, perhaps it's just awareness of the fact that that's the way it should be, if it isn't.

One must find a balance, in both the courage to be as oneself and the courage to be as a part (Tillich, 1952).

S. I remember long discussions with the one teacher who meant everything to me. Who still does. I just spent, as a matter of fact, a very long evening with her last weekend. Last weekend I spent my, the evening of my twenty-first birthday with her. But ah, ah, the ability to ah, to be able to have a sense of myself without, without feeling that the sense is based on other people, which has been very important, very, very important. Ah, of course, it's still based on other people in many, many ways, but it's, it's a little different now.

Integrity of purpose in Commitment, together with freedom from old external constraints, require the individual to decide for himself how much he will judge his performance on his own experience of it, and how much value he will put on external judgments and rewards.

S.   Some of the . . . ah, most important things that I could think of would be . . . just the matters of . . . well . . . some, some things are more or less a matter of proportion that come from trying to see things in their . . . in their places and . . . what sort of importance a thing really does have. Just trying to see things in proportion and . . . and analyzing them apart from the necess-, from the . . . conventional views of them that one might take. I found myself getting very annoyed at my parents who were very proud to ha-, receive quite accidentally the department's notice that they recommended me for a magna, because my parents haven't the slightest idea really of what I've been doing or whether it's any damn good, but they s-, just take this particular sign as something to be very proud for.

The challenge to self-trust, however, can be poignant. A senior looks back, and ahead:

I.   Do you view yourself as changed any way in the four years other than having satisfied desire to have a certain amount of direction? Have you changed in other ways? . . . too ambiguous a question . . . ?

S.   No, it's not ambiguous at all. Ah well fundamentally, probably not, in degree sort of, but-ah (*pause*) still the, the ah, inclination— well, I'll speak—I'll say this is before I decided, [I had the] inclination to really ah, live from day to day ah—the moment counts, and a real refusal to study for marks except at a certain minimum level, maybe, it might be a bit of wildness, a real rejection of anything imposed, doing what I have to and just getting whatever else I felt like, at whatever time. Often a flagrant disregard for consequences, and even with an awareness of what might happen . . . the lack of responsibility, so that I wind up feeling that I owe myself a lot more than I delivered, and not feeling particularly happy about this, but feeling now that perhaps I can deliver a little more. That having imposed a set of restrictions on my activities, and a set of requirements, that perhaps this is the answer, and quite frankly hoping that it is the answer. But still it's a tremendous guilty feeling about not having looked forward enough. (*Pause*) And, well, a lot of regret, regret of not having written a thesis, regrets about so many things that I didn't do. Well, that's true. It's, it's really very difficult, except that I somehow have the feeling that I could have reconciled the two outlooks.

But yet, not letting this particularly bog me down, there's still the feeling that "this is it," you know, and now I'm behind, and not too late, no feeling of real discouragement.

But then again somehow the doubt, the feeling that maybe this is an out, that really maybe it's just something that I've imposed on myself, this will dissipate itself sure.

But I, I do feel this, definitely.

Trust must rest in more than will alone. Perhaps in growth itself, or the meaning that will emerge from the unexpected:

S. I carefully avoided thinking of anything particular to say before I came in here because I figured people would want to catch me and see what I had to say about this and that, because it would be probably more valuable, whatever is being thought about. I like to be caught unawares because then I don't have a stock answer—say anything that comes to mind. May be disorganized but it's probably a lot more real.

Order and disorder may be seen as fluctuations in experience:

S. I sort of see this now as a natural thing—that you constantly have times of doubt and tension—a natural thing in existing and being open, trying to understand the world around you, the people around you.

The old feeling that a few big decisions would settle all gives way to a realization of the complexity of growth—and its slowness:

S. No, no big thing, lots and lots of little things which have, which have been influencing me really changed me so that I, in the sum of all these things, my direction is really strongly in, into the area of, of social relations, social action and, and, religious liberalism, which, in a big sense is broader than . . . all these sorts of liberalism, I guess. And partly you know, each thing causes some of the others, and, and, and is caused by each of the others. And it has been, it's like an amoeba which extends a pseudopodia in one direction and follows the whole thing and this is about what I've been doing.

And:

S.   I've come to a fairly settled idea of what I want to do as far as my career is concerned, and also my general values have become oriented, kind of settled to some degree. Also one thing I've noticed, I've finally become at home. I feel at home in this atmosphere here, and coming from out where I do it took me quite a long time to do that. One major thing has been the formation of a group of friends in my house. As far as my values are concerned, I guess in my junior year—hard to really pinpoint it—I really severely questioned my basic beliefs about things. Intellectually there hasn't been any big jump. Ever since I came here, slowly I've learned new things. Slowly.

In this complexity one senses reason's limit and the necessity it implies:

S.   Well, O.K., what is everybody doing here? What are we existing for? What I more or less came out with is that, well we're here, make the best of it you can. That was more or less answered, and then I thought that, I'll have to work from a point of faith. I mean, well, I like to reason things out, turn things over a lot in my head and try to think of reasons for things—and I do mistrust faith. I always have to some extent. But then I just about said, said to myself, "Well, that's the only thing you got left, and there isn't anything else." So I more or less left it at that, and that helped quite a bit. I mean, that was something.

Complexity, especially the conflict between value systems, demands a capacity to tolerate paradox in the midst of responsible action. A junior whose roommate's breakdown had faced him with the necessity for decisive action reports his integration of conflict:

S.   I don't know whether to pass judgment or not. That was one of the, you know, one of the real dilemmas. Excruciating kind of thing. Even then you're kind of frustrated in turning outside for advice, or hoping that somebody else is going to see it. It was just amazing that no one else saw it. . . . I mean I, I imagine even the psychiatrist didn't . . . which-ah, which is, you know, I guess it's not surprising, human beings are . . . what you say in an hour, and you'd seen it over weeks and months and years, well years. Still human beings are so fallible, is what you finally have to conclude. Like when doctors who should know these things don't, and we kind of still carry on somehow in our bumbling fashion. See this is in the way you get educated. (*Laughs*) This is right there, so that's the big surprise. See, I still am sort of ironical about it, 'cause that's about the only way you can be, 'cause ironic, being ironic handles both values at once.

Action itself, when it is not simply a "flight into reality," seems to provide in the end the most workable focus for sanity. Seniors appear less caught in metaphysics than sophomores. They often felt they had little to "say" in interviews—just that they were "in it." Most were willing to contemplate, but always with a sense of limit:

S.　I heard some freshman trying to discuss, whether or not you can have an objective morality, the other day, and my heavens, I haven't thought about whether you could have—if I ever thought about such basic questions as whether you could have an objective morality—I haven't thought about it for several years. All we discuss now is, is problems of, of administration or technical problems, not problems so basic. And really, what's more basic? (*Laughs*) Ah, like the old question of are we free or are we determined as individuals? Well you can argue that forever, and I've tried. And you just exhaust yourself on that topic, and then you go on to another topic, and then you'll exhaust yourself on that topic, and go on and on, until you reach some topic that you can discuss and, and reach some sort of accord on. And when you get to that level it seems to me you've had a more profitable educational experience, not because you solved all the problems that lie beneath it, necessarily. You've discussed them, of course, but you haven't solved anything. It's just that you've reached a certain level, using a certain amount of language that allows you to come to a conclusion, to reach agreement on something. And it's important to reach this level of agreement, if you see what I mean.

I.   Exactly.

It is, then, in the midst of such balances that our students seemed to search for some dynamic equilibrium expressive of their particular temperament, preferences, history, judgment, courage, understanding, and care. Indeed their reports suggest that they experience identity even more keenly in their style of Commitment than in the external forms or content to which they commit themselves. We see sense in this. In espousing a career such as medicine a student defines himself; however, in doing so he must allow the culturally established forms of the role a large say in the definition. He defines himself, but also he is defined. Stylistic decisions, however, remain more expressively his own. In finding some position between narrowness and breadth, stability and growth, certainty and doubt, the judgment and the risks are his own. Within broad limits, he can find no external guidelines for this ultimate self-expression—even when he feels such guidelines would be a comfort. There are, in short, other premedical students, but only he acquits the role in his particular way.

Previous excerpts have illustrated some of the stylistic qualities of Commitment, issue by issue. In the following passages a single student describes his groping for his own equilibrium in the matrix of many issues. The passages begin with the opening of his account of his junior year:

> I.   Looking back over three years, what seems to stand out now?
>
> S.   I don't know . . . it wasn't so plain, so clear last year but it's pretty clear now. Change takes place one way or another.
>
> I.   There's been a great change?
>
> S.   Oh, yes. I mean you just look at things differently. It's hard to say what. It's hard, I mean, because you can only put your finger on some of them. You feel that you're growing up. I mean, certain things become less important, certain things become more important. But on the whole, you don't (*pause*) find yourself getting quite so totally taken up in something as you might have. I think that this, of course, is purely my own, that the values that you start off with in this place definitely

change, one way or another. I mean, the things that you think are important drop out and new things take their place. Or the old values become transformed in some way. Into something better, a lot better. Something different.

I.   Different? But something that feels better?

S.   Well, when you first come here, you're confronted with this rainbow of different things. For some reason, you don't see at first that maybe it's kind of egotistical or something, as a value—but there is a value built into it—the feeling that you can do *whatever* you want to, if you just do it. And after a while maybe you don't feel that way. You *do* it, and it seems that you kind of do these things because there's so many, in a sort of indif-, well, not indifferent, but there's no *keenness* about the way you do most things, because whenever you do one thing there's something else on your mind. If you're working, then there's a social at the club. I never was in a club, but I should imagine that this would be how it was. Or if you're studying, then you have your job on your mind. I mean, you can't focus on any particular aspect of what you're confronted with. There was this idea that you have to get the full benefit of everything and there's so much to take advantage of that you have to spend 40 hours a day taking advantage of everything.

Maybe it's not that you take some new values up and drop others, but that some become more clear. I mean, because you certainly become more enthusiastic about the interests you take up.

I.   What would you say in your case, Mike? Realizing how hard it is to spell any of this out, what would you say within this range is becoming more important to you?

S.   I decided that I would like to teach in a college. What you're worried about when you make a decision like that initially is that, well, maybe you just decide that because you're in college. The people

Inclusiveness vs. intensity

Choice
vs.
external
influence

Intrinsic
values
vs.
external
symbols

who have the highest prestige that you come into contact with are your teachers. Values are in terms of knowledgeability rather than anything else. And after a certain number of years these are the values you take up. If you go someplace else, their values are stated in different terms. Then you'll just assimilate those values. That, so to speak, desire to teach is not something that you have come onto yourself, but something which has impressed itself upon you after three years of going to classes and going to lectures and taking exams. And that is really something to worry about, because if you're just doing it because it's been impressed on you after three years, then maybe there are other things that you would want to do just as well if you had a chance to see them and do them for a while.

But if you do decide that you want to teach, say government which is my field, then the desire to learn and to know about government becomes greater than just a mere desire to accumulate enough information to pass an examination. If as a freshman you measured your knowledge of the field in terms of your performance on an examination, because this meant living up to a certain standard, later on you become more aware of what your capabilities are and you don't judge yourself so exclusively in terms of examinations or grades. My grades aren't so poor that I think this is a rationalization. I get B grades, so I don't think that it's a rationalization for not getting A grades.

[And yet] maybe part of it is intellectual snobbery. I wouldn't deny that. I really think it is. Because you're part of this atmosphere. I mean, the values you're confronted with are the Harvard values. You can't help but judge in terms of the center of the circle, which is Harvard. And you can't help but get impatient once in a while. People are concerned with unimportant things. Well, I mean unimportant in terms of what *you* consider im-

Certainty
vs.
doubt

portant. (*Long pause*) There are things that you think about. For example: are these things really better or do you just think they're better? When you say that what is here is in any real sense better or more important than what goes on say in the real estate business or insurance business, is that right? Is what goes on here in any real sense more important or interesting or more lively than what goes on in a law firm or in a hospital? But even though you have these doubts you don't feel compulsive needs to resolve them—to present yourself with answers to them, I mean. Maybe that's one of the things that happens. If initially your value is to have answers, maybe that changes and becomes transformed into just having questions to think about rather than have answers to the questions.

I.   You feel that you can sustain an awful lot more ambiguity. . . .

Faith
vs.
external
reasons

S.   Probably, I mean in this particular problem. Is there any way to tell it when one career is better than another? You can state it in different ways, but it finally comes down to the fact that what you finally decide, you will have to decide independently of any absolute merit that some career has. You have to decide solely in terms of your own interest. (*Pause, speaks very softly*) But you accept that.

Gains in
focus
vs.
loss in
alternatives

   No matter what you finally choose, you don't really have to feel that it has intrinsic merit. (*Long pause*) In America today, it's very important as a value to do well financially. I don't think anybody will deny that. A person tends to be judged in terms of position. Not *solely* in financial terms, but a kind of equation of financial success with intelligence and merit. They kind of become synonymous, and then, you appreciate that in a place like this, it really isn't quite that way. But on the other hand, to decide to teach doesn't mean to reject all that. At first, it becomes kind of a dichotomy. Either you decide to teach and give up the material benefits that America certainly has in terms of comfort and leisure, or you decide not to teach and to give up the intellectual benefits and solely go for the other. It seems after a while that these things kind of merge. It's not stated in terms of taking one and leaving the other. If you decide to focus on one you're not necessarily bound to give up everything else. It's a matter more of focus than of pure choice.

Idealism
vs.
realism

[*He goes on to speak of his acceptance of limits within his old idealistic intent to improve the entire world.*] So it's not (*long pause*) so much a matter of getting into a rut and accepting it, as seeing that this is unchanging. I hate to call it "fatalism" because you don't accept it in the sense that you approve of it and you want it that way, but only in the sense that you can't change it.

[*The same student continues in his senior year.*] Well, one thing I have to say is that this year for the first time I moved into a House, after commuting for the first three years. So of course this was something entirely new. And in a way, the first surprise was that after three years here, I could still step into something so completely different; different types of people with different interests. And I guess the upshot of this has been to make me feel uncertain about how many more steps a person could possibly take and still go further.

Settledness
vs.
growth

I.   Anything come to mind with respect to the difference?

S.   When I was transposed into this from living at home, I was confronted with a great many more attitudes about ways of doing things than I had seriously considered before. Ah, for instance, the people who want to work hard—and the people who don't—in something like studies. One thing I've tried to do, which was a response to living in, was to think out much more carefully just where I wanted to stand. Because living in one of the houses, it was even more possible than it had ever been before to see the spectrum, and to make decisions. Some decisions seem to be easier than others, and some alternatives seemed to be easier than others, and some alternatives seemed to be more desirable than others. It seemed easier sometimes to work than not to work. Well in any case, the point was that decisions had to be made, and the relative merits of the alternatives were not always completely clear. One had to think out very carefully just what his position was, and where he wanted to stand—not that this was always possible. You couldn't say, "I stand here" and then live like that, because part of it was in a way, doing a little bit of everything, and then trying to come back to what you thought you should be doing. To try to enjoy everything that "living in" had to offer, /uhuh/ and nevertheless to come back to what I was serious about.

Stability vs. flexibility

I think also, along the lines of developing an awareness of your own position that you tend to be less reluctant and less fearful of questioning certain values, a certain aspect of activity that you see before you. I mean, initially, I think I mentioned that as a freshman you're confronted with this whole spectrum of possibilities or ways you can spend time, and interests you can develop. And at this time, it seems pretty much that they're almost all of equal validity. This is purely subjective, and therefore some of the decisions are difficult. Most of them were difficult for me. You really can't decide which way is better than another. But I think also as you become aware of your own position, certain decisions become easy. It becomes less difficult for you to reject certain aspects of what you're confronted with. If you don't enjoy social work, then it's not hard to give up, say, Phillips Brooks House. And if you don't like newspaper writing, then you don't have to ask yourself whether or not you should try out for the *Crimson*. The choice is

Confidence in identity vs. confusion

Developing
commitment

Dualism
vs.
relativism
in choice

broad in the sense that you have this great academic scope—anything from physics to political
science. Then you have to start making decisions,
and narrowing them down, and, you take courses.
If you consider this as a rainbow, as a kind of a
spectrum, then you select the academic section of
the spectrum, and within this you're confronted
again. . . . I used to think that you could evaluate
decisions in terms of a right and a wrong. The right
thing to do was associated with the more *difficult*
path, and the wrong was associated with the easy
way out. And I think lately I've been somehow rejecting this. I don't know. Not specifically, but more
or less discarding the idea that, that you can make
right and wrong decisions. You simply make decisions, and whichever way you go there's not going
to be any violent repercussion.

I.   How do you protect yourself, if there's any need
for protection, against this kind of relativism?

S.   Well-ah, God, this is really hard. I mean, this is
something I have been worrying about, and it
seems that if there is no right or wrong, and the
people who don't study, but who spend time going
out and enjoying four years of college as opposed
to the person who spends four years in his room
working, ah, if there is no clear right and wrong,
then I think what you *have* to do is to reject the
idea of right and wrong, and find out what *you*
want. You have to be introspective, in the sense that
you try to establish the way *you* want to live, carefully. And once having done this I think, you can

Own values
vs.
others'
values

proceed to look at everything else. You can be critical of it, and yet you say, "Well, this is one way to
do things." One trouble I'm having is that I'm making the ambiguities too clear. I mean, because the
way people live never confronts them in terms of a
clear opposition between one way of doing things
and another. There are people who spend more
time doing one thing and people who spend less,

so it's always a matter of shaving degrees. Once you find out where you stand, if you ever can find out where you stand, then you just have to say, if you're confronted with a person who doesn't do things like *you* do, "Well, *he* has decided to do things like this— *I wouldn't*. I don't think it's *right*." And yet you have to come back and say, "But this is only *subjective*— this is only my own way of looking at things. I can't say, in absolute terms, that this is immoral."

I.   And do you think you had stronger and clearer moral convictions when you arrived, in the sense that you felt you were able to make those distinctions?

S.   I think when I arrived, in the first couple of years, I wasn't quite as aware as I am now of the very different ways people do things. This awareness is something which I think has crept in very slowly. I think that when I came in—I had no real attitudes at all. I just hadn't thought about things. And in the first year I developed some very strong opinions about things. When I met this tutor, I seemed to judge everybody against him, and then judged myself against him. I tended to say, "Well, he works, therefore I will work." I tended to measure people against this . . . as a moral standard.

Certainty
vs.
doubt

I think more recently I have been less certain. When I rejected things then, it was very strong. I don't know how I want to put this exactly. I can still say "yes" or "no," but I'm still beset with these doubts. My position has become much more relative than it was. I don't think I had doubts as a freshman when I made a decision, and now I have. But lingering doubts. I think when I made a decision then, I tried to stick by it. And I think now, I, I shift back and forth much more. In a sense, I'm very much less certain about things now than I was then.

[*He goes on to speak of teachers and books in the development of his values.*] I think I was

Identification

particularly impressed by this book, because it criticized certain aspects of American society with the same basic assumptions that I had myself. I'm beginning to realize that the book was so striking to me because the author's unstated assumptions were similar to mine, or I should say, mine were so similar to his. And the basic assumptions of the course were very similar to mine. These were more or less academic values. Well, not academic, but sort of the idea that a person has to earn his bread in this world, and that you do it by working, and contributing something, spending most of your time reading or writing or doing research. In some sense leisure is secondary. Also, there was the idea embedded in the course, that there wasn't enough of this around. Too many people tend to take the easy road, not enough people do any real work, and there are too few people willing to sacrifice themselves somehow for some sort of higher good. In any case, the whole course more or less corresponded with certain very deep feelings I had about things, particularly with certain very deep academic values that I had. But what has become difficult since, is that when I try to make a decision about what I want to do in the future, I tend to think very highly of academic values and this involves neglecting my own capacity.

Self-centered
vs.
other-centered

Limits of
identification

[*He then speaks of students and others whose values he disapproves, and yet whom he has come to understand and respect.*] I think that as a freshman, it would have been much easier for me to reject these people than it is now, with much less lingering doubt. It would not have been at all possible for me as a freshman to set these people up and compare them to other people, which I think is possible now. All this comparing, of course, makes final decisions more and more difficult. The more you compare things and set up oppositions, the more difficult decisions become and the less sure you are of any right and wrong.

Both my roommates came from families somewhat better off economically than my own family. I think that I gave something to both. . . . I don't want to sound egotistical, but I think I gave something to both by being present and by presenting them with a different set of attitudes. I mean a kind of a "work ethic." If you can talk about my attitude as being a kind of work ethic, then in the House I moderated this more or less to conform to their designs. We had to live together, and some clear decisions had to be made, decisions like a cocktail party in the room *versus* studying in the room, on a Saturday night. In this case, there was a clear confrontation, and there was definite interaction taking place with moderation and compromise on both sides. This was about the clearest opposition that stands out in my mind, and also the clearest case of an impact perhaps I made.

I.   Using your own term, "work ethic," do I get the feeling that you brought it with you, and that it's been reformed and moderated, but that you're going away with it too . . . ?

S.   I think now, that while this is the way I should feel, and this is the way I *do* feel, I certainly have to keep thinking about it. Some of the plans I have for the summer involve thinking out my own ideas about this. Trying to figure it out once more. This year has been central so to speak. I came in with this idea and held it firmly. And this year all this diversity has subjected my attitude to considerable doubt. It no longer stands on the ground it once stood on. All that there is left of the idea is a kind of a vague feeling that maybe this is a better way to do things; that this is for *me* really *the* way to do things. But in any case, I certainly will have to spend a great many weeks, and perhaps never will come out with any more firm idea than I have now. I certainly feel that I will have to think about it a great deal.

The four years have contributed doubt, certainly. One thing I heard someone say about religion at Harvard was that people who came here, religiously committed, went out more confirmed in their attitudes than they came in. The impact of Harvard had been to cause them to rethink and reshuffle and reformulate, but that they came out as strongly committed in a different sense somehow as they had come in. And I wondered if this applied to my own general attitudes about things. It seemed to apply in the sense that I'm still going out with the idea that a better way to do things is to work hard and accomplish something. But I wouldn't conceive of myself as having anywhere near the religious attachment to this attitude that I had when I came in. When I came in, I felt a kind of almost—I don't want to use too strong words—but scorn, or contempt, for the people who had it easy and who took it easy.

Tolerance vs. contempt

One of the problems that confronts you in graduate school is commitment to academic values. Success in graduate school involves a very strong commitment, and a willingness to put in a great deal of work. Can I do well unless I somehow redevelop this old devotion I had? Again, this is something I've been thinking about in the last few weeks. When I say I've been thinking about something, of course I don't mean I sit down and *think* about something. I mean that scattered thoughts go through my mind during the most silly moments. While tying my shoe I'll think about something for a few seconds. I think I will probably have

Self-trust vs. self-doubt[19]

Action vs. contemplation

---

[19]The passage illustrates the poignancy with which the realization of a relative world requires the development of a new basis for self-trust. If one's previous endeavors were experienced in an absolute belief in their worth, one cannot be confident in advance that one will find in one's relative Commitments sufficient faith to balance sacrifice, or to counter despair.

to develop a new attitude, because I don't think you can find a way to work hard without the absolute conviction which I once had that this was the way to live. And this will be a new challenge.

Oddly, and I hate to confess something like this, but I think that just this last year my own doubts about the work ethic have been so great that my work has suffered a little bit. And just in the last

Limits of
reason

two months or so I was really in a process of thinking out this thing. I think one of the things I wanted to say before was that I had been wondering, if I were transposed into an atmosphere where more of a leisure ethic was the key, whether I would endure for long with the same old values? If I had lived in a House for two or three years and joined a Club, maybe I would have changed completely. I just don't know. I really don't. Because the other possibility is that my attitude would have weakened, and wavered for a time, but then that I might have simply gone back. I don't think I'll ever be able to find this out, since it's something you just don't know.

This last paragraph describes the purgatory of Relativism in which our students found themselves standing, outside of Eden. The university, compactly representing through "a liberal education" the diversity of the modern world and the contingency of modern knowledge, is revealed as Serpent. The students have eaten.

Doubt is now not limited to knowledge of the "out there," or to ancestral values. It is reflected back upon the individual. Can he claim to be who he thinks he is? He must, if he is to live heartily, but with how much certainty? Having reached the limits of reason, "faith is all you have left." But faith, in view of the investment, requires courage.

The students whose words have illustrated the main line of development in this report elected to move ahead from challenge to challenge. Their words suggest why this was for them, implicitly or explicitly, an act of moral courage.

The data in the following sections describe the alternatives that were open to them all along the way.

—⁓— Alternatives to Growth:
Temporizing—Retreat—Escape

In any of the Positions in the main line of development a person may suspend, nullify, or even reverse the process of growth as our scheme defines it: (1) He may pause for a year or more, often quite aware of the step that lies ahead of him, as if waiting or gathering his forces (*Temporizing*). (2) He may entrench himself, in anger and hatred of "otherness," in the me-they or we-other dualism of the early Positions (*Retreat*). (3) He may settle for exploiting the detachment offered by some middle Position on the scale, in the deeper avoidance of personal responsibility known as alienation (*Escape*).

The judges found themselves in far more agreement about the Position that expressed the structure of a student's world than about the tonality that expressed his involvement in growth. They even expressed a reluctance to make these latter judgments at all. They complained that the values built into the entire scheme put them in a moral bind. Any rating of a student's report as expressive of Temporizing, Retreat, and Escape became a negative moral judgment of his character. We acknowledged the reality of this dilemma.

At the same time, we could assure them that growth (as we saw it) was rarely linear and more usually wavelike. Growth, we felt, usually occurred in surges. Between the surges, a person might pause to explore the implications of his new position. Or he might lie fallow, waiting for the resurgence of strength to meet the next challenge. On occasion he might even have to detach himself from the whole business, or retreat to old positions, in order to assure himself that he was still his own man. Then, after having found that he was still free to choose, he could know any reengagement to be an authentic act, not an enslavement. Every such moment between surges, we acknowledged, involves risk, subjective and objective. The forces of growth may indeed be forever denied. It happens.

We pointed out, however, that even this formulation itself was said within the context of our scheme. In this context, a final settling for the attitudes described in "Escape" or "Retreat" is by definition a failure of growth and maturity. This is a value to which we ourselves were committed. If, then, we were true to the very struggles we were tracing in our students, we had to allow that others might hold quite different values. Someone might look on a life of what we called "alienation" as a triumph—we could disagree passionately, but we could not, as the students would say, call him wrong "in any absolute sense."

The judges were only mildly reassured. They used these categories a little more sparingly than we would have ourselves. When they did, however, their agreement was beyond anything one could reasonably attribute to chance. Very possibly our volunteer sample contained fewer instances of alienation than may occur in the student population at large, especially since the judged sample contained only students who had persevered through four years of college and who were willing to share their experience with us for four consecutive years. Yet our general experience of undergraduates causes us to doubt it. Most students, of course, do experience moments of alienation, even yearnings toward it—and when they speak from it, they shock adult ears. We tend, however, to look on entrenched alienation as the exception it shows itself to be in this study.

Temporizing

Temporizing, defined as a pause in growth over a full academic year, does not itself involve alienation, even though it may contain that potential. Sometimes it is even a time of what one might call lateral growth—a spreading out and a consolidation of the structure of a Position recently attained. At other times it seems more fallow, suspended, poised. Often enough a student will say, "I'm just not ready yet."

The destiny of such periods—whether they will terminate in a resumption of growth or in a drifting into Escape—seems to be foretold in the tone in which a student waits. He may speak as one waiting for agency to rise within himself, for himself to participate again in responsibility for his growth. Or he may speak as one waiting for something to happen to him, something to turn up that will interest him enough to solve all problems.

Temporizing can occur at any Position on our scale. Here, for example, a sophomore finds himself still wandering, after two years, in the diffuse relativism of Position 5 into which his opposition to Authority had led him in high school.

S.   I haven't basically changed any of my, sort of my underlying philosophic concepts, you might say . . . whatever rationalizations we use for the way we behave. These haven't particularly changed since my senior year in high school.

I.   Ah—how would you spell those out? . . .

S.   Well, I can't say much except a complete ah, relativistic outlook on everything. I used to be a very militant agnostic in high school, and though I'm no longer militant, I'm . . . still an agnostic. I don't do the debating with anybody any more, probably because I've come to the conclusion that in many respects the other side is quite worthwhile for a great many people . . . and . . . even for me perhaps thirty years from now. But not right at the moment. I've become, my whole dominant theme has been sort of just a pragmatic approach to everything. At times I feel this is highly inadequate and it perhaps is just all an excuse for . . . thinking what you want to think. (*Laughs*) If you want go be a pragmatist, you carry it in any direction you like (*laughs*) and you don't have to put very many checks on yourself.

But I can't see any other answer to the problem. It doesn't seem possible to, to, to determine any absolute, so . . . so I'm sort of stuck with the relativism that leaves me a little bit dissatisfied. . . . It's still basically the same relativism that I, that I had when I was back in high school.

The inner challenge of Commitment, and environmental demand for decision, combine to make Temporizing most vivid in Position 6. A senior:

S.   I'm not going on to graduate school, that's one thing for sure, not yet anyway, because I don't know what I want to do. I'd hate to go to law school for a year and spend two or three thousand dollars, and find out after the year that I hated law school and hated the study of law and I wished I hadn't spent the year or the three thousand dollars. So I felt maybe just a couple of years doing something else . . . going to France and, and the navy. A little bit of a background so that, you know, I may be able to get around a little more, have a few more experiences and then I could be better able to judge perhaps whether I wanted to go into law school or graduate school of arts and science or divinity school or what. Because it seems like I (*laughs*), instead of my interests narrowing down, you know, to two or three choices, it (*laughing*) seems like they're *mush*-rooming, expanding all over the place, in the last year or two, and so it's worse than it was when I was in high school.

A sophomore:

S.   No, no definite plan. It's . . . it's silly. Only twenty. . . . Just turned twenty and it's, it's just dumb to, to go off, run off committing yourself, I think probably what I'll do is go to law school, but I don't know . . . it might be good to go ahead and get, get the doctorate, you know, so . . . with these, with these sudden ideas coming in and these desires you can't make a decision.

Anyway-ah I can't, what, what can you do? You've gotta take all these things into account and kind of plan for them, but . . . getting all upset about a career this, this early, it's just not worth it. I imagine by my senior year I'll have switched around completely and be pretty panicky, but . . . this year it's just too, just too comfortable here to-ah, get all wrought up about that and there's nothing you can do about it.

Sheer competence in academic skills provides a resting place, and the temptation of escape. A senior:

S.   For example in history, that's what I've been doing in history, just hitting a few things on the surface, perhaps making a flashy paper with some cheap conjunctions. And I realize they're cheap. I realize that, ah, I'm not at any stage of the work where I'm going to the heart of a problem, trying to see if there is any real connection.

Temptation, indeed, can be vivid:

S.   Then of course there's the draft board to contend with. I would really hate to be drafted. So I don't know, I think I, I would like the navy if I went in for-ah, the OCS, that's four months and then another three years and I think it's a little more adventure . . . to the . . . to the navy. You're on a boat, and that's a vehicle, and you're going some place (*laughing*) and that's what I like to do, I like to be going some place all the time.

I'm really not that crazy about the water, actually, and ships. But . . . I don't know . . . I almost feel like drifting. I almost feel like ah leaving and then just going off, you know, for just a couple of months with a knapsack on my back or something or just a bicycle and just going through—I, I've never been any farther west than Buffalo, New York—just traveling around the country. I had a friend that did that once. I think it would be kind of fun. Maybe it wouldn't be. Maybe it would be horrid. So I don't know, I even, I've even thought of teaching. I've thought of going back and, and ah . . . teaching and, in New York State. They have a very good program, if you, if you ah—I wouldn't want to teach for good, but for a couple of years to make a little money. But there's a tremendous danger in that because ah, even my parents recog-recognize this ah, in my going back home because all my friends have said, "Oh, golly, if you go back there, you'll be buried," you know. And I, it's so, it so . . . easily could happen. Go back to a small town and find yourself there about thirty years later and wonder what happened.

Perhaps "something will turn up." But how? In foreseeing such an event, the felt balance between one's own agency and the agency of fate can be complex and precarious. A senior of oppositional temperament looks forward to a more "congenial" environment for self-definition:

S.   I think Cambridge is, is such a permissive place—you know, it lets you be whatever you want to be—that you really don't have to be anything. You have nothing, nothing to set yourself against—no, no particular codes of morality, or conformity, whatever you want to call it. There, there's nothing to take a stand in this community against, because someone will agree with you, and someone will disagree with you, but you'll always find someone. . . . Mr. Brower in English 162 is comparing Cambridge to, to the dilemma of, of Henry James between Europe and America, you know, Lambert Strether goes to Europe and sees a new type of, of morality, a certain visual and aesthetic awareness of, of Chad's affair with—with, ah, Madam—whatever her name is—and I think here that you have the chance for that sort of experience. But after you've had that, the real test is, is going on some place else, some place that doesn't have the permissiveness and . . . just perhaps the academic atmosphere and, and trying to test what you've learned. I think Cambridge has made me very eager to go away. In a way I am happy I'll be in Philadelphia next year because I know in Philadelphia I can, can *be* something, if you know what I mean. There'll be more pressure on me to tow the line and. . . .

I.   More definite shape to the expectations? . . .

S.   That other people have of me? Yeah, that's true.

I.   . . . in relation to which you can feel your own shape, and form, and stand better?

S.   Yeah, and see if I want to go against the, grain. I don't know now whether I do or not, because this, this community gives me no way of testing.

Waiting for experience to inform one can slip toward letting fate be responsible:

S.   Well, I've got a pretty—well my problem is that I've got a clear view of three or four things that I'd like to be doing. Can't for the life of me figure out which one I want to follow. Ah, foreign service, college teaching, politics. . . . I don't know which one I want to follow. Again here is the-ah . . . the problem, I think, is . . . one between activism and detached analysis, and I can't figure out which one, ah, I'm best for, and whether I can figure out a synthesis of both in some field. I don't know, perhaps I'll wait and see what, see what time brings, see if I pass the foreign service exam. Let that decide.

Followed a few steps further, the temptation leads into the style of alienation and irresponsibility we call Escape. "Temptation" and "irresponsibility" are moral terms, and I use them advisedly. In our records, as we shall show, students who speak from Escape express guilt—a malaise they experience not so much in regard to the social responsibilities from which they are alienated as in regard to their own failure toward themselves.

First, however, it is appropriate to consider the alternative of active Retreat.

Retreat

In the early years of this study we established the term "Retreat" to refer specifically to an entrenchment in the dualism of Position 2 or 3—an entrenchment undertaken in reaction to the complexities, envisioned or experienced, of more advanced Positions. We came to regret this specificity. We should have allowed the term the more general meaning of regression wherever regression might occur. In our early study of our records, however, we were so struck by the dramatic energy of regression into Position 2 or 3 that we failed to notice instances of regression at any other range of our scale.

General theory, and common observation, would suggest that one may retrogress at any point or range of development in our scheme. With the help of our judges, we did indeed learn to perceive the few instances in our records. For example (requoted):

> S.   I'm beginning to discover that I can't follow a reasoned argument at all. I've never had to. I can't read philosophy. It's a sad state of affairs, but . . . I tell myself that this is no way to-ah really prove anything, anyway—logic is really meaningless. I'm a great believer in intuition rather than science or logic.

As a brief statement reflecting the tonality of an entire report, the excerpt expresses a regression into Multiplicity in reaction against the intellectual efforts of Relativism. The rest of the report supports a reading to the effect that the student is describing a giving up, for the moment at least, of the responsibilities of reason (and of considered Commitment) and falling back on impulse.[20]

In our early thinking we did not distinguish this rather limp regression in the middle area of our scale from that lateral movement of evasive dissociation which we called Escape. They do share in com-

---

[20]Stated in more sophisticated terms, the proposition would be the common expression of the failure of courage in an intellectual community. A person may move through all those defeats of the hope for certainty demanded by Positions 3, 4, 5, and 6, only to forget his relinquishments. It is as if, in his expansion in the intellectual endeavors of Relativism, the old hope of certainty had crept into his labors, unnoticed. Then, confronted with the failure of reason to certify any Commitment, the person says in disillusion, "It's all up to the individual in the end," meaning: "so why not in the beginning? Why all this work for nothing?"

mon a loose abandonment of responsibility. Regression, however, involves a "retreat into previously prepared positions"; Escape achieves relief from involvement by exploiting the provision for detachment offered by advanced structures themselves.

The distinction could have been valuable, but its omission was not vital. Fortunately for this study, regression at higher levels was so rare in our records that our oversight caused the judges no disastrous trouble. When they saw regression at advanced levels, they coded it, with a note, as a variation of Escape.

"Retreat," in the narrow sense of our definition, is also rare in our records. When it occurs, however, it tends to take a dramatic form. It appears to require fight. Regression from higher levels back to Multiplicity defends itself by its very looseness: "There's no one to argue with; everyone has a right to his own opinion." Regression into dualism, however, calls for an enemy.

The first reason is intrinsic. The dichotomous structure itself divides the world into good and bad, we and they, friend and foe—and this on absolute grounds. As a point of origin in normal development, of course, the familial "good" in this Position may provide an embeddedness in which fight is unnecessary. The enemy of "bad others" is far away. In retrogression, however, the enemy has been sighted. At this point reactive adherence to Authority (the "reactionary") requires violent repudiation of otherness and of complexity. Similarly, reactive Opposition to Authority (the "dogmatic rebel") requires an equally absolutistic rejection of any "establishment." Threatened by a proximate challenge, this entrenchment can call forth in its defense hate, projection, and denial of all distinctions but one. In short, if the tendency of extreme regression at higher levels is toward the pathology of bland depersonalization, the tendency of extreme regression at Position 2 is toward paranoia.

The second reason for the dramatic quality of Retreat is environmental. One can hardly imagine a less congenial milieu for this entrenchment than a pluralistic university. Defense must be vigilant, and preoccupying. We found only one statement in which smugness alone seemed sufficient, and this was made in retrospect with a sense of the battle won.

S. Well you have to either, you either take what you've been-ah taught [in childhood] and use it as acceptable in the light of nothing better, or you assess what facts that you can find and construct something that will serve. Ah, typical in this way, is I suppose, is, is morality and belief in God, and this sort of thing, which no one seems to be able to prove to the satisfaction of anyone around here. I'm satisfied to accept most of what I've been raised with-ah, that there is a God in some form-ah. I have my own ideas, and there's no need to go into them, I mean the details, and just how strong, how closely connected the moral-ah, mores that are in effect, are to what actually ought to be according to His law, that's the matter for a lot of controversy. Certainly I've been subjected during these last three years to more oh, temptation and, I don't know if you can call it temptation, but there's different views I mean for extremely liberal views of sex and so forth.

I'm satisfied, I've gained in everything here: knowledge and self-confidence and everything. I haven't lost a thing here. I'm not a great one for the learning methods here. I tend to prefer the high school method of learning stuff. It's thrown at you here where you're left to cope too much on your own.

When you're talking about these things, you're thinking about them, you know, and in talking about them you clarify your own ideas, /mm/ and once you get them clarified, you just sort of let them stay that way, you know . . . and I, I feel pretty well settled in my ways now I know pretty much where I'm going and how I'm getting there, and a lot of things that-ah, have had questions raised about them junior year—that you have wondered about, relations with people-ah and stuff, the question as to the absolute nature of them, may still be there but they are founded for me—there is one answer. And that is the way it's going to be, you know. So . . . that's the way I look at it.

This is itself a relatively complex statement; out of context, its balance between Retreat and Commitment is surely arguable. Internally its significant cues may well be (1) the lumping of all pluralism under the term "temptation," and (2) the anxiety implied in the statement "you're left to cope too much on your own."

The main reason for entrenchment in dualism, indeed, seems to lie in a dependence on highly "authoritarian," all-or-none structures of emotional control. In view of the relative ease of Escape at higher levels, only these internal necessities would seem to account for Retreat. Such a personality structure can cause intellectual difficulties in dealing with the ambiguities of relativism, and if the situation is compounded by some natural limitation in academic aptitude, Retreat may be the only direction in which a student can go. The pain implied can be poignant.

The following excerpts from a single student express the structure and tonality of his interviews year by year.

Freshman year (*Voice is plaintive*):

S.   Ah, they, they-ah, keep throwing out questions. . . . I mean, we never seem to find an absolute answer to it. Of course, I guess Soc. Sci. isn't anything like science. I mean, maybe I like science more because there is a definite answer to certain things. There's a definite reason for certain, why certain things occur. . . . And Soc. Sci. seems to be left open; there seems to be too many ways. Well, "It might have happened because of this, and of course there was this and this and this . . . " (*laughs*) and you don't seem to get any real definite answer to why certain things came about. I don't say it's anything *bad* in Soc. Sci. My other schools, see, they gave you a book, and you read it, and you got the facts out, and that was it. And here, it's just the opposite. You've got to read a book, and they, they, they don't give you a question on the book. They, they give you a big generalization, big question to answer, and you pick out all the facts, and you form them into some kind of an answer which you can give them, why. *You* find out the "why." *You've* got to figure it out. And before, they give you the "why." At school, I mean, they told you exactly.

  There's too much, too much of a change to get from one to the other, I mean, all in one year. I haven't even been able to get hold of it yet. I can't get ahold of it. I mean I haven't even been able to-ah, I haven't had enough practice in being able to think that way. . . .

(Judges' rating: Position 2, Adherent, Defensive, Multiplicity resisted.)

Sophomore year (*The student is speaking of the one course in his college career in which he received an honor grade*):

S.   They could, they could bring out a ton of information. A guy could learn, oh, twice as much as I've learned, without much more trouble, if he, if the teachers would just push it out to him. And, and instead of trying to go out and. . . . You see, the student is not here to grope it out. He's trying to grope it out for himself, but he's got to have more help than he's getting. He's just not getting enough help. And, and, these fellows who hold back their information are just not, the right kind to, they're not developing the students' minds at all. 'Cause we certainly didn't, I don't think enough of us came out of that course with, with the-ah, with the real knowledge we were supposed to have and the real feelings. I mean, he's supposed to change your attitude and your feelings, too, and it has me, and it's a, it's a darned good course, just an invaluable source of information that you've got to develop or else you're going to be going around like a lot of these guys, just not understanding the other fellow at all, just kicking him around, and just kicking yourself or something like that, and, if you. . . . But as I say, the kids in our course could have understood it a lot better if they had, I mean they could have, I could have myself gotten a lot more information in the course. I'm just kind of sorry he didn't teach us some of it. It's a very, very good course.

(Judges' rating: Position 3, Adherent, Multiplicity subordinate.)

Junior year (*Plaintiveness of voice had hardened into complaint; there is a note of anger*):

S.   Some of the teachers—I mean, it's more like a battle here between the students and the teacher to find out. I mean, see, you're here to learn, as far as . . . and I don't care how you get the information; one way or another, you're supposed to be able to learn, how to get information, and how to study it, and acquire it. But the teachers sure, sure don't, don't-ah, go to the trouble, much. They seem to try, to try, sort of go over things, go over it very briefly and let you find out the rest which is good, in a way, but you feel as if they're trying to hide a lot of facts.

It's sort of like a little game. You see if you can guess what they're going to give you on an exam and, and, you know, just like that, a kid's game. I mean, when I talk, as I say, I like to be out in the open. I mean, I like to just, just come out with the facts and have them say, "Here's the information I want you to learn. This is the way I want you, this is what I want you to get out of the course when you come out." If I know what I want . . . I'm expected from a teacher . . . and what kind of questions he might ask, how thoroughly he wants you to read this material. . . . The big things are to get the basic principles. But he doesn't give you these! He ought to line them up right at the beginning; right at the first lecture he ought to tell you exactly what you're going to go over and what he wants us to basically get out of that course.

So that you, you won't be exceptionally smart when you get through here. The thing is to learn a technique. It's a method of learning that you're supposed to be doing here. It's a method of getting material across, and what to pick out that's important, you see; but a lot of the time you don't feel that, that is, put across to you as well as it could be.

(Judges' rating: Retreat, Position 3.)

Senior year (*Voice is angry*):

S.   What impresses you most sometimes around here is the way in which they-ah, the approach towards getting the grades is made here. The grades seems to be so impressed around here. They've-ah, I mean the student, and you get dragged into it too. It's more or less the law of the place to get the marks, no matter how you get it.

I have to work my pants off because I, I don't know how to read, well. That gets you mad. You can work your pants off, you can take fif-, a book of notes, or you can take a page. They only want to see what you put on that exam paper.

The big professor gives the course. You don't ever see them, I mean, you wouldn't—I mean, y-y-you—I don't think you could get an appointment with him for one thing, and you might be able to talk with him for a couple of minutes, but I mean it's just ridiculous to think you're gonna be buddy-buddy with him, get down and talk with him for an hour. You feel, well doggone now, I'll call him up here and have a whole hour's discussion on this course. Right now, every week, you know. You think he wants to see you? Not on your life.

And your section man, well, that'd be nice. But you feel you'd be a pain in the neck to him if you go in there for an hour and sit around and talk about the course, or try to discuss things. And it's pretty hard to get a lot of the other kids around here together for three or four hours. So they, they, they, it's a very competitive system. They, they don't want to help you out. Because everything's . . . on the almighty grade, and everything's on the, the degree, get that mark, don't matter how much work you do.

I've seen so many kids around here loafing. They've got the brains. They don't want to—they've got the idea that you can get something for nothing in this world. That's all the angles it seems. . . .

I'm one of the guys who puts in too much work, and gets out so little, but I've seen so many other guys who just put in so little work and get out a lot. I think they're in, in the most precarious position. I think if you—if you can put in a lot of work and get by with a C, or C pluses or B–, then they'd be I think not in as precarious a position. But if the guy doesn't pass with a C, let's say, what if he's sort of downed, let's say he gets a D, he gets kicked out, his whole life is gonna be, it's gonna be really. . . . If you make it, then everything's great, but brother if you miss!

I mean, you're gonna feel, "Man, you should have learned the *angles* around here. You shoulda *learned* how to, how to, how to *wangle* these courses, how to do a little bit of cheating around, and how to do things right, and you've got to learn the system—it's all angles," and, and-ah I was almost—I was beginning to think—well, I was—I might have gotten the attitude, man I'm gonna forget these lousy morals—they never get you anywhere. Learn the angles.

If you don't pass it's gonna mold you later on. If you make it, it's all roses, you might say and believe in your system. But if you don't make it, well, you're gonna turn to the *wrong* approach. I mean, i-in a way here, he is a, here is a lot of future-ah, possible delinq- . . . you might say, delinquent attitudes, only on higher levels.

(Judges' rating: Retreat, Position 2.)

It is of some interest to consider the validity of this student's complaint. In even the best of courses, once it has been given for several years, "they" do come to know the answer, if not "the answer." In presenting the same problems, without revealing the range of acceptable "answers," may it not be said, "They're hiding things"?[21]

---

[21]I am reminded of a brilliant freshman scientist who was so disgusted with "cook book" laboratory exercises that he took to playing variations on them and finally provoked his instructor into blurting: "See here, there'll be no experimenting in this laboratory!"

Where, however, this student construes all demand for independent thought as Authority's failure of its function—and as a temptation to immorality—he can be said to speak from a reactive dualism, and his desperate insistence on an imagined paternalistic ideal warranted the judges' rating of "Retreat, Position 2, defensive adherence, reactive anxiety."

A more Oppositional response directs anger at Authority in a disillusion that preserves no explicit image of the ideal Authority compared to whom immediate personages are derelict. A freshman makes a statement which may well spring from the "facts" of his program as well as from himself:

S.   I found out how bad the courses I was taking were, and how unworthy of any serious effort they were.

If, however, the qualification "courses *I was taking*" disappears, and revolt becomes totalistic, and indiscriminate, a rating of dualistic Oppositional Retreat may be appropriate. For such a rating, of course, an entire record must speak the same structure and tone. (Requoted):

S.   This place is full of bull. They don't want anything really honest from you. If you turn in something, a speech that's well written, whether it's got one single fact in it or not is beside the point. That's sort of annoying at times, too. You can put things over on people around here; you're almost given to try somehow to sit down and write a paper in an hour, just because you know that whatever it is isn't going to make any difference to anybody. If you make one good point in a paper, one ten-word sentence, somebody will think it's very nice, and that's so silly, really, because it's completely meaningless.

You know, I said I didn't like all this bull around here. On the other hand, I don't really—scholarship doesn't appeal to me, sitting in the library stacks, peering at birds and things like that outside. It makes no sense to me either. I think it's nice to know things and have the feeling when you do know it that you never learned it. I *hate* the feeling of learning something.

Clearly, the maintenance of such a stance requires considerable emotional effort. In more advanced structures, complexity offers avenues to a less strenuous dissociation.

Escape

Perhaps the clearest of the roads into Escape are those leading from Temporizing. There are two such roads, each leading to its special kind of disengagement, and to its special limitations of identity and responsibility. The following excerpts illustrate midpoints along each of these roads:

TOWARD DISSOCIATION

S.   It ah . . . Well, I really, I don't know, I just, I don't get particularly worked up over things. I don't react too strongly. So that I can't think. I'm still waiting for the event, you know, everyone goes through life thinking that something's gonna happen, and I don't think it happened this year. So we'll just leave that for the future. Mainly you're, you're waiting for yourself to change, see after you get a good idea, continued trial and effort, exactly how you're going to act in any period of time, once you get this idea, then you're constantly waiting for the big change in your life. And, it certainly didn't happen this year. . . .

Also:

S.   But-ah, I just, I don't, don't, don't have any-ah, consuming interest or burning desire or anything. I like Government probably better than I, I feel, that I'd like anything else. And on the whole it's fairly interesting to me. And I just, just drift along, I guess you might say.

On the one hand, I, I-am-um, having an, an-ah . . . ah, an extremely comfortable life here. But-ah, perhaps later, I'm, I may find out that I'm-ah . . . drifting and, and that I'm not happy in my drift.

I was discussing the problem with a few friends. I just, I just don't, don't know. I was thinking mainly of the Puritans, not for any of their doctrines really, but the fact that they did have a, a central commitment. And that, that might be a good idea, on the other hand it might not be a good idea for me. I was contrasting the Puritans with all their-um hard, and, and really painful approaches to life with some of the um-um more outright-um madmen, if that's a good enough term . . . who are sort of flitting about. And I was wondering if I might not be headed in that direction and, and it might turn out that when I get older I, I'll find that . . . um . . . I am living a, a hollow life.

I don't necessarily associate the comfortable life with a hollow existence. I'm not saying that to have a central commitment you, you have to-ah, live in the manner that the Puritans did. I imagine that you could be a Machiavelli, or, or Humanist, Renaissance, or, or any one of a dozen other. . . . It, it might be. I, I don't know. I've just been thinking about it.

Or:

S.   As I get interested in something I probably *will* like it. Right now I, I find it too easy to sort of goof around and not do anything. But I don't have any real interest in any of my courses . . . and, ah . . . and so it makes it sort of . . . I don't know.

Well, as I get older, I'll change values because I, ah, as soon as I get interested in something I, I'll probably start working, and then, then I'll probably start making plans about what I'm going to do when I get out—maybe even get a little ambition, you know.

I think it's similar to, before a war sometimes there is this peaceful, useless kind of an age and then the war comes and the decision is to go off to war; you have to do it, and they get fired up and enthusiastic about it—that's the kind of thing I'd almost be waiting for. Well, not—I'm not waiting for a war, but I'm waiting for something, some cause, but there's not any real cause.

"Dissociation," the term we used to denote the potential of this "drifting," refers to a passive delegation of all responsibility to fate. Its tone is depressed, even when pleasure is still possible in irresponsibility. The sense of active participation as an agent in the growth of one's identity is abandoned. Its final destiny lies in the depersonalized looseness of Multiplicity (Multiplicity Correlate, Position 4) dissociated from the challenge of meaning.

TOWARD ENCAPSULATION
The more strenuous intellectual demands of Relativism provide an escape in which a vestigial identity can be maintained in sheer competence. Here the self is a doer, or a gamesman, and its opportunism is defended by an encapsulation in activity, sealed off from the implications of deeper values.

S.   I know that I had trouble-ah first of all in just listening to the lectures, trying to make out what they meant. . . . These-ah-ah, the pursuit of the absolute first of all. . . . And then I . . . (*laughs*) sort of lost the absolute, and stuff like that. I think that gradually it sunk in, and, I don't know, maybe it's just. . . . Well, it came to me the other night: if relativity is true on most things, it's an easy way out. But I don't think that's . . . maybe that's just the way I think now. . . . Well, in, in a sense I mean that you don't have to commit yourself. And maybe that's just the push button I use on myself . . . right now, because I am uncommitted.

S.   I find myself using some of the Soc. Sci. 1 techniques, in examinations, because somehow, I don't know, they convinced me that this is the way to write an examination, how you see a question. Well, 95 percent of the time there's something wrong with the question, all right; criticize it. Well, this is . . . I suppose a good old healthy skepticism is fine, but then again it can be just an examsmanship technique. Because if you're as good at handling words as any English major is, I can take any question and I can get a lot of inconsistency out of it. And whether it's tenuous or not, it's good enough to start an essay.

On the Chart of our scheme, we divided Escape itself into a four-way box: (1) Dissociation in Multiplicity, (2) Encapsulation in Relativism, (3) Dissociation in Relativism, and (4) Encapsulation in Multiplicity. The last two we supposed to be rare, but possible, and the four combinations seemed to round out our characterology of alienation. The notes on the chart suggest the typology we had in mind.

Instances of alienation were so few in our sample that the judges could give no fair test of this nosology. In any case we looked on the four categories as classifying dominant strategies rather than people, just as do all categorizations of personality based on dynamics. Some persons, indeed, may favor one strategy over others sufficiently to appear as a "type." Close examination will usually discover a greater complexity.

In any case, a full record is necessary for any judgment, and the following excerpts illustrate only those partial expressions which would feed into an overall estimate. I have, therefore, refrained from categorizing them; they convey their messages most forcefully through the shadings of their tone.

S.   I never get particularly upset about anything, but my father feels I'm wasting my time and potential and his money, and all that.

But I don't know, I don't really see any way this thing can be resolved; I've just accepted it. . . . But I would like to make my peace with the family.

S.   I can always rationalize my way out of anything, I mean, if I ever start to feel this way, I feel that it's all sort of futile; I haven't done anything yet and it's too late, why start now? . . . defeated, and all that. Oh, I can always find something to do to forget about it, or just tell myself it's ridiculous, and it never really bothers me for any length of time.

S.   I've come to a, to a dilemma this year of, of-ah . . . what sort of work to go into; it was not a real question before, I always wanted to teach, and, and that was it, and if I couldn't make it as a teacher, I would be a journalist. Ah-ah, that's the way it is since-ah freshman year in high school. This year, because of all that I've learned, and a lot that I haven't learned, I, I have lost confidence in my-ah grasp of, of my chosen field, which is English. I seem to have a superfic-superficial knowledge of quite a lot but a profound knowledge of nothing. I, I don't seem to-ah . . . well, I picture a teacher as one who knows all the answers, I want to teach in, in high school . . . one who knows all the answers. I simply can't imagine myself as knowing all the answers on, in English literature, or, I do know grammar, but I, well, I've sort of lost my confidence in my-ah . . . knowledge of, of my chosen field.

S.   (*Discussing what he calls "intellectual things"*) I don't know how to express it, but I just, as I say, I just don't give too much of a damn anymore about them. There's nothing particularly stimulating to do much work, and I didn't. I sort of drifted along, and I will until something does stimulate me.

S.   Harvard it's, it's—I don't know if you—it's not really I'd say a practical education you'd get like . . . if you went to MIT you'd probably major in a certain field, come out and have a job, like that, see. Then you're stuck in that one field, see, and you probably—I don't know; sometimes you get a, get a Harvard grad and an MIT grad, and he graduates from MIT, in say, four years, with a Bachelor of Science or whatever it is, and he goes out and he's got himself a job, right off the bat with G.E. or something. So you get the

Harvard graduate, he graduates four years at Harvard, and he's got a B.A. But then he can go to grad. school, see, science and so forth, and if he wanted to go to work for G.E. . . . what would, I think, myself, how it would end up would be the MIT student would be working under him, see. In other words, he'd be the, have the general lookout for everybody in there, and I think the MIT student would be just one of the people working where he'd be supervising everything. And I think that's the, the advantages of Harvard and so forth. You get a liberal education, and get to know a lot about everything; well, probably not a lot, but a little anyway. But sometimes if you really take a course and really study hard you can get a lot out of the course, see. And you, before you know it, you know, you know something about a lot of things, you know. And you can go out into the world and—well, I mean, what they try to really, really try to teach you here is to develop your mind as well as thinking, and so forth. When you go out in the world and so forth, you can relax, and know you went to college.

S.   I'm very Machiavellian, I see the system there and I have to beat it, and I, I don't like it really. Ahh, I took, well, maybe the kind of courses I was taking this year, might reflect on this. One of them was (*names course*). Now certainly the reading matter in that course as you know is highly factual. And the amount of it you need for the examination on the other hand is relatively little. In other words, on one hand they're giving you the material, and on the other hand they want the generalizations on the examination. So that . . . you have this frustrating feeling. Sometimes if you feel that you're learning all the facts and then not doing well because of the examination. . . . So that what happens then is that inevitably a course like this will try to indoctrin-indoctrinate you to a particular way of writing examinations, or a particular way of looking at material, so that it's really the biggest propaganda course in, in the college.

S.   I've thought quite a bit about this: I've never really identified myself definitely with anything. I hadn't permitted myself to so far as grades were concerned or as far as friends—particularly in a few isolated cases. I had just a sort of "I'm me, and I just like to stand out there and look things over" attitude, and I don't know whether this is good or bad.

S.   It turns out to be tough because of the fact, that, that you have these courses that tempt you to, to not do anything at all about them and therefore you're apt to, ah, get slightly lower grades than you would anyway, and it was, you know, what the heck, I wasn't interested anyway—next year, you know, it'll all be different when I'll be able to take almost all courses that I want to take, and so forth and so forth.

S.   It seems to me that the security that you gain from knowing how you're going to handle . . . a situation which isn't really that important now . . . is completely overshadowed by the worry . . . that it causes if you try to ascertain what you're going to do. And I think . . . oh, if you have, if your development is such that you can handle situations as they arise . . . and that you have more or less an intelligent point of view and a rational outlook, that you could solve any problem that comes up with a minimum of time, trouble, and . . . I don't think that it's necessary to worry about things so far in the future. I mean, opportunities may present themselves, or completely change my life, and the, the, and of course my wife and baby's life, too. I may be offered who knows what, right after I graduate, you know, you never know, and there's no chance of really-ah . . . planning so far ahead as to take into account; you can't do it. . . .

It's just like, I mean, it's just like playing football. As long as you have the right position and the right balance now, you're ready for anything that may come . . . whereas, if you plan for one special move, a change of plan on the opponent's side and you're right off on left field, and get faked out. As long as you're ready for anything and, and, and, and in good condition, more or less, and in football it takes a good body and a clear mind, and the same thing applies to . . . anything in general and being alert you're ready to . . . handle any situation as it arises and that's more or less the "full philosophy," unquote, that, I've, that I've used throughout my life . . . if I may be so bold as to say that; and . . . since I, it has been successful for me, and I've, I've found it very satisfactory to me, I . . . that's, that's just the way it is with me. And I don't think I recommend it for anyone, of course. I, I'd be a fool to, but I do think it has its merits, and for me it's the, the one way to do things.

S.   I detest people who just lead *such* a drab existence. They may be Group I or Group II but to me they're a machine. They just crank things in and spit them out, and they never really sample life or experiences around here which they could. I think they're missing a lot. I want to experience things, and in the process of trying I probably go too far the other way.

S.   So the best thing I have to do is just forget about deciding, and try to . . . I mean, not give up on any scheming or any basic set of ideas . . . that'll give myself, they'll give me a direction. Just give up completely, and when it comes down to individual choices, make them on what I feel like doing emotionally at the moment.

S.   I don't really care much about it now. I just like people and like life, and I'd just as soon not cut out having lots of money or being able to play the country club stuff and also be able to be a bum. Maybe it's impossible to be both.

Maybe you start getting set values and things, and I sort of feel and that I'm not going to . . . Yeah, I don't think you have to grow old . . . (*laughs*) but you get old and you . . . things are just too happy, and joyous. And I don't, I don't see how people can possibly get old; it's a very bad habit . . .

And I just don't see any need to draw any conclusions towards it at the moment. I'm perfectly satisfied with all of it in ways. Not to say that I don't get depressed, but I'm sort of satisfied with that too; it's very nice to be able to sit and think and smoke and play pool. There are a lot of joys in that. And then you start feeling like painting, so you paint your depression, and then you get happy again, and then you go out and play a set of tennis, or you go to the country club, or something, and have a good time there. It's all very nice.

S.   It's funny, lots of these people who do things that-ah really are quite impressive, and the conclusions seem to be, seem to be ready-made, and there . . . but sometimes when you go into it, you really start thinking about it, sometimes you don't agree at all, no matter how thoroughly documented their conclusions are. I'm getting to feel very much now that studying and reading . . . and things are really not so relevant somehow, really. . . . I feel perfectly capable of drawing my own conclusions about just about anything, as far as getting along in life. . . .

S.   I don't feel that I am particularly good in history or, or literature. Even memorizing the history of interpreting the literature, and I'm not that interested in it at the moment, and I don't read on my own. There's not too much that I do on my own at the moment . . . mostly sitting around and talking. There's no, because there's nothing that I feel that I can do well, there's nothing that I feel that I can do well, there's nothing that I would apply myself to. It's not worth it to try and to try and to try, and draw or, or actually sit down and compose something. . . . I guess I'm very anxious to have some true beliefs. But then it goes away, very quickly; I can't really trust my beliefs. . . .

A particular form of Escape, long recognized by philosophers and theologians, is "escape into commitment." The distinction between Commitment as a step of growth *in* a relativistic world and commitment as an escape *from* complexity is usually quite clear in our records. In the latter, commitment is yearned for as a reinstitution of embeddedness. The hope seems to be that through intensity of focus, all ambivalences will be magically resolved. The event is envisaged either as something one hurls oneself into through despair of choosing, or as some "interest" that emerges from the environment to absorb one totally, and blessedly.

S.   If I could find something that I really liked-ah, take some interest in my courses—I enjoy doing them, but I really don't get into them, like, say, I'd get into a football game. If I could get into a course like that, and enjoy it, I think that's the thing I'd want to stay with the rest of my life. That's what I'm looking for. Maybe I'll have to make myself feel that way, I don't know. . . . But, ahh, I feel sort of like I'm, I'm not really getting into my courses now, and I feel like I'm saying, "Well, here I am, teach me." When I go to a course that's not the way I want to feel.

Or again:

S.   It would be great if a bolt of lightning comes down, in some way I could be tested, and find out that I have a great talent for music (*laughs*) and then really just drop everything and go into that. But I'm sure it won't happen, or I'm almost sure. But it could just as well be anything as music.

And more complexly:

S.   I mean if you're going into archeology and you aren't interested in the neolithic revolution, by the time you're finished, whatever your thesis is, you ought to just care about *nothing* but that for
a while, and you don't have to be an unbalanced human being but
you've got to, this (*names professor*), this paleolithic professor, he's
not exactly paleolithic, he's awfully big, but he teaches, he's an old
world archeologist, and he's interested in the paleolithic. He just
knows everything, that's his life. Well, monolithic people like that
get pretty threatening sometimes and you don't want to get into
their way, and naturally they judge everybody according to their
own little standards, but they get something done, and most graduate students around here are simply not that way, you don't need
to be quite as extreme as he is, but it's an admirable trait. Football
players, really good professional athletes, you've got to be a zealot
to accomplish anything, and these people, most of the graduate students I know aren't zealots, and I don't want to get started until I
am, until I can feel that, you know, I can really commit myself because I'll never, I haven't ever committed myself to anything.

A lot of the guys that go to Law School, I don't think are committed to being lawyers or committed to law and are interested in
law. And you've got to be. The only people I know who are suc-
cesses are people who really throw themselves completely into what
they're doing.

And yet, one can be aware of the irresponsibility of the principle
that *any* Commitment is *better* than *no* Commitments:

S.   Robert Frost seems to have the theme that whether what you
do is right or wrong, just do it, and if you do it in good faith, the
mere fact that you're doing something is worth, worth consideration. That has a certain value, I suppose. I mean, not just sitting
around like the donkey between the, the bales of hay. That has no
value. You have to get out and, and do something, make some, take
some stand. Certainly that's a necessary part.

You have to, of course, that may be just the choice; *between*
stands again, the various stands that you can take.

Or just plain easier:

S. I've seen this all along: withdraw into your shell; this is the easy way. I mean you could take a basic, just a fundamental commitment and be done with it.

I. And be done with it. Yes. There you are.

S. That's an easy out. The other way is pretty frustrating.

Where the full context supports the reading of any passage as expressive of Escape, the overall tonality usually suggests not only despair but personal guilt. As some of the excerpts above suggest, only Encapsulation in sheer competence—be it of intellect or of action—seems to be devoid of this pervasive malaise; and this very freedom from all values except that of competence feels, to us, almost sinister. Indeed the very pain of personal guilt, as one who is failing of his own life, is perhaps the most hopeful awareness in alienation.

A Note on Resumption of Growth

Alienation in Escape need not be permanent. It may be for some persons a vital experience in growth—part of the very temptation in the wilderness that gives meaning to subsequent Commitment. Emergence may start in any affirmation of responsibility, even, paradoxically, the responsibilities implicit in Escape itself.

Briefly put:

S. Just saying, "O.K., well, that's what I can do, and that's what I can't do," in a way, and to be satisfied with my potential and not dream about other things and to try to develop what I have found that I have and not to worry about the things I don't have.

S. You ought to start doing some thinking about it, so I looked at all the seniors I know and I said well, they do one of four things when they graduate: you go on to grad school; you go out and get a job; you go into the service; you get married. Ah, marriage is eliminated; I have no one in mind, and I have absolutely no desire to be married. I didn't really want to go on to graduate school. I do like Harvard, but after the four years is up, I've had it, I mean, I've done my four years. I want a change, a variety; a job I ruled out because I'm really not sure what I want to do, and if I went out and got a job, I'd probably go into electronics and computers somewhere, and I might be able to get a reasonably good job, but three or four years I'd be in a sense be in a rut. I'd be sufficiently committed so that I couldn't really get out of that kind of work, and the next thing you know I'd be married and, boy, then you can't, I mean, you've got, you've got to take the job you've got. You just can't up and move. And I wasn't that sure I really wanted it that way. So the service offered me a chance to work with people, find out what I could do as a leader—although that's a corny phrase. I can "see the world" and see a different kind of life. Harvard is fantastic for the amount of freedom it allows you and after a while you just get this great desire to be subjugated, and so now I'm going out and you know, everything is nice and neat and cut and dried, and so on, and that will be a change. . . .

I think I've, to some extent, not perhaps as well as I like, have risen up to be able to accept it, and the responsibility that goes with it, but it's one little change.

Often recovery occurs as a kind of "lifting" of depression, or a resurgence of care:

S.   Emotionally I think I was trying to find some sort of rationalization for my feeling that I wasn't going to achieve anything. These are certainly not the values I have now. They're not the goals I want now. I don't think I'm going to be happy unless I can feel I'm doing something in my work.

S.   Some people tend to think that, that [college] newspaper is the greatest thing in the world, and they'll really dedicate themselves to it. I, I have a fairly different feeling after being elected to it than I did before. Before it was just sort of something to do, you know, something to put on the record. But now that I feel a part of it and have the feel of it, I respect it more. I feel I can give it a lot and it's no longer really an obligation like it was once. I work on it because I want to, and because I want to improve the paper, and I suppose I have a feeling of dedication now to a certain extent, which is really the first time I've ever had something of this.

S.   I was sort of worried when I came back, wondering if, "Well, shucks, am I just going to lie down on the job or am I going to do it because it has to be done?" I found out that I wasn't doing it because it *had* to be, but because things interested me. Some things didn't interest me so much, but I felt I couldn't let them slide and I took them as best I could, in what order I could.

Alienation (let alone recovery) varies widely in complex ways from person to person. Yet for all, the pervasive underlying tone is of the defeat of care. Whether the person sees society as having failed, or despairs of his own efforts to sustain his purposes, or just damn well asserts that he doesn't give a damn, the speaker always conveys a nostalgia for a care and involvement that once was, or might have been, or might yet be . . . if only . . .

Alienation cannot be prevented. And indeed it should not be. If it could be prevented, so could that detachment which is man's last recourse of freedom and dignity *in extremis*. The educator's problem is therefore certainly not to prevent alienation, or even to make the option less available. His problem is to provide as best he can for the sustenance of care.

In the following chapter, on the implications of this study, I shall enlarge on a central inference we have drawn from all that our students had to say: We infer that the community's substantive provision of worthwhile things to care about is not enough. Nor is the provision of an expectation that the student *will* care. The student finds his greatest sustenance, we feel, in a sense of community *in the risks of caring.*

The educator's effort would be, then, to increase the student's experience of recognition and confirmation as a member of the community by virtue of the courage with which he undertakes the risks of care. The communication of this kind of recognition and confirmation would seem to be both the highest and most profound of social arts. While such a study as this one cannot commend to the educator specific means of communication, it may contribute to the educator's effort through the illumination of those expanding forms in which students appear to experience their risks and their cares in the progress of their education.

CHAPTER SIX

Critique

T his chapter consists of three parts. The first notes the location of the study in philosophical thought and psychological theory, and the second delimits the study by pointing to neighboring areas which the study does not explore. Against the background of these definitions, the third part of the chapter explores relevancies of the study to issues in education.

THE STUDY IN ITS SETTING

The study draws its assumptions and method from contemporary philosophical and psychological theories and procedures. It offers, then, the fruits of an exploration made in extant frames with available tools. Since the study is so much the child of its times, it would be beyond the scope of this report to specify its inheritances from all its progenitors or to point out the family resemblance it shares with all its contemporary relatives. I shall therefore make only the briefest acknowledgments of major derivations—sufficient only to locate the genre—and then remark on such individuality as emerges in the study from its own particular synthesis.

Philosophical Context

In the broadest sense the study shares the assumptions of modern contextualistic pragmatism (Dewey, 1958b; White, M., 1963; cf. also Quine, 1963). This is most evident in the priority given to *purpose*. The students' ultimate purpose is postulated to be to find those forms through which they may best understand and confront with integrity the nature of the human condition.[1] To the extent, too, that we regard the forms of our scheme to be forms of the students' lives, our study aligns as well with that branch of the post-Wittgensteinian inheritance which emphasizes the primary givenness of the Forms of Life themselves, as over against the Forms of Language which derivatively "mirror" or "reflect" them (Wittgenstein, 1953; Hampshire, 1960; cf. also Aiken, 1962b).[2]

Since in the latter half of our scheme, the student's purpose involves him in the activity of personal Commitment, our philosophical antecedents include the existentialists (Barrett, 1958; May, 1961; Laing, 1965), with special reference to Camus' position in respect to the dilemmas of hope and despair, reason and unreason (see esp. *The Myth of Sisyphus,* 1955). As our address to values, then, is expressive of the contextualistic-pragmatic and existential traditions, the synthesis of those traditions represented by the work of Polanyi (1958) is most relevant to our study. Polanyi's analysis considers precisely what our students address: the ultimate welding of epistemological and moral issues in the act of Commitment.

In our attempt to give a description of the "how" of development within this broad philosophical setting, we have emphasized the interweaving of hierarchies of values with hierarchies of thought, of

---

[1] The logical priority of such a purpose is evident in instances of conflict with other purposes or "motives." For instance, if we were to say that the students were motivated simply to "reduce dissonance or incongruity," we could not account for their distinguishing between those dissonances or incongruities which they construe as signals for revision of their assumptions and those which they undertake to espouse as part of the human condition.

[2] An outline of this philosophical setting, with special references to educational issues, is contained in Robert S. Jaffe, *Philosophical Foundations of the Concept of a Person,* Bureau of Study Council, Harvard University, Cambridge, Mass., 1967.

meta-valuing with meta-thinking. We regard this structural linking of valuing with thinking as providing a frame in which steplike degrees of ethical objectivity are possible, and in which detachment, choice, and Commitment may function at generalized levels.

Such structural generalization provided us with a degree of freedom from head-on collision with our students' particular values at concrete levels. For example, a student at an advanced position of development in our scheme might commit himself to a faith in a religion which includes a faith in an absolute order manifest in human affairs in Natural Law. Even if we ourselves disagreed at concrete levels, we would still be free to honor his values, since, in our context, he has elected them in a world which he has learned to consider, from another point of view, as relativistic. If he continues to respect the legitimacy of relativistic valuing in others, and also others' faiths in other absolutes, his Commitment to an absolute represents, for us, not a failure of logic (or a regression to earlier forms) but a considered and courageous acceptance of an unavoidable stress.[3]

As contextualistic pragmatists, we see our philosophical assumptions to be doubly reflexive. For one thing, at the highest point of development in our scheme, the majority of our students are portrayed as addressing the world in the very same general terms as our scheme's own philosophical outlook. For another, we apply the same general assumptions to our own relation, as investigators, to the data of the study. But since within our contextualistic-pragmatic and existential framework we see reasoning to be circular by ultimate necessity, we look upon this double reflexiveness as a manifestation of the virtue of coherence without looking upon circularity as necessarily a vice. We have cared only that the circle be of sufficient scope to illuminate more than its own return upon itself. That is to say, we have cared that the

---

[3]The alternative of "situation ethics" (Fletcher, *Situation Ethics,* 1966) would seem more coherent in a relativistic context and hence less stressful. However, it may offer only less *cognitive* stress. Fletcher's tone suggests that it offers a further reduction of stress through freedom from the shackles of "moral legalism." In our view, this freedom, if it is to be responsibly espoused, carries a heavy price. As compared with obeying some external law, it may be *more* stressful, *morally,* to take upon oneself the responsibility for constant self-examination and ethical decision.

circle make a sufficient sweep to generate propositions which integrate a variety of experience and which may be susceptible, in some instances at least, to test.

Psychological Context

Regular citation of our theoretical derivations in psychology would have overburdened this report almost phrase by phrase. The reader will have recognized our indebtedness. To drop the names of just a few pioneers in whose conceptual realms we have presumed to feel free: Jean Piaget, Robert W. White, Erik Erikson, Heinz Werner, Kurt Lewin, Fritz Heider, Gordon Allport, George Kelly, Peter Blos, R. J. Havighurst . . . there are others. I should add phenomenologists (Lyons, Merleau-Ponty, Van Kaam), existentialists (Rollo May), and researchers of moral development (Kohlberg). Since developmental psychology has not yet fully addressed the transition from adolescence to adulthood, I add here only N. Sanford (1956, 1962) and R. Heath (1958, 1964), on whose work in the college setting we drew in shaping this study.

This very partial list is intended only to "place" the study.[4] Other sources have already been cited, and others, either sources or comparisons, are listed in the bibliography for this volume. In place of listing numerous items of acknowledgment I shall briefly compare this study to the work of one major source, Jean Piaget, and one contemporary parallel, the work of Harvey, Hunt, & Schroder.

In comparing our study with the work of Piaget, more is involved than particulars. We do depend heavily on his particular concepts of assimilation of an experience to extant structure (or more broadly "schema") and of accommodation of structure by transformations and recombinations which can result in new and more differentiated structuring of experience. Somewhat more broadly, too, we make similar assumptions about the emergent, interactional ontogenesis of intelligence (cf. also Hunt, J. McV., 1961). Methodologically, also, we depend on self-report, as Piaget does to great extent with his older children, and though we pose our subjects less prestructured prob-

---

[4] A further placement of the study in relation to psychoanalytic theories of development, to "self" theories, and to theories of career development may be found in Lee, J. (1965).

lems, our request to our students to expand on their reactions to items of CLEV is analogous to his posing of moral situations as in *The Moral Judgment of the Child.* Together with Piaget, moreover, we may be accused of suggesting, even when we do not affirm, some pretty large-sized generalizations about human development in our culture on the basis of a few, homogeneous and specialized subjects in one highly specialized setting.

However, the most forceful way in which Piaget's framework could be used to delimit our scheme might be by attempting to assimilate our work directly to his frame and then to consider what distinctions would be revealed by the effort. In such a placement, we could suppose first that our developmental scheme reflects processes ascribed by Piaget to the "period of formal operations." It traces a recapitulation (by vertical *décalage*) of a centrifugal movement, evident in the earlier sensory-motor and concrete-operational periods. The movement is away from a naive egocentrism to a differentiated awareness of the environment. This awareness reflects back to create a new and differentiated awareness of self and to make possible a complex dynamic equilibrium between self and environment. Our scheme traces such a process, in the assimilations and accommodations that mediate it, with particular emphasis on the structural changes in a person's assumptions about the origins of knowledge and of value. Although Piaget and his co-workers have not yet traced in detail the articulation of this particular process at the level of late adolescence and early adulthood, they have pointed explicitly to it in describing the impact on the adolescent of his bringing to bear upon his ideals his new capacity to think not only of what "is" but of all that "might be" (Inhelder & Piaget, 1958, pp. 341–346).

Such a placement of our scheme is a useful first approximation. However, there are matters of content in which our scheme addresses developmental issues to which Piaget's framework does not yet extend, and there are matters of quality in which our scheme falls short not only of Piaget's precision but also of his looseness. These differences distinguish our scheme from Piaget's framework.

In deriving from the study of people beyond the age of 15, the scheme reflects processes not examined in Piagetian studies so far published. The powers of objectivity and detachment consequent on the ability to meta-think (which in our present culture appears to flower most noticeably after age 15) make it possible for the person to address an entirely new environment. He can now move from the moral environment to the ethical, from the formal to the existential. Positions 5 through 9 in our scheme describe in very general terms the course of orientation in this environment, or, to use Piaget's terms, the development of "equilibrium" in this dimension.

One could look on our scheme, then, as adding an advanced "period" to Piaget's outline. If so, I would call it the "period of responsibility." But there are difficulties. While the first half of our scheme does reveal processes paralleling those of motoric, cognitive, and moral "decentering" portrayed in each of Piaget's periods, the development of a personal style or equilibrium in Commitment in the second half seems qualitatively different. The shift is away from spatial-cognitive restructuring to emotional and aesthetic assessments. At this level, therefore, our study addresses issues which psychological science had not yet succeeded in differentiating conceptually, much less in documenting experimentally. Here, with little pretense at precision left to lose, the study extends its embrace to its subjects' style of humanistic and philosophical concern.

At this level, the differentiations presented by the second half of our scheme are indeed rough and crude, to an extreme appropriate to an initial endeavor. However, the success of our judges in rating students' reports reliably against these differentiations shows, we hope, that the area may be within the reach of more exacting exploration.

In respect to the first half of our scheme, I wish to refer briefly to parallels in the work of Harvey, Hunt, and Schroder (1961) and especially Hunt (in Harvey, 1966). This work was contemporaneous with our study, and publication prior. For us, a major significance of the parallels derives from the fact that we were ignorant of their publications until after our own formulation was complete in 1960. Rather than examine too closely the causes of so startling an oversight, we have focused on the confirmation provided for the findings of both studies. The confluence of these independent researches is to us a great encouragement.

The interested reader will wish to examine the parallels and differences for himself. Translation of vocabularies becomes clear in context and requires no comment here. The several schematic parallels, while in no case precise, are striking. Of additional significance are (1) these researchers' demonstration of the relevance of such a general outline to earlier age groups, (2) the support they provide through measurement with specially designed tests, and (3) Hunt's report of an experiment in grouping students by "stages" for instructional purposes.

THE STUDY'S BOUNDARIES

The study achieves its focus through a considered neglect of some major variables. Like the internal technical limits noted in Chapter 1, and the conceptual decisions discussed in Chapter 4, these omissions are relevant to any consideration of the study's significance.

In general, our abstraction of this particular scheme from our students' reports involved no presumption that we were exhausting the observations which could be made from such rich materials. Our discovery of this particular sequence of challenges as an element common to all our students' experience was a product of our own relation to our data. It was salient to us, and our judges confirmed its generality throughout the reports of our students. This is not to say, however, that other observers with other concepts might not find other common elements or developments. If they were to do so, then any question of which was most "important" or even "salient" would have to be considered in the purposes and values of a particular context.

More specifically, in focusing on a common scheme of development, we have reduced to a minimum the consideration of individual differences based on personality, temperament, ability, sociology, and personal history. The scheme allows for many such differences; indeed, we saw the scheme *through* them, but our exposition has emphasized the common core.

Since the generalized development was seen "through" individual reports, the imprints of certain major categories of individual differences appear on the scheme as variant facets. These find expression in such concepts as "A" (adherent tendency), "O" (oppositional tendency), the alternate structures of Positions 2 and 4, the concept of variable rate of growth, the concept of defensive closedness ("d"), the options of Temporizing, Escape, and Retreat (in varying forms), and most notably in the wide range of stylistic expression available in Positions 7, 8, and 9. In general, however, we attempted no nosology (contrast Heath, R., 1964) and no systematic tracing of differing developmental paths which might be characteristic of different "types" of students.

In a parallel choice, we have considered our students' milieu in terms of a generalized "liberal arts college." In view of the extensive differences among colleges (Jacob, 1957; Heist, 1960; Stern, 1960a,b; Riesman, 1958a,b), this may appear unimaginative. Yet with the qualification we have made—that we mean by a "liberal arts college" a pluralistic institution where the teaching of the procedures of rela-tivistic thought is to a large extent deliberate—we are confident that our findings would hold.

This confidence is supported by a curious sensation arising from a comparison of the students' reports, one with another. Although Har-vard is sometimes reputed to be a unique or idiosyncratic place, the re-ports reveal it to be many things to different people. In fact the students gave little evidence that they were talking about the same courses, much less the same college. It is our wager that if our students' reports were cleared of specific denotative clues and shuffled with reports elic-ited in a similar way from students in other leading colleges of liberal arts, it would be quite impossible to sort them out again. This wager, if won, would not of course say that all such colleges are the same, but only that their differences would not be detectable or essential in the students' consideration of the issues we have addressed.

We suppose, indeed, that the range of approach and of quality *within* any large and reputable college is probably greater than the overall differences from college to college. Section men in the same large course are reputed to differ markedly. It is this kind of difference which raises the more serious question, internal to our study. In ex-amining a student's report, our primary purpose has been to infer from it the structure through which he organizes his experience. But might he not be simply reporting "the truth," that is, the forms the en-vironment brings to him? When a student complains, for example, that a given instructor "talks all over the place" and is "hiding the an-swers," might this not represent the simple truth rather than a conflict of epistemologies? Such instructors exist.

Given the context of an entire report, our judges experienced sur-prisingly little difficulty with this question. In discussion of the infer-ences to be drawn from certain isolated statements, some judge might protest to another, "But I *agree* with this guy—that's the way things *are.*" However, the judges found they could regularly resolve such con-flicts by recourse to the broader context of the student's report and by a reconsideration of the transactional nature of human reality.

IMPLICATIONS OF THE STUDY
Contributions

In itself the study demonstrates that aspects of intellectual and ethi-cal development in late adolescence can be described in an orderly way. Within the limits of the population studied, it offers one such description which portrays (1) certain structural transformations in outlook through which the students moved from an all-or-none, right-or-wrong construal of knowledge and value to the outlook and skills of contextual relativism, (2) the ways in which they then went on to orient themselves in a relativistic world through the content and style of ongoing acts of Commitment, and (3) the forms of those options through which some students appeared to withdraw or retrench at various points in the development.

Within this general frame, we have conceptualized, in ways we believe to be new, two important processes in human development. First is that transformation which takes the form of exploiting a complex structure, first learned as a subordinate part of a more simplistically structured context, by transposing it to become the structure of a larger context which then subsumes the simpler structure that once was context (see pp. 121 ff.).[5]

The second conceptual contribution is that of Commitment as an activity involving stylistic equilibria. Here the reference extends beyond

---

[5]Good teachers have traditionally relied upon this sequence in the form (1) teach the student a simple thing until he can stand on it; (2) help him learn a complex thing by attaching it onto the simple thing he has learned, as if it were a small variant, intriguing puzzle, or ornament; (3) then say, "Now move over onto this, this is the real thing." Many debates about curricular strategies may be interpreted as centering on the propriety and wisdom of this sequence in particular subjects and situations. Since the sequence involves the risk that some students will find it difficult or impossible to "unlearn" the notion of the simple-as-context, the counterclaim states that it is preferable, wherever possible, for the learner to start out with the more complexity structured context. In the conceptualization of knowledge and value, however, it is hard to imagine how complex concepts of better and worse could be developed in advance of the simple dichotomy of right vs. wrong; the real question would seem to be how *early* the transposition could be productively achieved, and through what particular sequences of concrete illustrations. The many experimental efforts now being made in introducing relativism in various subjects in elementary and secondary school promise to be informative. However, the issues with which our students grappled, as reflected in our scheme, would seem to extend backward to involve child-rearing procedures in general, and outward to involve the forms of teacher-student interaction throughout the educational process at large (see below pp. 236 ff.).

the content of Commitment to embrace a process in which the person integrates the expressive and the instrumental through affirmations in which his standards are ultimately aesthetic. Because the flowing equilibria that an individual maintains among the stresses of coexistent incompatible states are so personal (e.g., wholeheartedness in the midst of tentativeness), our presentation of the anatomy of style in Commitment should be a contribution to the concept of identity. Furthermore, since what is at issue is the person's manner of experiencing and expressing responsibility, the concept forms a link between the individual and society, a link complementary to, and enlivening of, the concept of role.

In its social significance, the distinction between Commitment in which a hypothesis is accorded faith (Positions 6, 7, 8, and 9) and commitment in which a hypothesis is mistaken for the only truth (Positions 1, 2, 3, and 4) articulates a distinction between the foundations of considered conformity as against blind conformity, judicious revolt as against blindly reactive revolt.[6] This is hardly a new distinction, but in informal discussions with students we have found its articulation useful, especially in providing the prospect that integrity may be maintained in judicious effort as well as in polarized combat.

Educational Implications

Should our developmental scheme turn out to have the general validity which we believe it to have, the steps between its generalities and practical educational applications will remain many and arduous. It does, however, illuminate possibilities, and some urgencies. I shall mention briefly certain administrative and instructional implications and then turn to that more broadly social concern which the study has set most forcefully before us.

---

[6]The issue is currently viewed in the *forms* of thought in which the use of force and violence are "justified" in contemporary student protest in its extremes. In these forms, the conviction of absolute moral rightness is preemptive to the extent of according others no rights (see the status accorded "others" in Positions 1 and 2, and especially the discussion of the dilemma of oppositional revolt undertaken in advance of learning the tools of relativistic thought). The forms may be examined in the statements of those students emphasizing their "radical" as opposed to "liberal" position in *Students and Society* (Center for the Study of Democratic Institutions, 1968).

The existence of such a developmental sequence as that described in our scheme bears on administrative practice in such areas as grouping, selection, and guidance. In grouping it confirms the desirability of cultural diversity while pointing toward ways of identifying and supporting those most vulnerable to cultural shock. In selection and guidance (for example, curriculum tracking, college admissions, etc.) the study documents and specifies the ways in which certain differences among students which appear as differences of personality or ability may express developmental process. This documentation sharpens certain unresolved problems of prediction. For example, in considering students who have done well in a "traditional" schooling and who may evidence the outlook characterized by Position 1, 2, 3, or 4 in our scheme, differential prediction among them would require two related assessments: (1) the degree to which a student's preference for precise dualistic tasks is derivative of (*a*) personality structure (especially "closed" or "defensive" systems of emotional control) or (*b*) more superficial cultural experience more open to developmental change; (2) the extent of his measured achievements and abilities in the tasks such students have mastered as predictive of their aptitude for quite different intellectual operations.[7] A developmental scheme such as ours, therefore, while it cannot directly provide a basis for prediction of potentials for growth, does articulate both the limits of our present arts of prediction and the direction in which such arts may profitably move.

In the area of instruction, similarly, our scheme raises questions in regard to grouping, curriculum design, and teaching method. As it stands, the scheme may be of immediate solace to a teacher in that it explains on impersonal grounds how he can be so differently perceived by various students in his class. This solace can be of no mean value, in that it can free his thinking for a more differential address to individual students "where they are." The more general implications for differential grouping of students by developmental stage will require long-range exploration. The two most suggestive experiments we

---

[7]In the words of a freshman: "I feel it's a great mistake: to gauge by the College Boards, which, especially in our school, and in others, you're prepared ahead of time and you've memorized stuff by rote. And it's purely objective; they're multiple-choice—you've got a chance of hitting it. And then you get into college and it's so entirely different."

know of are those of Wispé (Wispé, 1951) and Hunt (Hunt, D. E., 1966). Wispé grouped students in relation to a concept of personality difference readily translatable into developmental level on our scheme, Hunt in relation to a scheme of development parallel to the early section of our own. Both researchers varied instructional procedures. Wispé administered, to different sections of each of his two "types" of students, methods congruent and incongruent with their preferences. The different responses of these two "types" to instruction incongruent with their preferences corresponds to what one would predict for students of Position 4 (and below) and students of Position 5 (and above) on our scheme. Hunt's teachers found that different procedures were necessary to keep the different stage-groups comfortable, but that the introduction of calculated incongruities was required to instigate movement in a group moving toward the next developmental stage.

In our reports, the most difficult instructional moment for the students—and perhaps therefore for the teacher as well—seems to occur at the transition from the conception of knowledge as a quantitative accretion of discrete rightnesses (including the discrete rightnesses of Multiplicity, in which everyone has a right to his own opinion) to the conception of knowledge as the qualitative assessment of contextual observations and relationships. In approaching this point of transition the student generally misconstrues what his teacher is doing, and both suffer. It is a crucial moment; and for intelligent action, the teacher requires the clearest understanding of his, and the student's, predicament. To judge from our students' reports, the teacher's most promising point of address is to the student's bewilderment about the grounds on which his work is evaluated. Our students' accounts suggest that an assist might come from explicit reference to analogies in those relativistic structures which the student has already developed at more concrete levels of experience. One of our students drew the analogy from his experience as a truck driver, in which he had been impressed by his foreman's qualitative rather than all-or-none evaluation of his errors. Another suddenly perceived his English instructor's encouragements as parallel to those of his baseball coach, thereby discovering that in the interpretation of a poem, qualitative, integrative improvement was possible. As this student put it: "So I figured the first thing is you gotta get in there and take a chance—start swinging. Maybe you're wild, but maybe he says 'close' and then you keep pulling things together."

This English instructor's encouragement of risk and his use of the word "close" carry educational implications leading back to the epistemological changes with which this study began. If one contrasts the definitions of knowledge implied by the examination questions of sixty years ago and those of today (see Chapter 1, p. 5) it becomes evident that education in these different kinds of knowledge would involve quite different relations of teacher and student, and place very different responsibilities upon each role. Where knowledge consisted of facts in a single frame of reference, the teacher's primary duties were to make the facts clear and to so correct his students in respect to the right or wrong of each fact as to allow of no error. The student, in turn, collected correct facts and procedures. Where knowledge is contextual and relative, the teacher's task is less atomistic as the student's is more integrational. The good teacher becomes one who supports in his students a more sustained groping, exploration, and synthesis. His acts of evaluation must subtend more than discrete rights and wrongs, and extend through time to assist discrimination among complex patterns of interpretation.

Where the extent of this difference is not clear and explicit in an instructor's mind he may attempt to serve both sets of values at once in ways that are conflicting rather than complementary. We have over the past several years received from young instructors several hundred recordings of their work in section meetings and in one-to-one tutorial. These offerings have come from earnest men who have courageously volunteered to record for the sake of their own learning. Typically, they enter their classrooms with the second set of values, looking at the section meeting or tutorial as an opportunity for the students to develop initiative and scope in their own thinking. No sooner do the students get started, however, and some error or inexactness is voiced, than the older form of responsibilities imposes on the instructor the imperative of "correcting." In the hours where this tendency gets in motion, three to five corrections of this kind appear sufficient to defeat the students' initiative for search and the flow of their exploration. The initiative for conversation then falls back upon the instructor, who then finds himself in a monologue or lecture, with the sensation of being somehow trapped, compelled, by powerful forces, in himself and the students, to do what he had never intended to do.[8]

---

[8]The problem is not, of course, the correction of errors; the question is *which* correction *when*. Timing, in the new epistemology, must be contingent on the dynamics of search, analysis, and integration in the student.

This comic tragedy dramatizes, we feel, a lag between the intellectual revolution of this century and the revolution in social expectations and actions required to support it. It also welds together the issues of these revolutions and the issues of the students' development portrayed by this study.

This latter welding points to more than the improvement of the teaching of intellectual competence in the new forms of thought. The efficient fostering of competence in the skills and disciplines of contextual meta-thinking does of course require, in itself, the further development of those ways of teaching which encourage risking, groping, analytic detachment, and synthetic insight. But our students' reports reveal that this competence alone would tend to result in a development no further than that expressed in our scheme by Position 5.

The failure of the diffuse relativism of Position 5 to provide orientation for the individual makes its structure highly unstable. No students in our study maintained themselves in it for more than a year, even those who found the sheer elaboration of skills most intriguing. Amidst such kaleidoscopic possibilities they felt a necessity to orient themselves somehow, moving either toward Commitment, on the one hand, or toward the detached, alienated orientation of Escape on the other. The exigency of this developmental crisis seems to us to impose a profound responsibility on the educator, a responsibility which is no longer a separable moral task like "building character," which was once somehow "tacked on" to regular teaching.

It appears, then, that it is no longer tenable for an educator to take the position that what a person does with his intellectual skills is a moral rather than intellectual problem and therefore none of the scholar's business. Epistemologically the knower and the known are now inseparable. The forms of knowing entwine with the forms of the known, and this involvement includes the forms of the knower's responsibility. The alienated student (whom we have carefully distinguished from the student who is committed to productive revolt) may imitate or parody the forms of other people's knowledge, but he is as sterile intellectually as he is socially.

The most pressing problem emerging from our study is therefore the question: *What environmental sustenance most supports students in the choice to use their competence to orient themselves through Commitments*—as opposed to using it to establish a nonresponsible alienation? Our study was not designed to produce hard data in answer to this question, but the students' reports provide for a general inference.

To be sure, some of our students probably arrived with a disposition toward responsibility so strong that it would have fulfilled itself in the most barren environment; a few, also, may have come with so fixed a resentment or terror of involvement that they would have refused the most nourishing support. For the majority, however, the most important support seemed to derive from a special realization of community. This was the realization that in the very risks, separateness, and individuality of working out their Commitments, they were in the same boat not only with each other but with their instructors as well. (See excerpts, Positions 6, 7, 8, and 9.)

Like any other sense of community this one seemed to derive from reciprocal acts of recognition and confirmation (Erikson, 1964). The individual may himself derive a sense of community by observing that others are like himself in that their cares and quandaries are like his own. His sense of membership is enormously strengthened, however, if in addition he experiences himself as *seen* by others in the same way.

The first of these requirements enjoins upon educators a certain openness—a visibility in their own thinking, groping, doubts, and styles of Commitment. Most of our students seemed to have found one or more models of this kind, and to be appreciative of them.

The second requirement enjoins on educators the duty of confirming the student in his community with them—a membership he achieves (at the very least as an apprentice or colleague-to-be) through his own making of meaning, his daring to take risks, and his courage in committing himself. In respect to the adequacy of this educational function our students' reports are equivocal. Putting what the students said and did not say into the setting of other observations of our own, we feel that educational mores have not kept up with this century's changes in the nature of knowledge or with the demands the new relativism places upon the learner. How usual, for example, is the student's experience that his paper has been read with primary attention to his meaning and only secondary attention to establishing his grade? It is a difficult experience to convey, especially in large courses backed by a corps of anonymous "graders." One student, not of this study, spontaneously reported *as the standout experience of four years* a grader's marginal note beside a paragraph the student had felt to be especially meaningful: "Nice point."

The one hard datum which our records do supply on this vital matter is equally appalling. A search of the records for some single specific educational recommendation put forward by any large number of the students reveals only one: "Every student should have an interview each year like this."

We are reluctant to suppose that these students meant such words to be taken literally; on the face of it the recommendation seems trivial. We doubt, too, that the students were merely being flattering, or even particularly gracious; such a compliment, when made to members of the establishment, is at least double-edged. The message, we believe, is more general: that students should experience themselves more vividly as recognized in the eyes of their educators in their efforts to integrate their learning in the responsible interpretation of their lives.

In the tone of this message we sense no plea for mere attention for its own sake. Much less do we hear a wish to escape the unavoidable in human separateness. Rather, we hear the students as hungering for a nutriment essential to growth and meagerly supplied within the conventions of present-day education. The growth demanded of them, and for which they yearn, involves a new kind of responsibility. Fifty years ago, our researches suggest, a college senior might achieve a world view such as that of Position 3 or Position 4 on our scheme and count himself a mature man. Now he must go beyond the assertion of his individualism in certainty to affirm his individuality in doubt. To be viable, the new aloneless requires a new realization of community.

How many educators provide more of this realization? Confirmation of the growing person in any community is of course an art and in large part implicit. Beyond its provisions in ritual, it is most effective where its spontaneity conveys the conviction that membership is assumed, and "goes without saying." For the fostering of a sense of community in the committing of intellect and care, therefore, we would be reluctant to recommend particular procedures or rituals. We could, of course, conceive of many institutional procedures and forms which might emerge as useful provisions, but to start with them would be to invite the spirit to go elsewhere.

This is why we feel that this study, if it is found to have a general relevance, leads more indirectly than directly to educational applications. We are content if the study illuminates certain of the issues of student development which educational policies address. As we see it, in summary, our study highlights two major issues:

First, the study sketches sequential forms of a major personal development occurring as late as the college years. At each step in this development the student sees himself, his instructors, and even truth itself in very different terms. Clearly, the community's efforts to instruct, recognize, and confirm the student must take forms that are generally relevant to the student's construal of the world, and of himself in it, at different points in his growth. Our records show, for example, that when the only pluralism a student sees is one in which any opinion is as good as another, an effort to encourage him in a relativistic Commitment will be simply misperceived. In any optimal sense, even a good estimate of "where the student is" in his structuring of the world is not enough. Has he just arrived there? If so, confirmation should aim at assisting him in firming up and expanding his discoveries. Is he ready to move on? If so, instruction should present him with those incongruities which best challenge him at the leading edge of his growth.

As a contribution toward these ideals, our scheme of development presents in their major outlines those structures through which students in a liberal arts college appear sequentially to construe the world. Ironically, our contribution points also to the distance between the ideal and current practice. Our students must be considered a relatively homogeneous group, in intelligence and academic ability, and yet our study reveals the wide range, in any one college year, of the ways in which they construed the nature of knowledge, the origin of values, the intentions of instructors, and their own responsibilities. The implications for the conduct of education are appalling, but there they are.

Finally, the study makes salient the courage required of the student in each step in his development. This demand upon courage implies a reciprocal obligation for the educational community: to recognize the student in his courage and to confirm the membership he achieves as he assumes the risks of each forward movement. This is a creative obligation: to find ways to encourage. At each step the student senses his option of taking up new responsibilities or of pulling out in retreat or alienation. He must make the decision himself, but if he feels not only alone, but alone in the experience of aloneness, he can draw his only strength from his past—if he has had a good past. In our reports, the issues of this dubious battle are revealed as cumulative, reaching their crisis in the student's emergence into a world perceived as relative and as one in which he must either affirm his own convictions and values or entrench himself in opportunism, proprietary absolutism, or despair. At this advanced moment of maturity he would seem to require not less support but more—and of a particular kind. He needs not only models to emulate but the experience of community with them. Our study makes clear enough why this experience cannot be fostered by the educational customs appropriate to the epistemology of fifty years ago. We hope it also articulates the nature of the experience which emerging customs must address if they are to confirm the young adult in his membership in this new and precarious community.

⁓ Bibliography

Adams, H. B. *The education of Henry Adams.* (1st ed.: 1907) New York: Modern Library, 1931.

Adorno, T. W.; Frenkel-Brunswik, E.; Levinson, D. J.; & Sanford, R. N. *The authoritarian personality.* New York: Harper, 1950.

Aiken, H. D. The fate of philosophy in the twentieth century. In H. D. Aiken & W. Barrett (Eds.), *Philosophy in the twentieth century.* Vol. 1. New York: Random House, 1962a. Pp. 3–18.

Aiken, H. D. Moral philosophy and education. In *Reason and conduct.* New York: Knopf, 1962. Pp. 3–32.

Aiken, H. D. *Reason and conduct.* New York: Knopf, 1962b.

Alexander, F. "The voice of the intellect is soft . . . " *Psychoanalytic Review,* 1941, *28,* 12–29.

Allard, M., & Carlson, E. The generality of cognitive complexity. *Journal of Social Psychology,* 1963, *59,* 73–75.

Allinsmith, W. A. Moral standards: II. The learning of moral standards. In D. R. Miller & G. E. Swanson (Eds.), *Inner conflict and defense.* New York: Holt, 1960. Pp. 141–176.

Allport, F. *Theories of perception and the concept of structure.* New York: Wiley, 1955.

Allport, G. W. The ego in contemporary psychology. *Psychological Review,* 1943, *50,* 451–478.

Allport, G. W. What units shall we employ? In G. Lindzey (Ed.), *Assessment of human motives.* New York: Holt, Rinehart and Winston, 1958. Pp. 239–262.

Allport, G. W. *Pattern and growth in personality.* (1st ed.: 1937) New York: Holt, Rinehart and Winston, 1961.

Allport, G. W. Psychological models for guidance. In R. L. Mosher, R. F. Carle, & C. D. Kehas, *Guidance: An examination.* New York: Harcourt, Brace & World, 1965. Pp. 13–23.

Alston, W. *Philosophy of language.* Englewood Cliffs, N.J.: Prentice Hall, 1964.

American Academy of Arts and Sciences. *Creativity and learning*. Boston: Daedalus, 1965.

American Psychological Association. Statement on report of joint commission on mental illness and health. *American Psychologist*, 1963, *18*, 307–308.

Anderson, A., & Dvorak, B. Differences between college students and their elders in standards of conduct. *Journal of Abnormal and Social Psychology*, 1928, *23*, 286–292.

Angyal, A. *Foundations for a science of personality*. New York: The Commonwealth Fund, 1941.

Angyal, A. *Neurosis and treatment: A holistic theory*. New York: Wiley, 1965.

Aronfreed, J. The origin of self-criticism. *Psychological Review*, 1964, *71*, 193–218.

Arsenian, S. Change in evaluative attitudes during four years of college. *Journal of Applied Psychology*, 1943, *27*, 338–349.

Attneave, F. *Applications of information theory to psychology*. New York: Holt, Rinehart and Winston, 1959.

Attneave, F. Perception and related areas. In S. Koch (Ed.), *Psychology: A study of a science*. Vol. 4. *Biologically oriented fields: Their place in psychology and in biological science*. New York: McGraw-Hill, 1962. Pp. 619–659.

Ayer, A. J. *Language, truth and logic*. (1st ed.: 1936) New York: Dover, no date.

Baldwin, J. M. *Social and ethical interpretations in mental development*. New York: Macmillan, 1906.

Barker, R. G. Ecology and motivation. In M. R. Jones (Ed.), *Nebraska symposium on motivation*. Lincoln: University of Nebraska Press, 1960. Pp. 1–50.

Barker, R. G. Explorations in ecological psychology. *American Psychologist*, 1965, *20*, 1–14.

Barrett, W. *Irrational man*. Garden City, N.Y.: Doubleday, 1958.

Barrett, W., & Aiken, H. D. (Eds.) *Philosophy in the twentieth century*. Vol. 1. New York: Random House, 1962.

Barron, F. Complexity-simplicity as a personality dimension. *Journal of Abnormal and Social Psychology*, 1953, *48*, 163–172.

Barron, F. The needs for order and for disorder as motives in creative activity. In C. W. Taylor & F. Barron (Eds.), *Scientific creativity: Its recognition and development*. New York: Wiley, 1963. Pp. 153–160.

Bartlett, F. C. *Remembering*. London: Cambridge University Press, 1932.

Barton, A. H. *College education: A methodological examination of changing values in college*. New Haven: Hazen Foundation, 1959.

Bay, C. A social theory of higher education. In N. Sanford (Ed.), *The American college*. New York: Wiley, 1962.

Beardslee, D. C., & Wertheimer, M. (Eds.) *Readings in perception*. Princeton, N.J.: Van Nostrand, 1958.

Bell, D. Twelve modes of prediction—a preliminary sorting of approaches in the social sciences. *Daedalus*, Summer 1964, 845–880.

Bell, D. *The reforming of general education*. New York: Columbia University Press, 1966.

Benedict, R. Continuities and discontinuities in cultural conditioning. (1938) In C. Kluckhohn, H. Murray, & D. Schneider (Eds.), *Personality in nature, society, and culture*. (2nd ed.) New York: Knopf, 1961. Pp. 522–531.

Bereiter, C., & Freedman, M. B. Personality differences among college curricular groups. Paper read at the American Psychological Association, 68th Annual Convention, Chicago, 1960. (Abstract in *American Psychologist*, 1960, *15*, 435.)

Bereiter, C., & Freedman, M. B. Fields of study and the people in them. In N. Sanford (Ed.), *The American college*. New York: Wiley, 1962.

Bergmann, G. *Philosophy of science*. Madison: University of Wisconsin Press, 1957.

Bergson, H. *The two sources of morality and religion*. (1st French ed.: 1932) Garden City, N.Y.: Doubleday, 1935.

Berlyne, D. E. Toward a theory of epistemic behavior: Conceptual conflict and epistemic curiosity. In R. J. C. Harper, C. C. Anderson, C. M. Christensen, & S. M. Hunka (Eds.), *The cognitive processes: Readings*. Englewood Cliffs, N.J.: Prentice Hall, 1964. Pp. 563–581.

Bidwell, C. E. (Ed.). *The American college and student personality: A survey of research progress and problems*. New York: Social Science Research Council, 1960.

Bidwell, C. E.; King, S. H.; Finnie, B.; & Scarr, H. A. Undergraduate careers: Alternatives and determinants. *The School Review*, 1963, *71*, 299–316.

Bidwell, C. E., & Vreeland, R. S. College education and moral orientations: An organizational approach. *Administrative Science Quarterly*, 1963, *8*, 166–191.

Birney, R. C., & Taylor, M. J. Scholastic behavior and orientation to college. *Journal of Educational Psychology*, 1959, *50*, 266–274.

Black, M. *Models and metaphors*. Ithaca, N.Y.: Cornell University Press, 1962.

Blaine, G., & McArthur, C. *Emotional problems of the student*. New York: Appleton, 1961.

Blake, R. R., & Ramsey, G. V. (Eds.) *Perception—An approach to personality.* New York: Ronald Press, 1951.

Bloomgarden, L. Our new elite colleges. *Commentary,* 1960, *29,* 150–154.

Blos, P. Aspects of mental health in teaching and learning. *Mental Hygiene,* 1955, *37,* 555–569.

Blos, P. *On adolescence, A psychoanalytic interpretation.* New York: Free Press, 1962.

Boldt, W. J., & Stroud, J. B. Changes in the attitudes of college students. *Journal of Educational Psychology,* 1934, *25,* 611–619.

Boring, E. G. A history of introspection. *Psychological Bulletin,* 1953, *50,* 169–189.

Braen, B. B. The measurement and validation of theoretically derived manifest rigidity in a group of college students. Unpublished doctoral dissertation. Abstract in *Dissertation Abstracts,* 1955, *15,* 2573–2574.

Bramson, L. (Ed.) *Examining in Harvard College: A collection of essays by members of the Harvard faculty.* Cambridge, Mass.: Faculty of Arts and Sciences, Harvard University, 1963.

Bridgman, P. W. *The way things are.* Cambridge, Mass.: Harvard University Press, 1959.

Bronowski, J. The discovery of form. In G. Kepes (Ed.), *Structure in art and in science.* New York: Braziller, 1965. Pp. 55–60.

Brown, D. R. Some educational patterns. In N. Sanford (Ed.), Personality development during the college years. *Journal of Social Issues,* 1956, *12,* 44–60.

Brown, D. R. Non-intellective qualities and the perception of the ideal student by college faculty. *Journal of Educational Sociology,* 1960, *33,* 269–278.

Brown, D. R. Personality, college environments, and academic productivity. In N. Sanford (Ed.), *The American college.* New York: Wiley, 1962.

Brown, D. R., & Bystryn, D. College environment, personality, and social ideology of three ethnic groups. *Journal of Social Psychology,* 1956, *44,* 279–288.

Brown, D. R., & Datta, L-E. Authoritarianism, verbal ability, and response set. *Journal of Abnormal and Social Psychology,* 1959, *58,* 131–134.

Brown, R. W. A determinant of the relationship between rigidity and authoritarianism. *Journal of Abnormal and Social Psychology,* 1953, *48,* 469–476.

Brown, R. W. Language and categories. In J. S. Bruner, J. J. Goodnow, & G. A. Austin, *A study of thinking.* New York: Wiley, 1956.

Brown, R. W. Models of attitude change. In R. W. Brown, E. Galanter, &

E. H. Hess, *New directions in psychology.* New York: Holt, Rinehart and Winston, 1962. Pp. 1–85.

Brown, R. W. How shall a thing be called? In R. J. C. Harper, C. C. Anderson, C. M. Christensen, & S. M. Hunka (Eds.), *The cognitive processes: Readings.* Englewood Cliffs, N.J.: Prentice Hall, 1964. Pp. 647–654.

Brown, R. W.; Galanter, E.; & Hess, E. H. *New directions in psychology.* New York: Holt, Rinehart and Winston, 1962.

Brumbaugh, A. J. *Research designed to improve institutions of higher learning.* Washington, D.C.: American Council on Education, 1960.

Bruner, J. S. Personality dynamics and the process of perceiving. In R. R. Blake & G. V. Ramsey (Eds.), *Perception: An approach to personality.* New York: Ronald Press, 1951.

Bruner, J. S. Discussion of L. Festinger's The relation between behavior and cognition. In H. Gruber, K. Hammond, & R. Jessor (Eds.), *Contemporary approaches to cognition.* Cambridge, Mass.: Harvard University Press, 1957a. Pp. 151–156.

Bruner, J. S. Going beyond the information given. In H. Gruber, K. Hammond, & R. Jessor (Eds.), *Contemporary approaches to cognition.* Cambridge, Mass.: Harvard University Press, 1957b. Pp. 41–69.

Bruner, J. S. On perception readiness. In D. C. Beardslee & M. Wertheimer (Eds.), *Readings in perception.* Princeton, N.J.: Van Nostrand, 1958. Pp. 686–729.

Bruner, J. S. Inhelder and Piaget's *The growth of logical thinking.* I. A psychologist's viewpoint. *British Journal of Psychology,* 1959, *50,* 363–370.

Bruner, J. S. *The process of education.* Cambridge, Mass.: Harvard University Press, 1960.

Bruner, J. S. *Toward a theory of instruction.* Cambridge, Mass.: Harvard University Press, 1966.

Bruner, J. S., & Goodman, C. Value and need as organizing factors in perception. *Journal of Abnormal and Social Psychology,* 1947, *42,* 33–44.

Bruner, J. S.; Goodnow, J. J.; & Austin, G. A. *A study of thinking.* New York: Wiley, 1956.

Bruner, J. S., & Postman, L. On the perception of incongruity: A paradigm. In D. C. Beardslee & M. Wertheimer (Eds.), *Readings in perception.* Princeton, N.J.: Van Nostrand, 1958. Pp. 648–663.

Brunswik, E. *Perception and the representative design of psychological experiments.* (2nd ed.) Berkeley: University of California Press, 1956.

Brunswik, E. Scope and aspects of the cognitive problem. In H. Gruber,

K. Hammond, & R. Jessor (Eds.), *Contemporary approaches to cognition.* Cambridge, Mass.: Harvard University Press, 1957. Pp. 5–31.

Brunswik, E. The conceptual framework of psychology. In O. Neurath (Ed.), *International encyclopedia of unified science* (1st ed.: 1950), 1962, *1* (10).

Brunswik, E. The conceptual focus of systems. In M. H. Marx (Ed.), *Theories on contemporary psychology.* New York: Macmillan, 1963. Pp. 226–237.

Buchanan, S. *Poetry and mathematics.* (1st ed.: 1929) Philadelphia: Lippincott, 1962.

Buck, P. Introduction. In P. Buck (Ed.), *Social sciences at Harvard, 1860–1920.* Cambridge, Mass.: Harvard University Press, 1965. Pp. 1–17.

Buck, P. (Ed.) *Social sciences at Harvard, 1860–1920.* Cambridge, Mass.: Harvard University Press, 1965.

Bugelski, R., & Lester, O. Changes in attitudes in a group of college students during their college course and after graduation. *Journal of Social Psychology,* 1940, *12,* 319–332.

Burke, K. *A grammar of motives.* Englewood Cliffs, N.J.: Prentice Hall, 1945.

Burke, K. *Permanence and change.* (1st ed.: 1935) Los Altos, Calif.: Hermes, 1954.

Camus, A. *The myth of Sisyphus, and other essays.* J. O'Brien (Tr.). New York: Knopf, 1955.

Carlson, H. B. Attitudes of undergraduate students. *Journal of Social Psychology,* 1934, *5,* 202–212.

Carnap, R. Empiricism, semantics, and ontology. (1950) In E. Nagel & R. Brandt (Eds.), *Meaning and knowledge: Systematic readings in epistemology.* New York: Harcourt, Brace & World, 1965. Pp. 298–305.

Carroll, J. B. *The study of language.* Cambridge, Mass.: Harvard University Press, 1959.

Carroll, J. B. *Language and thought.* Englewood Cliffs, N.J.: Prentice Hall, 1964a.

Carroll, J. B. Words, meanings and concepts. *Harvard Educational Review,* 1964b, *34,* 178–202.

Cartwright, D. Lewinian theory as a contemporary systematic framework. In S. Koch (Ed.), *Psychology: A study of a science.* Vol. 2. *General systematic formulations, learning, and special processes.* New York: McGraw-Hill, 1959. Pp. 7–91.

Cassirer, E. *An essay on man.* New Haven, Conn.: Yale University Press, 1944.

Center for the Study of Democratic Institutions. *Students and society.* Santa Barbara, 1968.

Chapanis, A. Men, machines, and models. *American Psychologist,* 1961, *16,* 113–131.

Chomsky, N. *Syntactic structures.* The Hague: Mouton, 1957.

Chomsky, N. A review of B. F. Skinner's *Verbal behavior.* In J. A. Fodor & J. J. Katz (Eds.), *The structure of language.* Englewood Cliffs, N.J.: Prentice Hall, 1964a. Pp. 547–578.

Chomsky, N. A transformational approach to syntax. In J. A. Fodor & J. J. Katz (Eds.), *The structure of language.* Englewood Cliffs, N.J.: Prentice Hall, 1964b. Pp. 211–245.

Chomsky, N. *Aspects of the theory of syntax.* Cambridge, Mass.: M.I.T. Press, 1965.

Chomsky, N., & Miller, G. A. Introduction to the formal analysis of natural languages. In R. D. Luce, R. R. Bush, & E. Galanter (Eds.), *Handbook of mathematical psychology.* Vol. 2. New York: Wiley, 1963. Pp. 269–321.

Cohen, B. D.; Kalish, H. I.; Thurston, J. R.; & Cohen, E. Experimental manipulation of verbal behavior. *Journal of Experimental Psychology,* 1954, *47,* 106–110.

Cohen, M. R. *A preface to logic.* (1st ed.: 1944) New York: Meridian, 1956.

Cooley, W. W., & Lohnes, P. R. *Multivariate procedures for the behavioral sciences.* New York: Wiley, 1962.

Cronbach, L. The two disciplines of scientific psychology. *American Psychologist,* 1957, *12,* 67–184.

Crutchfield, R. Conformity and character. *American Psychologist,* 1955, *10,* 191–198.

Danto, A., & Morgenbesser, S. (Eds.) *Philosophy of science.* Cleveland: World Publishing, 1960.

Deutsch, K. Autonomy and boundaries according to communications theory. In R. Grinker (Ed.), *Toward a unified theory of human behavior.* New York: Basic Books, 1956. Pp. 278–297.

Deutsch, M. Field theory in social psychology. In G. Lindzey (Ed.), *Handbook of social psychology.* Vol. 1. *Theory and method.* Reading, Mass.: Addison-Wesley, 1954. Pp. 181–222.

Dewey, J. *Essays in experimental logic.* (1st ed.: 1916) New York: Dover, no date.

Dewey, J. *Art as experience.* (1st ed.: 1934) New York: Capricorn, 1958a.

Dewey, J. *Experience and nature.* (2nd ed.) New York: Dover, 1958b.

Dewey, J. *Logic: The theory of inquiry.* (1st ed.: 1938) New York: Holt, Rinehart and Winston, 1960a.

Dewey, J. *On experience, nature, and freedom.* Representative selections. R. J. Bernstein (Ed.) New York: Liberal Arts, 1960b.

Dewey, J. Context and thought. In J. Dewey, *On experience, nature, and freedom.* Representative selections. R. J. Bernstein (Ed.). New York: Liberal Arts, 1960. Pp. 88–110.

Dewey, J. *Philosophy, psychology and social practice.* J. Ratner (Ed.) (2nd ed.) New York: Capricorn, 1965a.

Dewey, J. The reflex arc concept in psychology. In J. Ratner (Ed.), *Philosophy, psychology and social practice.* (2nd ed.) New York: Capricorn, 1965b. Pp. 252–266b.

Dewey, J., & Bentley, A. F. *Knowing and the known.* (1st ed.: 1944) Boston: Beacon Press, 1960.

Dressel, P. L.; Lehmann, I. J.; and Ikenberry, S. O. Critical thinking, attitudes and values in higher education, a preliminary report. East Lansing: Michigan State University Press, 1959.

Dressel, P. L., & Mayhew, L. *General education: Explorations in evaluation.* Washington, D.C.: American Council on Education, 1954.

Dressel, P. L. (and associates). *Evaluation in higher education.* Boston: Houghton Mifflin, 1961.

Eddy, E. D., Jr. *The college influence on student character.* Washington, D.C.: American Council on Education, 1959.

Eisenstadt, S. *From generation to generation.* New York: Free Press, 1956.

Ekstein, R., & Motto, R. Psychoanalysis and education—past and future. Unpublished paper read at Panel on psychic development and the prevention of mental illness, Midwinter meeting of the American Psychoanalytic Association, New York, December, 1961.

Engel, M. Psychological theory and guidance. In E. Landy & P. Perry (Eds.), *Guidance in American education: Backgrounds and prospects.* Cambridge, Mass.: Harvard University Graduate School of Education, 1964.

Erikson, E. H. *Childhood and society.* New York: Norton, 1950a.

Erikson, E. H. Growth and crises of the healthy personality. In M. J. E. Senn (Ed.), *Symposium on the healthy personality,* Supplement II; Transactions of the 4th conference. New York: Josiah Macy, Jr., Foundation, 1950b.

Erikson, E. H. Identity and the life cycle. In G. S. Klein (Ed.), *Psychological Issues.* Vol. 1 (1). New York: International Universities Press, 1959.

Erikson, E. H. Youth: Fidelity and diversity. *Daedalus,* Winter, 1962, 5–27.

Erikson, E. H. *Insight and responsibility.* New York: Norton, 1964.

Erikson, E. H. The nature of clinical evidence. In *Insight and responsibility.* New York: Norton, 1964. Pp. 47–80.

Erikson, E. H. Psychological reality and historical actuality. In *Insight and responsibility*. New York: Norton, 1964. Pp. 159–215.

Eron, L. D., & Walder, L. O. Test burning: II. *American Psychologist,* 1961, *16,* 237–244.

Farnsworth, D. *Mental health in college and university.* Cambridge, Mass.: Harvard University Press, 1957.

Farnsworth, D. *Psychiatry, education, and the young adult.* Springfield, Ill.: Thomas, 1966.

Faterson, H. F. Articulateness of experience: An extension of the field-dependence-independence concept. In S. Messick & J. Ross (Eds.), *Measurement in personality and cognition.* New York: Wiley, 1962. Pp. 171–181.

Fay, P. J., & Middleton, W. C. Certain factors related to liberal and conservative attitudes of college students: Sex, classification, fraternity membership, major subject. *Journal of Educational Psychology,* 1939, *30,* 378–390.

Feigl, H. Philosophical embarrassments of psychology. *American Psychologist,* 1959, *14,* 115–128.

Fenichel, O. *The Psychoanalytic theory of neurosis.* New York: Norton, 1945.

Festinger, L. The relation between behavior and cognition. In H. Gruber, K. Hammond, & R. Jessor (Eds.), *Contemporary approaches to cognition.* Cambridge, Mass.: Harvard University Press, 1957a. Pp. 127–150.

Festinger, L. *A theory of cognitive dissonance.* Evanston, Ill.: Row, 1957b.

Fingarette, H. *The self in transformation.* New York: Harper & Row, 1965.

Finnie, B. Interests of Harvard students as freshmen and seniors. Paper read at the American Psychological Association, September, 1966.

Finnie, B. Satisfaction and its relationship to other variables: A preliminary report. Paper read at the American College Health Association, Washington, March, 1967.

Finnie, B.; Scarr, H. A.; & King, S. H. Changes in personality variables among college students. Paper read at the New England Psychological Association, November, 1963.

Fishman, J. A. Unsolved criterion problems in the selection of college students. *Harvard Educational Review,* 1958, *28,* 340–349.

Fishman, J. A. Non-intellective factors as predictions, as criteria, and as contingencies in selection and guidance of college students: A sociopsychological analysis. In Center for the Study of Higher Education (Ed.), *Selection and educational differentiation: Proceedings.* Berkeley, Calif.: Editor, 1960a. Pp. 55–73a.

Fishman, J. A. Why are the values of college students changing? *Educational Record,* 1960b, *41,* 342–346b.

Flavell, J. H. *The developmental psychology of Jean Piaget.* Princeton, N.J.: Van Nostrand, 1963.

Fletcher, J. *Situation ethics.* Philadelphia: Westminster Press, 1966.

Florence, L. M. Mental growth and development at the college level. *Journal of Educational Psychology,* 1947, *38,* 65–82.

Fodor, J. A. Explanations in psychology. In M. Black (Ed.), *Philosophy in America.* Ithaca, N.Y.: Cornell University Press, 1965. Pp. 161–179.

Fodor, J. A., & Katz, J. J. (Eds.) *The structure of language.* Englewood Cliffs, N.J.: Prentice Hall, 1964.

Freedman, M. B. The passage through college. In N. Sanford (Ed.), Personality development during the college years. *Journal of Social Issues,* 1956, *12,* 13–28.

Freedman, M. B. The impact of college. In W. R. Hatch (Ed.), *New dimensions in higher education.* No. 4. Washington, D.C.: U.S. Department of Health, Education, and Welfare, 1960a.

Freedman, M. B. Some observations on personality development in college women. *Student Medicine,* 1960b, *8,* 228–245b.

Frenkel-Brunswik, E. Personality theory and perception. In R. R. Blake & G. V. Ramsey (Eds.), *Perception—An approach to personality.* New York: Ronald Press, 1951. Pp. 356–419.

Frenkel-Brunswik, E. Intolerance of ambiguity as an emotional and perceptual personality variable. In D. C. Beardslee & M. Wertheimer (Eds.), *Readings in perception.* Princeton, N.J.: Van Nostrand, 1958. Pp. 664–685.

Freud, A. Regression as a principle in mental development. *Bulletin of the Menninger Clinic,* 1963, *27,* 126–139.

Freud, A. *Normality and pathology in childhood.* New York: International Universities Press, 1965.

Freud, S. *An outline of psychoanalysis.* New York: Norton, 1949.

Frick, F. C. Information theory. In S. Koch (Ed.), *Psychology: A study of a science.* Vol. 2. *General systematic formulations, learning, and special processes.* New York: McGraw-Hill, 1959. Pp. 611–636.

Friedenberg, E. *The vanishing adolescent.* Boston: Beacon Press, 1959.

Fromm, E. *Escape from freedom.* New York: Avon Books, 1965.

Frost, R. Education by poetry: A meditative monologue. *Amherst Alumni Council News,* 1931, *4,* Supplement, 6–13.

Frost, R. The constant symbol. *Atlantic Monthly,* 1946, *178,* 50–52.

Fuller, R. B. Conceptuality of fundamental structures. In G. Kepes (Ed.), *Structure in art and in science.* New York: Braziller, 1965. Pp. 66–88.

Fullmer, D. W. Success and perseverance of university students. *Journal of Higher Education,* 1956, *27,* 445–447.

Gardner, R. W. Cognitive styles in categorizing behavior. *Journal of Personality,* 1953, *22,* 214–233.

Gardner, R. W. Cognitive controls in adaptation: Research and measurement. In S. Messick & J. Ross (Eds.), *Measurement in personality and cognition.* New York: Wiley, 1962. Pp. 183–198.

Gardner, R. W.; Holzman, P. S.; Klein, G. S.; Linton, H. B.; & Spence, D. P. Cognitive control: A study of individual consistencies in cognitive behavior. In G. S. Klein (Ed.), *Psychological Issues.* Vol. 1 (4). New York: International Universities Press, 1959.

Gardner, R. W.; Jackson, D. N.; & Messick, S. J. Personality organization in cognitive controls and intellectual abilities. In G. S. Klein (Ed.), *Psychological Issues.* Vol. 2 (4). New York: International Universities Press, 1960.

Gardner, R. W., & Schoen, R. A. Differentiation and abstraction in concept formation. *Psychological Monographs,* 1962, *76* (Whole No. 560).

Garner, W. R. *Uncertainty and structure as psychological concepts.* New York: Wiley, 1962.

George, F. H., & Handlon, J. H. A language for perceptual analysis. *Psychological Review,* 1957, *64,* 14–25.

Gibson, J. J. *The perception of the visual world.* Boston: Houghton Mifflin, 1950.

Gibson, J. J. Constancy and invariance in perception. In G. Kepes (Ed.), *The nature and art of motion.* New York: Braziller, 1965. Pp. 60–70.

Gill, M. M. The present state of psychoanalytic theory. *Journal of Abnormal and Social Psychology,* 1959, *58,* 1–8.

Gill, M. M., & Brenman, M. *Hypnosis and related states.* New York: International Universities Press, 1959.

Gillespie, J. M., & Allport, G. W. *Youth's outlook on the future: A cross-national study.* Garden City, N.Y.: Doubleday, 1955.

Gladstein, G. A. The relationship between study behavior and personality for academically successful students. Unpublished doctoral dissertation, University of Chicago, Chicago, Ill., 1957.

Gladstein, G. A. Study behavior of gifted stereotype and non-stereotype college students. *Personnel and Guidance Journal,* 1960, *38,* 470–474.

Goldsen, R. K.; Rosenberg, M.; Williams, R. M., Jr.; & Suchman, E. A. *What college students think.* Princeton, N.J.: Van Nostrand, 1960.

Goldstein, K. *The organism.* New York: American Book Co., 1939.

Gombrich, E. H. *Art and illusion.* (1st ed.: 1960) New York: Pantheon, 1965.

Goodman, P. *Growing up absurd.* New York: Vintage, 1962.

Goodstein, L. Institutional research on students: A summing up. In H. T. Sprague (Ed.), *Research on college students.* Boulder, Colo.: Western Interstate Commission for Higher Education, & Berkeley, Calif.: Center for Higher Education, 1960. Pp. 124–132.

Gough, H. G. Clinical versus statistical prediction in psychology. In L. Postman (Ed.), *Psychology in the making.* New York: Knopf, 1963. Pp. 526–584.

Greenberg, R. A., & Hepburn, J. G. (Eds.) *Robert Frost: An introduction.* New York: Holt, Rinehart and Winston, 1961.

Greenspoon, J. The effect of verbal and non-verbal stimuli on the frequency of members of two verbal response classes. Unpublished doctoral dissertation. Indiana University, 1951.

Gruber, H.; Hammond, K.; & Jessor, R. (Eds.) *Contemporary approaches to cognition.* Cambridge, Mass.: Harvard University Press, 1957.

Guilford, J. The three faces of intellect. *American Psychologist,* 1959, *14,* 469–479.

Guntrip, H. *Personality structure and human interaction.* New York: International Universities Press, 1961.

Hall, C. S., & Lindzey, G. *Theories of personality.* New York: Wiley, 1957.

Hall, E. W. *What is value? An essay in philosophical analysis.* New York: Humanities Press, 1952.

Hallowell, A. I. Cultural factors in the structuralization of perception. In D. C. Beardslee & M. Wertheimer (Eds.), *Readings in perception.* Princeton, N.J.: Van Nostrand, 1958. Pp. 552–564.

Hampshire, S. *Thought and action.* New York: Viking, 1960.

Hanfmann, E.; Jones, R.; & Baker, E. *Psychological counseling in a small college.* Cambridge, Mass.: Schenkman, 1963.

Hanley, C., & Rokeach, M. Care and carelessness in psychology. *Psychological Bulletin,* 1956, *53,* 183–186.

Hanson, N. R. *Patterns of discovery.* Cambridge, England: University Press, 1961.

Hare, R. M. *The language of morals.* New York: Oxford University Press, 1952.

Harlow, H. F. Mice, monkeys, men, and motives. *Psychological Review,* 1953, *60,* 23–32.

Harper, R. J. C.; Anderson, C. C.; Christensen, C. M.; & Hunka, S. M. (Eds.) *The cognitive processes: Readings.* Englewood Cliffs, N.J.: Prentice Hall, 1964.

Harris, D. B. (Ed.) *The concept of development.* Minneapolis: University of Minnesota Press, 1957.

Hartmann, H. *Ego psychology and the problem of adaptation.* New York: International Universities Press, 1939.

Hartshorne, E. Y. Undergraduate society and college culture. *American Sociological Review,* 1943, *8,* 321–332.

Harvard University. *General education in a free society.* Cambridge, Mass.: Harvard University Press, 1945.

Harvey, O. J. (Ed.) *Experience, structure and adaptability.* New York: Springer, 1966.

Harvey, O. J.; Hunt, D. E.; & Schroder, H. M. *Conceptual systems and personality organization.* New York: Wiley, 1961.

Havemann, E., & West, P. S. *They went to college.* New York: Harcourt, Brace, 1952.

Havighurst, R. J., & Taba, H. *Adolescent character and personality.* New York: Wiley, 1949.

Hawkins, D. Design for a mind. *Daedalus,* Summer 1962, 560–577.

Hawkins, D. *The language of nature.* San Francisco: Freeman, 1964.

Hawkins, D. The informed vision: An essay on science education. *Daedalus,* Summer 1965, 538–552.

Heath, D. H. *Explorations of maturity: Studies of mature and immature college men.* New York: Appleton-Century-Crofts, 1965.

Heath, R. Personality and student development. In University of Pittsburgh (Ed.), *New dimensions of learning in a free society.* Pittsburgh. Editor, 1958. Pp. 225–245.

Heath, R. *The reasonable adventurer.* Pittsburgh: University of Pittsburgh Press, 1964.

Hebb, D. O. A neuropsychological theory. In S. Koch (Ed.), *Psychology: A study of a science.* Vol. 1. *Sensory, perceptual, and physiological formulations.* New York: McGraw-Hill, 1959. Pp. 622–643.

Hebb, D. O. *The organization of behavior.* (1st ed.: 1949) New York: Science Editions, 1961.

Hebb, D. O. The mammal and his environment. In R. W. White (Ed.), *The study of lives.* New York: Atherton, 1963. Pp. 127–135.

Hebb, D. O. The American revolution. In R. J. C. Harper, C. C. Anderson, C. M. Christensen, & S. M. Hunka (Eds.), *The cognitive processes: Readings.* Englewood Cliffs, N.J.: Prentice Hall, 1964. Pp. 1–16.

Heidbreder, E. The attainment of concepts—A psychological interpretation. *Transactions of the New York Academy of Sciences,* 1945a, *7,* 171–188a.

Heidbreder, E. Toward a dynamic psychology of cognition. *Psychological Review,* 1945b, *52,* 1–22b.

Heidbreder, E. The attainment of concepts. I. Terminology and methodology. II. The problem. *Journal of General Psychology,* 1946, *35,* 173–189, 191–223.

Heidbreder, E. The attainment of concepts. III. The process. *Journal of Psychology,* 1947, *24,* 93–138.

Heider, F. Environmental determinants in psychological theories. *Psychological Review,* 1939, *46,* 383–410.

Heider, F. Social perception and phenomenal causality. *Psychological Review,* 1944, *51,* 358–374.

Heider, F. *The psychology of interpersonal relations.* New York: Wiley, 1958.

Heider, F. On perception, event structure, and psychological environment. In G. S. Klein (Ed.), *Psychological Issues.* Vol. 1 (3). New York: International Universities Press, 1959.

Heider, F. The gestalt theory of motivation. In M. R. Jones (Ed.), *Nebraska symposium on motivation.* Lincoln: University of Nebraska Press, 1960. Pp. 145–172.

Heisenberg, W. *Philosophic problems of nuclear science.* F. C. Hayes (Tr.). New York: Pantheon, 1952.

Heisenberg, W. The representation of nature in contemporary physics. *Daedalus,* Summer 1958, 95–108.

Heist, P. Diversity in college student characteristics. *Journal of Educational Sociology,* 1960, *33,* 279–291.

Heist, P., & Webster, H. Differential characteristics of student bodies—Implications for selection and study of undergraduates. In Center for the Study of Higher Education (Ed.), *Selection and educational differentiation: Proceedings.* Berkeley, Calif.: Editor, 1960a. Pp. 91–106a.

Heist, P., & Webster, H. A research orientation to selection, admission, and differential education. In H. T. Sprague (Ed.), *Research on College Students.* Boulder, Colo.: Western Interstate Commission for Higher Education, & Berkeley, Calif.: Center for Higher Education, 1960b. Pp. 21–40.

Helson, H. Adaption-level as a basis for a quantitative theory of frames of reference. *Psychological Review,* 1948, *55,* 297–313.

Hildum, D., & Brown, R. Verbal reinforcement and interviewer bias. *Journal of Abnormal and Social Psychology,* 1956, *53,* 108–111.

Hoffer, E. *The true believer.* (1st ed.: 1951) New York: Mentor, 1962.

Holt, R. R. Clinical and statistical prediction: A reformulation and some new data. *Journal of Abnormal and Social Psychology,* 1958, *56,* 1–12.

Holt, R. R. A clinical-experimental strategy for research in personality. In S. Messick & J. Ross (Eds.), *Measurement in personality and cognition.* New York: Wiley, 1962. Pp. 199–218.

Holt, R. R. Two influences on Freud's scientific thought. In R. W. White (Ed.), *The study of lives*. New York: Atherton, 1963. Pp. 365–387.

Holt, R. R. Review of R. W. White's Ego and reality in psychoanalytic theory. *Contemporary Psychology*, 1964, *9*, 433–434.

Holt, R. R. A review of some of Freud's biological assumptions and their influence on his theories. In N. S. Greenfield & W. C. Lewis (Eds.), *Psychoanalysis and current biological thought*. Madison: University of Wisconsin Press, 1965.

Holton, G. Science and the deallegorization of motion. In G. Kepes (Ed.), *The nature and art of motion*. New York: Braziller, 1965. Pp. 24–31.

Horwitz, L. Theory construction and validation in psychoanalysis. In M. Marx (Ed.), *Theories in contemporary psychology*. New York: Macmillan, 1963. Pp. 413–434.

Hunt, D. E. A conceptual systems change model and its application to education. In O. J. Harvey (Ed.), *Experience, structure and adaptability*. New York: Springer, 1966. Pp. 277–302.

Hunt, E. L. *The revolt of the college intellectual*. New York: Human Relations Aids, 1963.

Hunt, J. McV. *Intelligence and experience*. New York: Ronald Press, 1961.

Hunter, E. C. Changes in general attitudes of women students during four years in college. *Journal of Social Psychology*, 1942, *16*, 243–257.

Husserl, E. *Ideas: General introduction to pure phenomenology*. New York: Crowell-Collier, 1962.

Hymes, D. (Ed.) *Language in culture and society*. New York: Harper & Row, 1964.

Inhelder, B., & Piaget, J. *The growth of logical thinking from childhood to adolescence*. New York: Basic Books, 1958.

Inkeles, A. Personality and social structure. In R. Merton, L. Broom, & L. Cottrell (Eds.), *Sociology today*. New York: Basic Books, 1959. Pp. 249–276.

Ittelson, W. H. Perception and transactional psychology. In S. Koch (Ed.), *Psychology: A study of a science*. Vol. 4. *Biologically oriented fields: Their place in psychology and in biological science*. New York: McGraw-Hill, 1962. Pp. 660–704.

Jackson, D. N. Intellectual ability and mode of perception. *Journal of Consulting Psychology*, 1957, *21*, 458.

Jacob, P. E. *Changing values in college*. New York: Harper, 1957.

Jacob, P. E. Social change and student values. *Educational Record*, 1960, *41*, 338–342.

Jaffe, R. S. *Philosophical foundations of the concept of a person*. Cambridge, Mass.: Bureau of Study Counsel, Harvard University, 1967.

Jahoda, M. *Current concepts of positive mental health.* New York: Basic Books, 1958.

Jencks, C., & Riesman, D. Patterns of residential education: A case study of Harvard. In N. Sanford (Ed.), *The American college.* New York: Wiley, 1962.

Jervis, F. M., & Congdon, R. G. Student and faculty perceptions of educational values. *American Psychologist,* 1958, *13,* 464–466.

Jessor, R. The problem of reductionism in psychology. In M. H. Marx (Ed.), *Theories in contemporary psychology.* New York: Macmillan, 1963. Pp. 245–256.

Jones, K. J. *The multivariate statistical analyzer.* Privately printed, 1964.

Jones, M. R. (Ed.) *Nebraska symposium on motivation.* Lincoln: University of Nebraska Press, 1960.

Jones, R. M. *Ego synthesis in dreams.* Cambridge, Mass.: Schenkman, 1962.

Jones, V. A. Attitudes of college students and the changes in such attitudes during four years in college. *Journal of Educational Psychology,* 1938, *29,* 14–25, 114–134.

Jordan, J. A self that can whistle. *Harvard Educational Review,* 1964, *34,* 22–32.

Josselyn, I. The ego in adolescence. *American Journal of Orthopsychiatry,* 1954, *24,* 223–237.

Kagan, J., & Moss, H. A. *From birth to maturity.* New York: Wiley, 1962.

Kahl, J. A. Educational and occupational aspirations of "common man" boys. *Harvard Educational Review,* 1953, *23,* 186–203.

Kaplan, A. *The conduct of inquiry.* San Francisco: Chandler, 1964.

Katz, J., & Sanford, N. The curriculum in the perspective of the theory of personality development. In N. Sanford (Ed.), *The American college.* New York: Wiley, 1962.

Kelly, G. A. *The psychology of personal constructs.* Vol. 1. A theory of personality. New York: Norton, 1955.

Kelly, G. A. Man's construction of his alternatives. In G. Lindzey (Ed.), *Assessment of human motives.* New York: Holt, Rinehart and Winston, 1958. Pp. 33–64.

Keniston, K. Inburn: An American Ishmael. In R. W. White (Ed.), *The study of lives.* New York: Atherton, 1963. Pp. 40–70.

Keniston, K. *The uncommitted: Alienated youth in American society.* New York: Harcourt, Brace & World, 1965.

Kenny, D. T., & Ginsberg, R. Authoritarian submission attitudes, intolerance of ambiguity, and aggression. *Canadian Journal of Psychology,* 1958, *12,* 121–126.

Kepes, G. (Ed.) *The nature and art of motion.* New York: Braziller, 1965a.

Kepes, G. (Ed.) *Structure in art and in science.* New York: Braziller, 1965b.

Kepes, G. Introduction. In G. Kepes (Ed.), *Structure in art and in science.* New York: Braziller, 1965. Pp. i–vii.

Kimball, S. T., & McClellan, J. E., Jr. *Education and the new America.* New York: Random House, 1962.

King, S. H. Emotional problems of college students: Facts and priorities. *American Association of University Professors Bulletin,* Winter, 1964, 327–332.

King, S. H. Characteristics of students seeking psychiatric help during college. Paper read at the American College Health Association, Washington, D.C., March, 1967a.

King, S. H. Personality stability: Early findings of the Harvard Student Study. Paper read at the American College Personnel Association, Dallas, March, 1967b.

King, S. H.; Bidwell, C. E.; Finnie, B.; & Scarr, H. A. Values and personality development among college men. Paper read at the American Psychological Association, New York, September, 1961.

Klein, G. S. The personal world through perception. In R. R. Blake & G. V. Ramsey (Eds.), *Perception—An approach to personality.* New York: Ronald Press, 1951. Pp. 328–355.

Klein, G. S. Cognitive control and motivation. In G. Lindzey (Ed.), *Assessment of human motives.* New York: Holt, Rinehart and Winston, 1958. Pp. 87–118.

Klein, G. S. Perception, motives and personality. In J. L. McCary (Ed.), *Psychology of personality: Six modern approaches.* (1st ed.: 1956) New York: Grove Press, 1959. Pp. 121–200.

Klein, G. S. Need and regulation. In M. R. Jones (Ed.), *Nebraska symposium on motivation.* Lincoln: University of Nebraska Press, 1960. Pp. 224–274.

Klein, G. S. On hearing one's own voice: An aspect of cognitive control in spoken thought. In N. S. Greenfield & W. C. Lewis (Eds.), *Psychoanalysis and current biological thought.* Madison: University of Wisconsin Press, 1965.

Klein, G. S., & Bruner, J. The functions of perceiving. In B. Kaplan & S. Wapner (Eds.), *Perspectives in personality theory.* New York: International Universities Press, 1960. Pp. 61–77.

Klein, G. S., & Krech, D. The problem of personality and its theory. In G. S. Klein & D. Krech (Eds.), *Theoretical models and personality theory.* Durham, N.C.: Duke University Press, 1952. Pp. 2–23.

Klein, G. S., & Schlesinger, H. Where is the perceiver in perceptual theory? *Journal of Personality*, 1949, *18*, 32–47.

Kluckhohn, C. Have there been discernible shifts in American values during the past generation? In E. E. Morison (Ed.), *The American style.* New York: Harper, 1958. Pp. 145–217.

Kluckhohn, F. R., & Strodtbeck, F. L. *Variations in value orientations.* Evanston, Ill.: Row, Peterson, 1961.

Knoell, D. Institutional research on retention and withdrawal. In H. T. Sprague (Ed.), *Research on college students.* Boulder, Colo.: Western Interstate Commission for Higher Education, & Berkeley, Calif.: Center for Higher Education, 1960. Pp. 41–66.

Koch, S. (Ed.) *Psychology: A study of a science.* New York: McGraw-Hill, 1959–1963. 5 vols.

Koch, S. Psychological science versus the science-humanism antinomy. *American Psychologist*, 1961, *16*, 629–639.

Koffka, K. *Principles of Gestalt psychology.* New York: Harcourt Brace, 1935.

Kohlberg, L. The development of children's orientations toward a moral order: I. Sequence in the development of moral thought. *Vita Humana*, 1963a, *6*, 11–33a.

Kohlberg, L. Moral development and identification. In H. W. Stevenson (Ed.), *Child psychology 62nd Yearbook, National Society for the Study of Education*, Part 1. Chicago: University of Chicago Press, 1963b.

Kohlberg, L. Psychological analysis and literary form: A study of the doubles in Dostoevsky. *Daedalus*, 1963c, *92*, 345–363c.

Kohlberg, L. Development of moral character and moral ideology. *Review of Child Development Research*, 1964, *1*, 383–431.

Köhler, W. *The place of value in a world of facts.* New York: Liveright, 1938.

Köhler, W. *Gestalt psychology: An introduction to new concepts in modern psychology.* New York: Liveright, 1947.

Kris, E. On preconscious mental processes. In *Psychoanalytic explorations in art.* New York: International Universities Press, 1952. Pp. 303–318.

Kris, E. The psychology of caricature. In *Psychoanalytic explorations in art.* New York: International Universities Press, 1952. Pp. 173–188.

Kroeber, A. L. *Style and civilizations.* Ithaca, N.Y.: Cornell University Press, 1957.

Kroeber, T. C. The coping functions of the ego mechanisms. In R. W. White (Ed.), *The study of lives.* New York: Atherton, 1963. Pp. 178–198.

Kubie, L. S. *Neurotic distortion of the creative process.* Lawrence: University of Kansas Press, 1958.

Kuhn, T. S. *The structure of scientific revolutions.* Chicago: University of Chicago Press, 1962.

Kuhn, T. S. The essential tension: Tradition and innovation in scientific research. In C. W. Taylor & F. Barron (Eds.), *Scientific creativity: Its recognition and development.* New York: Wiley, 1963. Pp. 341–354.

Lachman, R. The model in theory construction. (1960) In M. H. Marx (Ed.), *Theories in contemporary psychology.* New York: Macmillan, 1963. Pp. 78–89.

Laing, R. D. *The divided self.* Baltimore: Pelican, 1965.

Lampl-de Groot, J. On defense and development: Normal and pathological. In J. Lampl-de Groot, *The development of the mind.* New York: International Universities Press, 1965. Pp. 273–285.

Lampl-de Groot, J. Remarks on genesis, structuralization, and functioning of the mind. In J. Lampl-de Groot, *The development of the mind.* New York: International Universities Press, 1965. Pp. 364–373.

Landis, P. H. *Adolescence and youth: The process of maturing.* New York: McGraw-Hill, 1945.

Langer, S. *Philosophy in a new key.* (3rd ed.) Cambridge, Mass.: Harvard University Press, 1957.

Lashley, K. S. The problem of stimulus equivalence. VII. Theoretical consideration. In M. H. Marx (Ed.), *Psychological theory: Contemporary readings.* New York: Macmillan, 1951. Pp. 448–452.

Lashley, K. S. The problem of serial order in behavior. In S. Saporta (Ed.), *Psycholinguistics: A book of readings.* New York: Holt, Rinehart and Winston, 1961. Pp. 180–198.

Leach, E. Anthropological aspects of language: animal categories and verbal abuse. In E. Lenneberg (Ed.), *New directions in the study of language.* Cambridge, Mass.: M.I.T. Press, 1964. Pp. 23–63.

Lecky, P. *Self-consistency.* New York: Island Press, 1945.

Lee, D. *Freedom and culture.* Englewood Cliffs, N.J.: Prentice Hall, 1959.

Lee, J. Commitment: Its nature and development in late adolescence. Unpublished qualifying paper, Graduate School of Education, Harvard University, Cambridge, Mass., 1965.

Leeper, R. W. Cognitive processes. In S. S. Stevens (Ed.), *Handbook of experimental psychology.* New York: Wiley, 1951. Pp. 730–757.

Leeper, R. W. Learning and the fields of perception, motivation, and personality. In S. Koch (Ed.), *Psychology: A study of a science.* Vol. 5. *The process areas, the person, and some applied fields.* New York: McGraw-Hill, 1963a. Pp. 365–487.

Leeper, R. W. Theoretical methodology in the psychology of personality. In M. H. Marx (Ed.), *Theories in contemporary psychology.* New York: Macmillan, 1963b. Pp. 389–413b.

Lehmann, I. J., & Ikenberry, S. O. Critical thinking, attitudes and values in higher education. East Lansing: Michigan State University, 1959.

Lenneberg, E. H. The capacity for language acquisition. In J. A. Fodor & J. J. Katz (Eds.), *The structure of language.* Englewood Cliffs, N.J.: Prentice Hall, 1964a. Pp. 579–603a.

Lenneberg, E. H. (Ed.) *New directions in the study of language.* Cambridge, Mass.: M.I.T. Press, 1964b.

Lenneberg, E. H., & Roberts, J. M. The language of experience. In S. Saporta (Ed.), *Psycholinguistics: A book of readings.* New York: Holt, Rinehart and Winston, 1961. Pp. 493–502.

Lerner, E. The problem of perspective in moral reasoning. *American Journal of Sociology,* 1937, *43,* 249–269.

Leventhal, H. Cognitive processes and interpersonal predictions. *Journal of Abnormal and Social Psychology,* 1957, *55,* 176–180.

Levinson, D. Role, personality, and social structure. In L. Coser & B. Rosenberg (Eds.), *Sociology theory.* New York: Macmillan, 1959. Pp. 284–297.

Levy, L. H. *Psychological interpretation.* New York: Holt, Rinehart and Winston, 1963.

Lewin, K. *A dynamic theory of personality.* New York: McGraw-Hill, 1935.

Lewin, K. Comments concerning psychological forces and energies, and the structure of the psyche. In D. Rapaport (Ed.), *Organization and pathology of thought.* New York: Columbia University Press, 1951a. Pp. 76–94.

Lewin, K. *Field theory in social science.* Collected papers. D. Cartwright (Ed.). New York: Harper, 1951b.

Lewin, K. Intention, will and need. In D. Rapaport (Ed.), *Organization and pathology of thought.* New York: Columbia University Press, 1951c. Pp. 95–153c.

Lindzey, G. (Ed.) *Handbook of social psychology.* Vol. 1. *Theory and method.* Reading, Mass.: Addison-Wesley, 1954.

Lindzey, G. (Ed.) *Assessment of human motives.* New York: Holt, Rinehart and Winston, 1958.

Littman, R. Psychology: The socially indifferent science. *American Psychologist,* 1961, *16,* 232–236.

Loevinger, J. A theory of test response. *Proceedings of the Invitational Conference on Testing Problems.* Princeton, N.J.: Educational Testing Service, 1959.

Loevinger, J. Conflict of commitment in clinical research. *American Psychologist,* 1963, *18,* 241–251.

Loomis, S. D., & Green, A. N. The pattern of mental conflict in a typical state university. *Journal of Abnormal and Social Psychology,* 1947, *42,* 342–355.

Lord, F. M. The measurement of growth. *Educational and Psychological Measurement,* 1956, *16,* 421–437.

Lord, F. M. Further problems in the measurement of growth. *Educational and Psychological Measurement,* 1958, *18,* 437–451.

Louise, Sister M. F. Mental growth and development at the college level. *Journal of Educational Psychology,* 1947, *38,* 65–83.

Luce, R. D.; Bush, R. R.; & Galanter, E. (Eds.) *Handbook of mathematical psychology.* Vol. 2. New York: Wiley, 1963.

Lyons, J. *Psychology and the measure of man: A phenomenological approach.* New York: Free Press of Glencoe, 1963.

McArthur, C. Subculture and personality during the college years. *Journal of Educational Sociology,* 1960, *33,* 6.

McCary, J. L. (Ed.) *Psychology of personality: Six modern approaches.* (1st ed.: 1956) New York: Grove Press, 1959.

McClelland, D. C. Personality: An integrated view. In J. McCary (Ed.), *Psychology of personality: Six modern approaches.* New York: Logos, 1956. Pp. 321–366.

McClelland, D. C. The calculated risk: An aspect of scientific performance. In C. W. Taylor & F. Barron (Eds.), *Scientific creativity: Its recognition and development.* New York: Wiley, 1963. Pp. 184–192.

McConnell, T. R., & Heist, P. The diverse college student population. In N. Sanford (Ed.), *The American college.* New York: Wiley, 1962.

McCullers, J. C., & Plant, W. T. Personality and social development: Cultural influence. *Review of Educational Research,* 1964, *34,* 599–610.

McFee, A. The relation of students' needs to their perception of a college environment. *Journal of Educational Psychology,* 1961, *52,* 25–29.

McGuigan, F. J. Psychological changes related to intercultural experiences. *Psychological Reports,* 1958, *4,* 55–60.

McNemar, Q. On growth measurement. *Educational and Psychological Measurement,* 1958, *18,* 47–55.

MacRae, R., Jr. A test of Piaget's theories of moral development. *Journal of Abnormal and Social Psychology,* 1954, *49,* 14–18.

Mandelbaum, M. *The phenomenology of moral experience.* Glencoe, Ill.: Free Press, 1954.

Mandler, G., & Kessen, W. *The language of psychology.* New York: Wiley, 1964.

Martin, E. D. *The meaning of a liberal education.* New York: Norton, 1926.

Marx, M. H. (Ed.) *Psychological theory: Contemporary readings.* New York: Macmillan, 1951.

Marx, M. H. The general nature of theory construction. In M. H. Marx (Ed.), *Theories in contemporary psychology.* New York: Macmillan, 1963. Pp. 4–46.

Marx, M. H. (Ed.) *Theories in contemporary psychology.* New York: Macmillan, 1963.

Marx, M. H., & Hillix, W. A. *Systems and theories in psychology.* New York: McGraw-Hill, 1963.

Maslow, A. *Toward a psychology of being.* New York: Van Nostrand, 1962.

May, R. (Ed.) *Existential psychology.* New York: Random House, 1961.

Mayhew, L. B. And in attitudes. In P. L. Dressel (Ed.), *Evaluation in the basic college.* New York: Harper, 1958.

Mead, G. H. Language and the development of the self. In G. E. Swanson, T. M. Newcomb, & E. L. Hartley (Eds.), *Readings in social psychology.* New York: Holt, 1952, 44–54.

Medalie, J. D. Commitment to work as an aspect of personal development in college students. Unpublished doctoral thesis, Graduate School of Education, Harvard University, Cambridge, Mass., 1964.

Meehl, P. When shall we use our heads instead of the formula? In H. Feigl, M. Scriven, & G. Maxwell (Eds.), *Minnesota studies in the philosophy of science.* Vol. II: *Concepts, theories, and the mind-body problem.* Minneapolis: University of Minnesota Press, 1958. Pp. 498–506.

Merleau-Ponty, M. *The structure of behavior.* (1942) A. L. Fisher (Tr.). Boston: Beacon Press, 1963.

Merton, R. K.; Fiske, M.; & Kendall, P. *The focussed interview: A manual.* New York: Bureau of Applied Social Research, Columbia University, 1952.

Messick, S. J., & Jackson, D. N. Reinterpreting personality correlates of authoritarian attitudes: Some methodological problems. Paper read at Symposium: Redefining authoritarianism, the American Psychological Association, 64th Annual Convention, Chicago, 1956.

Messick, S. J., & Ross, J. (Eds.) *Measurement in personality and cognition.* New York: Wiley, 1962.

Michaels, J. Character structure and character disorders. In S. Ariet (Ed.), *American handbook of psychiatry.* New York: Basic Books, 1959.

Miller, D. R. The study of social relationships: Situation, identity, and social interaction. In S. Koch (Ed.), *Psychology: A study of a science.* Vol. 5. *The process areas, the person, and some applied fields.* New York: McGraw-Hill, 1963. Pp. 639–737.

Miller, G. A. The magical number seven, plus or minus two: Some limits on our capacity for processing information. In D. C. Beardslee & M. Wertheimer (Eds.), *Readings in perception.* Princeton, N.J.: Van Nostrand, 1958. Pp. 90–114.

Miller, G. A. *Language and communication.* New York: McGraw-Hill, 1963.

Miller, G. A. Language and psychology. In E. H. Lenneberg (Ed.), *New directions in the study of language.* Cambridge, Mass.: M.I.T. Press, 1964a. Pp. 89–107a.

Miller, G. A. *Mathematics and psychology.* New York: Wiley, 1964b.

Miller, G. A. Some preliminaries to psycholinguistics. *American Psychologist,* 1965, *20,* 15–20.

Miller, G. A., & Chomsky, N. Finitary models of language users. In R. D. Luce, R. R. Bush, & E. Galanter (Eds.), *Handbook of mathematical psychology.* Vol. 2. New York: Wiley, 1963. Pp. 419–491.

Miller, G. A.; Galanter, E.; & Pribram, K. H. *Plans and the structure of behavior.* New York: Holt, 1960.

Miller, G. A., & Selfridge, J. A. Verbal context and the recall of meaningful material. In S. Saporta (Ed.), *Psycholinguistics: A book of readings.* New York: Holt, Rinehart and Winston, 1961. Pp. 198–206.

Miller, J. Toward a general theory for the behavioral sciences. *American Psychologist,* 1955, *10,* 513–531.

Mooney, R. L. A conceptual model for integrating four approaches to the identification of creative talent. In C. W. Taylor & F. Barron (Eds.), *Scientific creativity: Its recognition and development.* New York: Wiley, 1963. Pp. 331–340.

Morris, C. *Paths of life.* New York: Harper, 1942.

Morris, C. *Signs, languages, and behavior.* (1st ed.: 1946) New York: Braziller, 1955.

Morris, C. *Varieties of human value.* Chicago: University of Chicago Press, 1956.

Morris, C. *Signification and significance.* Cambridge, Mass.: M.I.T. Press, 1964.

Murphy, G. *Personality: A biosocial approach to origins and structure.* New York: Harper, 1947.

Murphy, L. B. Coping devices and defense mechanisms in relation to autonomous ego functions. *Bulletin of the Menninger Clinic,* 1960, *24,* 144–153.

Murphy, L. B., & Raushenbush, E. (Eds.) *Achievement in the college years.* New York: Harper, 1960.

Murray, H. A. et al. *Explorations in personality: A clinical and experimental study of fifty men of college age.* New York: Oxford University Press, 1938.

Murray, H. A. Drive, time, strategy, measurement, and our way of life. In G. Lindzey (Ed.), *Assessment of human motives.* New York: Holt, Rinehart and Winston, 1958. Pp. 183–196.

Murray, H. A. The meaning and content of individuality in contemporary America. In H. M. Ruitenbeek (Ed.), *Varieties of modern social theory.* New York: Dutton, 1963. Pp. 151–175.

Murray, H. A., & Kluckhohn, C. Outline of a conception of personality. In C. Kluckhohn, H. Murray, & D. Schneider (Eds.), *Personality in nature, society, and culture.* (2nd ed.) New York: Knopf, 1961. Pp. 3–49.

Nagel, E. *The structure of science.* New York: Harcourt, Brace & World, 1961.

Nagel, E., & Newman, J. R. *Gödel's proof.* New York: New York University Press, 1958.

Neisser, U. The multiplicity of thought. *British Journal of Psychology,* 1963, *54,* 1–14.

Nettler, G. Test burning in Texas. *American Psychologist,* 1959, *14,* 682–683.

Newcomb, T. M. *Personality and social change: Attitude formation in a student community.* New York: Dryden Press, 1943.

Newcomb, T. M. Individual systems of orientation. In S. Koch (Ed.), *Psychology: A study of a science.* Vol. 3. *Formulations of the person and the social context.* New York: McGraw-Hill, 1959. Pp. 384–422.

Newcomb, T. M. Exploiting student resources. In H. T. Sprague (Ed.), *Research on college students.* Boulder, Colo.: Western Interstate Commission for Higher Education, & Berkeley, Calif.: Center for Higher Education, 1960. Pp. 6–20.

Newell, A.; Shaw, J. C.; & Simon, H. A. Elements of a theory of human problem-solving. In R. J. C. Harper, C. C. Anderson, C. M. Christensen, & S. M. Hunka (Eds.), *The cognitive processes: Readings.* Englewood Cliffs, N.J.: Prentice Hall, 1964. Pp. 339–356.

Nixon, R. E. Approach to the dynamics of growth in adolescence. *Psychiatry,* 1961, *24,* 18–31.

Ogden, C. K., & Richards, I. A. *The meaning of meaning.* New York: Harcourt, Brace, 1956.

O'Hara, R. P., & Tiedeman, D. V. Vocational self concept in adolescence. *Journal of Counseling Psychology,* 1959, *6,* 292–301.

Olafson, F. A. Meta-ethics and the moral life. *Philosophical Review,* 1956, *65,* 159–178.

Olafson, F. A. Two views of pluralism: Liberal and Catholic. *Yale Review,* 1962, *51,* 519–531.

Oppenheimer, R. Analogy in science. *American Psychologist,* 1956, *11,* 127–135.

Pace, C. R. Five college environments. *College Board Review,* 1960, *41,* 24–28.

Pace, C. R., & Stern, G. G. An approach to the measurement of psychological characteristics of college environments. *Journal of Educational Psychology,* 1958, *49,* 269–277.

Palubinskas, A. L. Personality changes in college women during four years of college experience. *Proceedings of the Iowa Academy of Science,* 1952, *59,* 389–391.

Parsons, T. An approach to psychological theory in terms of the theory of action. In S. Koch (Ed.), *Psychology: A study of a science.* Vol. III. New York: McGraw-Hill, 1959. Pp. 612–712.

Paul, I. H. Studies in remembering. In G. S. Klein (Ed.), *Psychological Issues.* Vol. 1 (2). New York: International Universities Press, 1959.

Peck, R. F., with Havighurst, R. J. *The psychology of character development.* New York: Wiley, 1960.

Peckham, M. *Beyond the tragic vision.* New York: Braziller, 1962.

Peirce, C. S. *Values in a universe of chance.* P. P. Wiener (Ed.). Stanford, Calif.: Stanford University Press, 1958.

Pepper, S. *World hypothesis.* Berkeley: University of California Press, 1942.

Perry, W. G., Jr. Examsmanship and the liberal arts: A study in educational epistemology. In L. Bramson (Ed.), *Examining in Harvard College: A collection of essays by members of the Harvard Faculty.* Cambridge, Mass.: Faculty of Arts and Sciences, Harvard University, 1963. Pp. 125–135.

Perry, W. G., Jr. *Patterns of development in thought and values of students in a liberal arts college: A validation of a scheme.* U.S. Department of Health, Education, and Welfare, Office of Education, Bureau of Research, Final Report, Project No. 5–0825, Contract No. SAE–8973, April 1968.

Piaget, J. *The child's conception of the world.* London: Routledge & Kegan Paul, 1928.

Piaget, J. *The psychology of intelligence.* New York: Harcourt, Brace, 1950.

Piaget, J. *Logic and psychology.* New York: Basic Books, 1957.

Piaget, J. *The moral judgment of the child.* (1st ed.: 1932) New York: Collier, 1962.

Pikas, A. *Abstraction and concept formation.* Cambridge, Mass.: Harvard University Press, 1966.

Pike, K. L. Towards a theory of the structure of human behavior. In D. Hymes (Ed.), *Language in culture and society.* New York: Harper & Row, 1964. Pp. 54–62.

Planck, M. *The philosophy of physics.* W. H. Johnston (Tr.). (1st ed.: 1936) New York: Norton, 1963.

Plant, W. T. Changes in ethnocentrism associated with a four-year college education. *Journal of Educational Psychology,* 1958a, *49,* 162–165a.

Plant, W. T. Changes in ethnocentrism associated with a two-year college experience. *Journal of Genetic Psychology,* 1958b, *92,* 189–197b.

Poincaré, H. *Science and method.* F. Maitland (Tr.). New York: Dover, 1952.

Polanyi, M. *Personal knowledge: Towards a postcritical philosophy.* Chicago: University of Chicago Press, 1958.

Postman, L. Toward a general theory of cognition. In J. H. Rohrer & M. Sherif (Eds.), *Social psychology at the crossroads.* New York: Harper, 1951. Pp. 242–272.

Postman, L. (Ed.) *Psychology in the making.* New York: Knopf, 1963.

Postman, L., & Tolman, E. C. Brunswik's probabilistic functionalism. In S. Koch (Ed.), *Psychology: A study of a science.* Vol. 1. *Sensory, perceptual, and physiological formulations.* New York: McGraw-Hill, 1959. Pp. 502–564.

Pötzl, O.; Allers, R.; & Teler, J. Preconscious stimulation in dreams, associations, and images. In G. S. Klein (Ed.), *Psychological Issues.* Vol. 2 (3). New York: International Universities Press, 1960.

Prelinger, E. Identity diffusion and the synthetic function. In B. Wedge (Ed.), *Psychosocial problems of college men.* New Haven, Conn.: Yale University Press, 1958. Pp. 214–241.

Prelinger, E., & Zimet, C. N. *An ego-psychological approach to character assessment.* New York: Free Press, 1964.

Prentice, W. C. H. Recent social change and its impact on higher education. *Educational Record,* 1960, *41,* 329–335.

Privette, P. G. Factors associated with functioning which transcends modal behavior. Unpublished doctoral dissertation, University of Florida, 1964. (Abstract: *Dissertation Abstracts,* 1964, *25,* 3406.)

Quine, W. van O. *From a logical point of view.* (1st ed.: 1953) New York: Harper & Row, 1963.

Quine, W. van O. On what there is. In *From a logical point of view.* (1st ed.: 1953) New York: Harper & Row, 1963. Pp. 1–19.

Quine, W. van O. Two dogmas of empiricism. In *From a logical point of view.* (1st ed.: 1953) New York: Harper & Row, 1963. Pp. 20–46.

Quine, W. van O. *Word and object.* (1st ed.: 1960) Cambridge, Mass.: M.I.T. Press, 1964.

Rapaport, D. Dynamic psychology and Kantian epistemology. Unpublished paper presented at the staff seminar of the Menninger Foundation School of Clinical Psychology, 1947.

Rapaport, D. (Ed.) *Organization and pathology of thought.* New York: Columbia University Press, 1951.

Rapaport, D. Toward a theory of thinking. In D. Rapaport (Ed.), *Organization and pathology of thought.* New York: Columbia University Press, 1951. Pp. 689–730.

Rapaport, D. Some metapsychological considerations concerning activity and passivity. Unpublished paper, Austin Riggs Center, Stockbridge, Mass., 1953.

Rapaport, D. Cognitive structures. In H. Gruber, K. Hammond, & R. Jessor (Eds.), *Contemporary approaches to cognition.* Cambridge, Mass.: Harvard University Press, 1957. Pp. 157–200.

Rapaport, D. The theory of ego autonomy: A generalization. *Bulletin of the Menninger Clinic,* 1958, *22,* 13–35.

Rapaport, D. A historical survey of psychoanalytic ego psychology. In G. S. Klein (Ed.), *Psychological Issues.* Vol. I (1). New York: International Universities Press, 1959. Pp. 5–17.

Rapaport, D. On the psychoanalytic theory of motivation. In M. R. Jones (Ed.), *Nebraska symposium on motivation.* Lincoln: University of Nebraska Press, 1960a. Pp. 173–247a.

Rapaport, D. The structure of psychoanalytic theory. In G. S. Klein (Ed.), *Psychological Issues.* Vol. 2 (2). New York: International Universities Press, 1960b.

Rapaport, D., & Gill, M. The points of view and assumptions of metapsychology. *International Journal of Psycho-Analysis,* 1959, *40,* 1–10.

Rapoport, A. *Fights, games, and debates.* Ann Arbor: University of Michigan Press, 1960.

Raushenbush, E. *The student and his studies.* Middletown, Conn.: Wesleyan University Press, 1964.

Redl, F., & Wineman, D. *Controls from within.* Glencoe, Ill.: Free Press, 1952.

Reich, W. *Character analysis.* (1933) New York: Noonday, 1949.

Richards, I. A. Structure and communication. In G. Kepes (Ed.), *Structure in art and in science.* New York: Braziller, 1965. Pp. 128–136.

Rickey, G. The morphology of movement: A study of kinetic art. In G. Kepes (Ed.), *The nature and art of motion.* New York: Braziller, 1965. Pp. 81–114.

Riesman, D. *The lonely crowd.* New Haven, Conn.: Yale University Press, 1950.

Riesman, D. *Constraint and variety in American education.* New York: Doubleday Anchor, 1958a.

Riesman, D. A review of the Jacob Report. *American Sociological Review,* 1958b, *23,* 732–739.

Riesman, D. The academic career: Notes on recruitment and colleagueship. *Daedalus,* 1959a, *88,* 147–169.

Riesman, D. The influence of student culture and faculty values in the American college. In G. Z. F. Bereday & J. A. Lauwerys (Eds.), *The year book of education 1959*. Higher Education. Yonkers-on-Hudson, N.Y.: World Book, 1959b.

Riesman, D. The uncommitted generation. *Encounter,* 1960, *15,* 25–30.

Roe, A. Man's forgotten weapon. *American Psychologist,* 1959, *14,* 261–266.

Rogers, C. *On becoming a person.* Boston: Houghton Mifflin, 1961.

Rokeach, M. A method for studying individual differences in "narrow-mindedness." *Journal of Personality,* 1951, *20,* 219–233.

Rokeach, M. The nature and meaning of dogmatism. *Psychological Review,* 1954, *61,* 194–204.

Rokeach, M. *The open and closed mind.* New York: Basic Books, 1960.

Rokeach, M.; McGovney, W. C.; & Denny, M. R. A distinction between dogmatic and rigid thinking. *Journal of Abnormal and Social Psychology,* 1955, *51,* 87–93.

Royce, J. *The encapsulated man.* Princeton, N.J.: Van Nostrand, 1964.

Rubin, E. Figure and ground. In D. C. Beardslee & M. Wertheimer (Eds.), *Readings in perception.* Princeton, N.J.: Van Nostrand, 1958. Pp. 194–203.

Ryle, G. *The concept of mind.* (1st ed.: 1949) New York: Barnes & Noble, 1962.

Sanders, M. Intellectual activity as adaptive behavior. Unpublished qualifying paper, Graduate School of Education, Harvard University, Cambridge, Mass., 1962.

Sanford, F. Creative health and the principle of *Habaes Mentem. American Psychologist,* 1955, *10,* 829–835.

Sanford, N. (Ed.) Personality development during the college years. *Journal of Social Issues,* 1956, *12*(4).

Sanford, N. The approach of the authoritarian personality. In J. L. McCary (Ed.), *Psychology of personality: Six modern approaches.* (1st ed.: 1956) New York: Grove Press, 1959.

Sanford, N. Motivation of high achievers. In O. David (Ed.), *The education of women.* Washington, D.C.: American Council on Education, 1959. Pp. 34–38.

Sanford, N. (Ed.) *The American college.* New York: Wiley, 1962.

Sanford, N. Developmental status of the entering freshman. In N. Sanford (Ed.), *The American college.* New York: Wiley, 1962.

Sanford, N. Research and policy in higher education. In N. Sanford (Ed.), *The American college.* New York: Wiley, 1962.

Saporta, S. (Ed.) *Psycholinguistics: A book of readings.* New York: Holt, Rinehart and Winston, 1961.

Sarbin, T. R.; Taft, R.; & Bailey, D. C. *Clinical inference and cognitive theory.* New York: Holt, Rinehart and Winston, 1960.

Sargent, H. Intrapsychic change: Methodological problems in psychotherapy research. *Psychiatry,* 1961, *24,* 93–108.

Schachtel, E. *Metamorphosis.* New York: Basic Books, 1959.

Schafer, R. Regression in the service of the ego: The relevance of a psychoanalytic concept for personality assessment. In G. Lindzey (Ed.), *Assessment of human motives.* New York: Holt, Rinehart and Winston, 1958. Pp. 119–148.

Scheerer, M. Cognitive theory. In G. Lindzey (Ed.), *Handbook of social psychology.* Vol. 1. *Theory and method.* Reading, Mass.: Addison-Wesley, 1954. Pp. 91–142.

Scheffler, I. Explanation, prediction, and abstraction. In A. Danto & S. Morgenbesser (Eds.), *Philosophy of science.* Cleveland: World Publishing, 1960a. Pp. 274–287.

Scheffler, I. *The language of education.* Springfield, Ill.: Thomas, 1960b.

Scheffler, I. Theoretical terms and a modest empiricism. In A. Danto & S. Morgenbesser (Eds.), *Philosophy of science.* Cleveland: World Publishing, 1960c. Pp. 159–173.

Scheffler, I. *The anatomy of inquiry.* New York: Knopf, 1963.

Schiller, F. *On the aesthetic education of man.* New York: Ungar, 1954.

Schrödinger, E. C. *Science theory and man.* (1st ed.: 1935) New York: Dover, 1957.

Schrödinger, E. C. *What is life?* (1st ed.: 1944) Cambridge, England: Cambridge University Press, 1962.

Scott, W. Research definitions of mental health and mental illness. *Psychological Bulletin,* 1958, *55,* 29–45.

Scott, W. Cognitive complexity and cognitive flexibility. *Sociometry,* 1962, *25,* 405–414.

Seward, J. The structure of functional autonomy. *American Psychologist,* 1963, *18,* 703–710.

Shils, E. A. Authoritarianism: "Right" and "left." In R. Christie & M. Jahoda (Eds.), *Studies in the scope and method of the authoritarian personality.* Glencoe, Ill.: Free Press, 1954. Pp. 24–49.

Simon, H. A., & Newell, A. The uses and limitations of models. In M. H. Marx (Ed.), *Theories in contemporary psychology.* New York: Macmillan, 1963. Pp. 89–104.

Skinner, B. F. *Cumulative record.* New York: Appleton, 1961a.

Skinner, B. F. A functional analysis of verbal behavior. In S. Saporta (Ed.), *Psycholinguistics: A book of readings.* New York: Holt, Rinehart and Winston, 1961b. Pp. 67–74.

Smith, H. *Purposes of higher education.* New York: Harper & Row, 1955.

Smith, J. E. *Value convictions and higher education.* New Haven, Conn.: Hazen Foundation, 1958.

Smith, M. B. Mental health reconsidered: A special case of the problem of values in psychology. *American Psychologist,* 1961, *16,* 299–306.

Smith, M. B.; Bruner, J. S.; & White, R. W. *Opinions and personality.* New York: Wiley, 1964.

Snygg, D. The phenomenological field. II. Inadequacy of the objective approach for prediction of human behavior. III. The characteristics of a phenomenological system. In M. H. Marx (Ed.), *Psychological theory: Contemporary readings.* New York: Macmillan, 1951. Pp. 324–330.

Solley, C., & Murphy, G. *Development of the perceptual world.* New York: Basic Books, 1960.

Soskin, W. F. Influence of four types of data on diagnostic conceptualization in psychological testing. *Journal of Abnormal and Social Psychology,* 1959, *58,* 69–78.

Spiegel, J. P. A model for relationships among systems. In R. Grinker (Ed.), *Toward a unified theory of human behavior.* New York: Basic Books, 1956. Pp. 16–26.

Spitz, R. A. *A genetic field theory of ego formation.* New York: International Universities Press, 1959.

Sprague, H. T. (Ed.) *Research on college students.* Boulder, Colo.: Western Interstate Commission for Higher Education, & Berkeley, Calif.: Center for Higher Education, 1960.

Stein, M., & Heinze, S. *Creativity and the individual: Summaries of selected literature in psychology and psychiatry.* New York: Free Press, 1960.

Stern, G. G. *Inventory of beliefs.* University of Chicago, 1953.

Stern, G. G. Assessing theological student personality structure. *Journal of Pastoral Care,* 1954, *18,* 76–83.

Stern, G. G. Congruence and dissonance in the ecology of college students. *Student Medicine,* 1960a, *8,* 304–339.

Stern, G. G. Student values and their relationship to the college environment. In H. T. Sprague (Ed.), *Research on college students.* Boulder, Colo.: Western Interstate Commission for Higher Education, & Berkeley, Calif.: Center for Higher Education, 1960b. Pp. 67–104.

Stern, G. G. Continuity and contrast in the transition from high school to college. In N. F. Brown (Ed.), *Orientation to college learning—A reappraisal.* Washington, D.C.: American Council on Education, 1961.

Stern, G. G. Environments for learning. In N. Sanford (Ed.), *The American college.* New York: Wiley, 1962a.

Stern, G. G. The measurement of psychological characteristics of students and learning environments. In S. Messick & J. Ross (Eds.), *Measurement in personality and cognition.* New York: Wiley, 1962b. Pp. 27–68.

Stern, G. G., & Cope, A. H. Differences in educability between stereopaths, non-stereopaths, and rationals. Paper read at the American Psychological Association, 64th Annual Convention, Chicago, September, 1956. (Abstract in *American Psychologist,* 1956, *11*, 362.)

Stern, G. G.; Stein, M. I.; & Bloom, B. S. *Methods in personality assessment.* Glencoe, Ill.: Free Press, 1956.

Sternberg, C. Personality trait patterns of college students majoring in different fields. *Psychological Monographs,* 1955, *69* (Whole No. 403).

Stevens, S. S. (Ed.) *Handbook of experimental psychology.* New York: Wiley, 1951a.

Stevens, S. S. Psychology and the science of science. In M. H. Marx (Ed.), *Psychological theory.* New York: Macmillan, 1951b. Pp. 21–54.

Stevens, S. S. On the theory of scales of measurement. (1946) In A. Danto & S. Morgenbesser (Eds.), *Philosophy of science.* New York: World, 1960. Pp. 141–149.

Stevenson, C. L. *Facts and values. Studies in ethical analysis.* New Haven, Conn.: Yale University Press, 1963.

Suchman, E. A. The values of American college students. In A. E. Traxler (Ed.), *Long range planning for education.* Washington, D.C.: American Council on Education, 1958.

Taylor, C. W., & Barron, F. (Eds.) *Scientific creativity: Its recognition and development.* New York: Wiley, 1963.

Taylor, D. W. Thinking. In M. H. Marx (Ed.), *Theories in contemporary psychology.* New York: Macmillan, 1963. Pp. 475–493.

Taylor, H. Freedom and authority on the campus. In N. Sanford (Ed.), *The American college.* New York: Wiley, 1962. Pp. 774–804.

Thistlethwaite, D. L. College press and student achievement. *Journal of Educational Psychology,* 1959, *50,* 183–191.

Tiedeman, D. V., & O'Hara, R. P. *Career development: Choice and adjustment.* New York: College Entrance Examination Board, 1963.

Tillich, P. *The courage to be.* New Haven: Yale University Press, 1952.

Tolman, E. C. *Purposive behavior in animals and men.* New York: Century, 1932.

Tolman, E. C. A psychological model. In T. Parsons & E. A. Shils (Eds.), *Toward a general theory of action.* Cambridge, Mass.: Harvard University Press, 1951a. Pp. 279–342.

Tolman, E. C. The intervening variable. In M. H. Marx (Ed.), *Psychological*

theory: Contemporary readings. New York: Macmillan, 1951b.
Pp. 87–102.

Tolman, E. C. Principles of purposive behavior. In S. Koch (Ed.), *Psychology: A study of a science.* Vol. 2. *General systematic formulations, learning, and special processes.* New York: McGraw-Hill, 1959.
Pp. 92–157.

Townsend, A. *College freshmen speak out.* New York: Harper, 1956.

Tripodi, T., & Bieri, J. Cognitive complexity as a function of own and provided constructs. *Psychological Reports,* 1963, *13,* 26.

Trow, M. The campus viewed as a culture. In H. T. Stern (Ed.), *Research on college students.* Boulder, Colo.: Western Interstate Commission for Higher Education, & Berkeley, Calif.: Center for Higher Education, 1960a. Pp. 105–123.

Trow, M. Cultural sophistication and higher education. In Center for the Study of Higher Education (Ed.), *Selection and educational differentiation: Proceedings.* Berkeley, Calif.: Editor, 1960b.

Tuddenham, R. D. The nature and measurement of intelligence. In L. Postman (Ed.), *Psychology in the making.* New York: Knopf, 1963. Pp. 469–525.

Tymieniecka, A. *Phenomenology and science in contemporary European thought.* New York: Noonday, 1962.

Van Bertalanffy, L. The theory of open systems in physics and biology. *Science,* 1950, *3,* 23–29.

Van de Geer, J., & Jaspars, J. Cognitive functions. In P. R. Farnsworth, O. McNemar, & Q. McNemar (Eds.), *Annual Review of Psychology.* Vol. XVII, 1966. Pp. 145–176.

Vannoy, J. S. Generality of cognitive complexity-simplicity as a personality construct. *Journal of Personality and Social Psychology,* 1965, *2,* 385–396.

Vreeland, R. S. Patterns of heterosexual relations among Harvard men. *Journal of American College Health Association,* April, 1968.

Vreeland, R. S., & Bidwell, C. E. Organizational effects on student attitudes: A study of the Harvard houses. *Sociology of Education,* 1965, *38,* 233–250.

Vreeland, R. S., & Bidwell, C. E. Classifying university departments: An approach to the analysis of their effects upon undergraduates' values and attitudes. *Sociology of Education,* 1966, *39,* 237–254.

Vygotsky, L. Thought and speech. (1934) In S. Saporta (Ed.), *Psycholinguistics.* New York: Holt, Rinehart and Winston, 1961. Pp. 509–536.

Waelder, R. The principle of multiple function: Observations on overdetermination. (1930) *Psychoanalytic Quarterly,* 1936, *5,* 45–62.

Waelder, R. *Basic theory of psychoanalysis.* New York: International Universities Press, 1960.

Walker, H. M., & Lev, J. *Statistical inference.* New York: Holt, 1953.

Wallach, M. A. Commentary: Active-analytical vs. passive-global cognitive functioning. In S. Messick & J. Ross (Eds.), *Measurement in personality and cognition.* New York: Wiley, 1962. Pp. 199–215.

Wallach, M. A. On psychological similarity. In R. J. C. Harper, C. C. Anderson, C. M. Christensen, & S. M. Hunka (Eds.), *The cognitive processes: Readings.* Englewood Cliffs, N.J.: Prentice Hall, 1964. Pp. 256–271.

Webster, H. Some quantitative results. In N. Sanford (Ed.), Personality development during the college years. *Journal of Social Issues,* 1956, *12,* 29–43.

Webster, H. Changes in attitudes during college. *Journal of Educational Psychology,* 1958, *49,* 109–117.

Webster, H.; Freedman, M. B.; & Heist, P. Personality changes in college students. In N. Sanford (Ed.), *The American college.* New York: Wiley, 1962.

Webster, H.; Sanford, N.; & Freedman, M. A new instrument for studying authoritarianism in personality. *Journal of Psychology,* 1955, *40,* 73–84.

Wedge, B. M. (Ed.) *Psychosocial problems of college men.* New Haven, Conn.: Yale University Press, 1958.

Weiss, P. The logic of the creative process. In P. P. Wiener & F. H. Young (Eds.), *Studies in the philosophy of Charles Sanders Peirce.* Cambridge, Mass.: Harvard University Press, 1952.

Weisskopf-Joelson, E. Some suggestions concerning Weltanschauung and psychotherapy. *Journal of Abnormal and Social Psychology,* 1953, *48,* 601–604.

Werner, H. Process and achievement: A basic problem of education and developmental psychology. *Harvard Educational Review,* 1937, 353–368.

Werner, H. Abnormal and subnormal rigidity. *Journal of Abnormal and Social Psychology,* 1948, *41,* 15–24.

Werner, H. *Comparative psychology of mental development.* (1st ed.: 1948) New York: Science Editions, 1961.

Werner, H., & Kaplan, B. *Symbol formation.* New York: Wiley, 1963.

Werner, H., & Wapner, S. Toward a general theory of perception. In D. C. Beardslee & M. Wertheimer (Eds.), *Readings in perception.* Princeton, N.J.: Van Nostrand, 1958. Pp. 491–512.

Wertheimer, M. *Productive thinking.* New York: Harper, 1945.

Wertheimer, M. Principles of perceptual organization. In D. C. Beardslee & M. Wertheimer (Eds.), *Readings in perception.* Princeton, N.J.: Van Nostrand, 1958. Pp. 115–135.

Wheelwright, P. *Metaphor and reality.* Bloomington: Indiana University Press, 1962.

White, M. *Toward reunion in philosophy.* (1st ed.: 1956) New York: Atheneum, 1963.

White, R. W. *Lives in progress.* New York: Dryden Press, 1952.

White, R. W. Motivation reconsidered: The concept of competence. *Psychological Review,* 1959, *66,* 297–333.

White, R. W. Competence and the psychosexual stages of development. In M. R. Jones (Ed.), *Nebraska symposium on motivation.* Lincoln: University of Nebraska Press, 1960. Pp. 97–144.

White, R. W. Ego and reality in psychoanalytic theory. In G. S. Klein (Ed.), *Psychological Issues.* Vol. 3 (3). New York: International Universities Press, 1963a.

White, R. W. (Ed.) *The study of lives.* New York: Atherton, 1963b.

Whitehead, A. N. *Modes of thought.* (1st ed.: 1938) New York: Macmillan, 1957.

Whitehead, A. N. *Science and the modern world.* (1st ed.: 1925) New York: Macmillan, 1957.

Whitehead, A. N. *The function of reason.* (1st ed.: 1929) Boston: Beacon Press, 1962.

Whitla, D. K. Life style study. Progress report. Harvard University, January, 1965. Mimeo.

Whyte, L. L. Atomism, structure and form. In G. Kepes (Ed.), *Structure in art and in science.* New York: Braziller, 1965. Pp. 20–28.

Wiener, P. P., & Young, F. H. (Eds.) *Studies in the philosophy of Charles Sanders Peirce.* Cambridge, Mass.: Harvard University Press, 1952.

Winer, B. J. *Statistical principles in experimental design.* New York: McGraw-Hill, 1962.

Wise, W. M. *They come for the best of reasons: college students today.* Washington, D.C.: American Council on Education, 1958.

Wispé, L. G. Evaluating section teaching methods in the introductory course. *Journal of Educational Research,* 1951, *45,* 161–186.

Witkin, H. A. *Personality through perception.* New York: Harper, 1953.

Witkin, H. A. The nature and importance of individual differences in perception. In D. C. Beardslee & M. Wertheimer (Eds.), *Readings in perception.* Princeton, N.J.: Van Nostrand, 1958. Pp. 513–524.

Witkin, H. A.; Dyk, R. B.; Faterson, H. F.; Goodenough, D. R.; & Karp,

S. A. *Psychological differentiation: Studies of development.* New York: Wiley, 1962.

Wittgenstein, L. *Philosophical investigations.* New York: Macmillan, 1953.

Zigler, E. Metatheoretical issues in developmental psychology. In M. H. Marx (Ed.), *Theories in contemporary psychology.* New York: Macmillan, 1963. Pp. 341–369.

━ Index

A

Absolute truth: as distinct from Authority, 74–76, 99; as domain of Authority, 102, 107; presumed existence of, 74

Action versus contemplation, 196–197

Adams, H. B., 5, 6, 39–40

Adolescent revolt, and modern liberal education, 80–81

Adorno, T. W., 8

Aiken, H. D., 226

Alienation, 18; findings on, 199, 214; prevention of, 223; and resumption of growth, 221–223. *See also* Escape

Allport, F., 59

Alternatives to Positions. *See* Escape; Retreat; Temporizing

Analysis versus synthesis, 163–164

Angyal, A., 58

Anti-intellectualism, 44

Anxiety, 58

Authority: anger at, 208–211; as distinct from Absolute truth, 74–76, 99; as mediator, 74–75; omniscience of, 66, 68–69, 71, 74, 95–96, 99, 102; presumed ignorance of, 108; relations to, in relativistic epistemology, 135–140; true versus fraudulent, 74, 76–77

Authority-oriented structure, modification of, 68, 72–73

B

Barrett, W., 226

Brown, R., 27

C

Camus, A., 226

Checklist of Educational Views (CLEV), 8, 17–18

Choice, dualism versus relativism in, 192

Cohen, B. D., 27

Cohen, E., 27

Commitment: as act of affirmation, 38–39; acting versus contemplating in, 196–197; analysis versus synthesis and, 163–164; certainty versus doubt and, 189, 193; choice versus external influence in, 188; to Commitment, 165–167; competing values in, 192–193; concept of, 151–152; confidence in identity versus confusion and, 191–192; considered conformity versus blind conformity and, 234; continuity versus breaking with past in, 164–165; detachment versus involvement and, 164, 178–179, 181; development of, 192; faith versus external reasons and, 189; gains in focus versus loss in alternatives and, 189–190; idealism versus realism and, 190;

identification and, 194–196; identity and, 152; inclusiveness versus intensity and, 187;

initial, 170–171, 172–176; intrinsic values versus external symbols and, 188; limits of reason and, 197; narrowness versus breadth of

GLOSSARY

The following glossary is reproduced from the *Judge's Manual*. It provides a reference for certain terms appearing in the text, and on the Chart, to which a particular meaning is assigned.

Absolute

The established Order; The Truth, conceived to be the creation and possession of the Deity, or simply to exist, as in a Platonic world of its own; The Ultimate Criterion, in respect to which all propositions and acts are either right or wrong.

Accommodation

The modification or reorganization of a structure in response to incongruities produced by assimilations.

Adherence   Chart code: A (contrast Opposition)

1. Alignment of self with Authority in a Dualistic structuring of the world; or
2. In parentheses: (A), a "conservative" preference in a relativistic structuring of the world.

Assimilation   Chart code: parentheses ( )

The connection of a new percept to an extant structure. This may require various degrees of subordination of the implications of the new percept to the demands of an extant structure, and/or various degrees of accommodation of the structure.

On the Chart, the quantity within the parentheses is to be read as assimilated to the structure preceding the parenthesis; for example, 4A(M) reads "Multiplicity assimilated to Adherence in structure of Position 4."

Authority   (upper-case A)

The possessors of the right answers in the Absolute, or the mediators of same (as viewed in Adherence); or the false or unfair pretenders to the right answers in the Absolute (as viewed in Opposition).

authority   (lower-case a)

An aspect of social organization and interaction in a relative world, with many differentiations (e.g., power, expertise, etc.).

Commitment   Chart code: C

An affirmation of personal values or choice in Relativism. A conscious act or realization of identity and responsibility. A process of orientation of self in a relative world.

The word Commitment (capital C) is reserved for this integrative, affirmative function, as distinct from 1) commitment to an unquestioned or unexamined belief, plan, or value, or 2) commitment to negativistic alienation or dissociation.

defensive   (adjective descriptive of Adherence or Opposition)   Chart code: Ad or Op

Adherence or Opposition functioning in internal structures of emotional control so as to produce high resistance to qualification, ambiguity, or change.

Dualism or Duality   (upper-case D)

A bifurcated structuring of the world between Good and Bad, Right and Wrong, We and Others.

Complex Dualism—a Dualism in which one element is itself dualistically structured.

dualism or duality   (lower-case d)

Any binary function in a relative world, e.g., the right/wrong quality of a proposition in a specified context.

Escape

The denial of the implications for growth in Positions 4 and 5 by Dissociation or Encapsulation in the structure of these Positions.

Dissociation   Chart code: D

Sustained opportunistic denial of responsibilities implied for the self in Multiplicity or Relativism.

Encapsulation   Chart code: E

Consolidated assimilation of Multiplicity or Relativism to a Dualistic structure, projecting responsibility on Authority.

Growth

Progression from one structure to a higher structure as defined in the scheme.

Multiplicity   Chart code: M

A plurality of "answers," points of view, or evaluations, with reference to similar topics or problems. This plurality is perceived as an aggregate of discretes without internal structure or external relation, in the sense, "Anyone has a right to his own opinion," with the implication that no judgments among opinions can be made. (compare Relativism)

Opposition   Chart code: O (contrast Adherence)

1. Alignment vs. Authority in a Dualistic structuring of the world; or
2. In parentheses: (O), a preference for change and experimentation, as opposed to conservatism, in a relativistic structuring of the world.

Position   (1 to 9 etc. on the Chart)

That structure representing the mode, or central tendency, among the forms through which an individual construes the world of knowledge and values at a given time in his life.

Relativism   Chart code: R

A plurality of points of view, interpretations, frames of reference, value systems, and contingencies in which the structural properties of contexts and forms allow of various sorts of analysis, comparison, and evaluation in Multiplicity.

Retreat

An active rejection of the implications for Growth by entrenchment in a defensive variant of Position 2 or 3.

Structure

The relational properties of a world view, with special reference to the forms in which the nature of knowledge and value are construed.

Temporizing

A suspension of Growth (for a year) without recourse to the structurings of Escape.

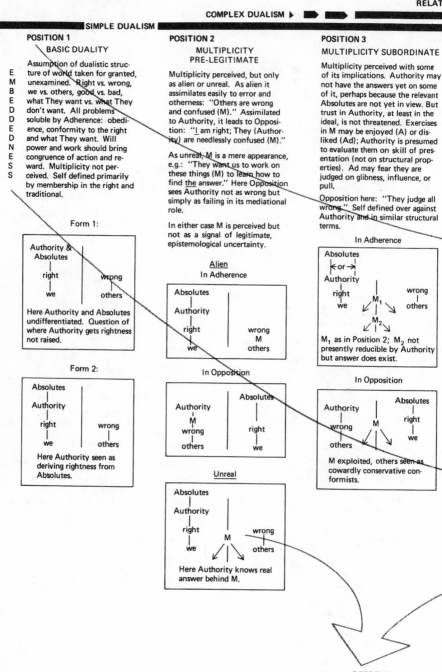

POSITION 1

BASIC DUALITY

E M B E D D E D N E S S

Assumption of dualistic structure of world taken for granted, unexamined. Right vs. wrong, we vs. others, good vs. bad, what They want vs. what They don't want. All problems soluble by Adherence: obedience, conformity to the right and what They want. Will power and work should bring congruence of action and reward. Multiplicity not perceived. Self defined primarily by membership in the right and traditional.

Form 1:

Authority & Absolutes
right — wrong
we — others

Here Authority and Absolutes undifferentiated. Question of where Authority gets rightness not raised.

Form 2:

Absolutes
Authority
right — wrong
we — others

Here Authority seen as deriving rightness from Absolutes.

POSITION 2

MULTIPLICITY
PRE-LEGITIMATE

Multiplicity perceived, but only as alien or unreal. As alien it assimilates easily to error and otherness: "Others are wrong and confused (M)." Assimilated to Authority, it leads to Opposition: "I am right; They (Authority) are needlessly confused (M)."

As unreal, M is a mere appearance, e.g.: "They want us to work on these things (M) to learn how to find the answer." Here Opposition sees Authority not as wrong but simply as failing in its mediational role.

In either case M is perceived but not as a signal of legitimate, epistemological uncertainty.

Alien
In Adherence

Absolutes
Authority
right — wrong M
we — others

In Opposition

Absolutes
Authority
M
wrong — right
others — we

Unreal

Absolutes
Authority
right — wrong
we — M — others

Here Authority knows real answer behind M.

POSITION 3

MULTIPLICITY SUBORDINATE

Multiplicity perceived with some of its implications. Authority may not have the answers yet on some of it, perhaps because the relevant Absolutes are not yet in view. But trust in Authority, at least in the ideal, is not threatened. Exercises in M may be enjoyed (A) or disliked (Ad); Authority is presumed to evaluate them on skill of presentation (not on structural properties). Ad may fear they are judged on glibness, influence, or pull.

Opposition here: "They judge all wrong." Self defined over against Authority and in similar structural terms.

In Adherence

Absolutes
←or→
Authority
right — wrong
we — M_1 — others
— M_2

M_1 as in Position 2; M_2 not presently reducible by Authority but answer does exist.

In Opposition

Authority — Absolutes
wrong — M — right
others — we

M exploited, others seen as cowardly conservative conformists.

RETREAT
Active Denial of Potential of Legitimacy in Otherness

(for variants, see box)